36.95
80E

Development Banking
In Mexico

Development Banking
In Mexico

The Case of the Nacional Financiera, S.A.

Miguel D. Ramirez

PRAEGER SPECIAL STUDIES • PRAEGER SCIENTIFIC

New York • Philadelphia • Eastbourne, UK
Toronto • Hong Kong • Tokyo • Sydney

Library of Congress Cataloging in Publication Data

Ramirez, Miguel D.
    Development banking in Mexico.

    Bibliography: p.
    Includes index.
    1. Nacional Financiera, S.A. (Mexico)
2. Development banks--Mexico.   I. Title.
HG2718.N33R35   1985   332.2   85-16700
ISBN 0-03-005334-X (alk. paper)

Published and Distributed by the
Praeger Publishers Division
(ISBN Prefix 0-275)
of Greenwood Press, Inc.,
Westport, Connecticut

Published in 1986 by Praeger Publishers
CBS Educational and Professional Publishing, a Division of CBS Inc.
521 Fifth Avenue, New York, NY 10175 USA

INTERNATIONAL OFFICES

Orders from outside the United States should be sent to the appropriate address listed below. Orders from areas not listed below should be placed through CBS International Publishing, 383 Madison Ave., New York, NY 10175 USA

Australia, New Zealand
Holt Saunders, Pty, Ltd., 9 Waltham St., Artarmon, N.S.W. 2064, Sydney, Australia

Canada
Holt, Rinehart & Winston of Canada, 55 Horner Ave., Toronto, Ontario, Canada M8Z 4X6

Europe, the Middle East, & Africa
Holt Saunders, Ltd., 1 St. Anne's Road, Eastbourne, East Sussex, England BN21 3UN

Japan
Holt Saunders, Ltd., Ichibancho Central Building, 22-1 Ichibancho, 3rd Floor, Chiyodaku, Tokyo, Japan

Hong Kong, Southeast Asia
Holt Saunders Asia, Ltd., 10 Fl, Intercontinental Plaza, 94 Granville Road, Tsim Sha Tsui East, Kowloon, Hong Kong

Manuscript submissions should be sent to the Editorial Director, Praeger Publishers, 521 Fifth Avenue, New York, NY 10175 USA

To My Wife and Parents

Preface

Development banks or corporations are usually thought
of as supplying long-term capital to prospective entrepreneurs.
Although this characterization is essentially correct, it is also
misleading when applied to multipurpose banks such as
Nacional Financiera, S.A. (NAFIN). Besides assuming this traditional function, the latter institution has been actively engaged throughout its history in promotional activities such as
enterprise creation and equity participation—operations that
defy efforts to pigeonhole the bank into any clear-cut category.

The purpose of this book is to provide a survey of
development banking in Mexico, with emphasis on NAFIN's
financing and promotion of the industrial sector since its creation in 1934. It also assesses the performance of both NAFIN
and private *financieras* in fostering the growth and development
of the financial sector. Throughout the analysis, particular
attention is given to the changing role of these development
banks within the limits set by the financial and industrial policies pursued by the Mexican government. Thus, this book
should prove to be of considerable interest to development
officials, scholars, and businessmen interested in the relationship between the public and private sectors in a developing
economy.

No volume can claim adequate coverage of every aspect of
a subject as complex as development banking in Mexico. Nevertheless, I hope this book will provide the reader with a framework of analysis for further study of the well-recognized, but
elusive, relationship between Mexico's financial development
and its economic growth.

Acknowledgments

The author wishes to express his gratitude to Prof. Werner Baer for the direction, encouragement, and valuable insights he provided through the writing of this work. Sincere thanks are extended to Prof. Peter Schran and Prof. Fred Gottheil, who gave many valuable comments and suggestions. Thanks are also due to Prof. Thomas A. Yancey for his technical assistance.

This study would not have been possible without the assistance of the Mexican government agencies that supplied much of the data used in this work. In particular, special thanks go to Lic. Luis Arturo Nava Hernández, senior representative of Nacional Financiera, S.A.

Finally, special thanks are due to Cindy A. Jacobs, my wife, who processed the many versions of my draft manuscript with patience, efficiency, and good cheer. Carol Stafford deserves much credit for undertaking the typing of the manuscript and executing it so well on top of an already heavy work load. Any errors or inconsistencies in the final product are, of course, entirely attributable to me.

Contents

List of Tables

List of Figures

Development Banking
In Mexico

1
Introduction

THE STUDY OF DEVELOPMENT BANKS

The desire of nations to industrialize has led to the creation
of financial institutions that will bridge the often-encountered
gap between savers and investors in the real economy. Development banks or corporations have usually fulfilled this role in
developing economies by supplying long-term capital to prospective entrepreneurs. Many Latin American governments, for
example, have created these institutions in response to the
pressing financial and technical requirements of their respective
countries during times of economic crisis. In this regard,
Mexico has been a leader in channeling private and public
funds, via development banks, to expand its infrastructure and
basic industry. Besides assuming this traditional function,
these institutions were among the first in Latin America to
implement promotional or innovative activities, such as enterprise creation and equity participation. These dual activities of
development and banking are best exemplified by the institutional and economic evolution of Nacional Financiera, S.A.
(NAFIN), since its creation in 1934. During this span of time,
the development bank not only has provided the building blocks
for a viable capital market but also, since 1941, has engaged
in a multitude of other activities ranging from equity investments in public and private enterprises to acting as fiduciary
for the federal government. It is the latter activities that will
be of primary concern to this study.

In a broader context, the discussion that follows will suggest that in the initial phases of industrialization, a country's economic development is constrained not only by a lack of accumulated savings but also by an inadequate effective demand for these funds due to a lack of viable investment projects and/or entrepreneurs. It is here, according to Joseph Kane, that the development bank can play an important role by ". . . identifying potential entrepreneurs, helping them identify viable investment projects, and finally, assisting them with back-up services during their early efforts."[1] Even though one case study cannot fully substantiate a theory, it is the author's opinion that multipurpose banks such as NAFIN, CORFO,* and BNDE** have demonstrated throughout their respective histories that they are much more than just "entrepreneurs of last resort." Put differently, they act as Gerschenkron's "substitutes for missing factors" in the full sense of that term.[2]

Besides this study's immediate objectives, particular attention is paid to the reorientation of NAFIN's operations within the parameters set by the general strategy of industrialization and financial development pursued by the public sector. It is shown, for example, that during the period of "stabilizing development" the public sector's deliberate efforts to promote the growth of the private sector resulted in NAFIN's assuming a purely passive role. This was followed, some years later, by a renewed entrepreneurial phase in the bank's history owing to the state's overall promotion of the petrochemical and capital goods industries. Throughout the analysis, a special effort is made to relate the activities of NAFIN to that of other private credit institutions, particularly private *financieras*. This leads to a better understanding of the relationship between the public and private sectors in the context of a developing economy.

NAFIN AND THE HYPOTHESIS OF LIMITED IMPACT

In formulating our framework for evaluating the economic and financial performance of Nacional Financiera, it will be expedient to follow the lead of Hugh Patrick and distinguish between the "demand-following" and the "supply-leading" financing of economic development. In the former, the economic

---

*Chilean Production Development Corporation.
**Brazilian National Development Enterprise.

system develops when modern financial institutions arise ". . .
in response to the demand for these services by investors and
savers in the real economy."[3] In other words, a demand-
following path of financial development is an automatic, spon-
taneous process responding to nonfinancial stimuli; it assumes
that the necessary preconditions or factors, such as accumulated savings, entrepreneurial ability, and a legal-institutional
structure conducive to business activity, are more or less present on the eve of industrialization. England and possibly Germany are countries that come to mind when we try to relate
the demand-following paradigm to actual events. What is significant here is that such a system develops under the impetus of
the private sector.

Quite the contrary is the case in a supply-leading system,
where ". . . the . . . financial instituions and . . . their
financial assets, liabilities, and related services is [sic] created
in advance of demand for them."[4] Put differently, the necessary preconditions for industrial takeoff are missing, and must
be created by the public sector in order to stimulate industrial development and to prevent a sectorally unbalanced growth.
A good example of this pattern of development is provided by
Japan, where the government established a commercial and
banking system well in advance of significant industrial development. This, in a nutshell, has also been the path of economic
development taken by a number of developing economies—
Mexico is a prime example of a country where nonmonetary
institutions have been created to provide long-term capital.[5]
However, as mentioned earlier, these financial intermediaries
did not only passively supply credit; they also engaged in a
variety of entrepreneurial operations, activities that earn them
the general designation "demand-leading institutions." Furthermore, it is hypothesized that these promotional functions will be
more prevalent in the initial phase of industrialization; once the
level of economic development becomes greater, and a viable
capital market comes into existence, the entrepreneurial services
of the development bank will be needed to a lesser extent. A
similar situation will exist with the long-term funds the development bank provides, for alternative sources of funds and
mechanisms for the reallocation and spreading of risk should
become available to domestic entrepreneurs.

The foregoing proposition can be made operational in the
case of NAFIN by formulating it in terms of what Joseph Kane
calls the "hypothesis of limited impact":[6] during initial industrialization the operations of the development bank—whether

they are in the area of supplying funds or of creating an
effective demand for the funds' productive use—are deemed to
have a minimal effect on the rate of capital formation. This
hypothesis can be reduced to either of the following conditions:

1. Low level of promotional activity. During initial industrialization the promotional and innovative activities of the
bank, whether they are in enterprise creation and/or the provision of risk capital to industry, are deemed to be unneces-
sary, since viable investment projects and/or entrepreneurs are
found in the domestic economy.

2. Alternative-funds condition. Private entrepreneurs
need not apply for medium- to long-term credits with the development bank during initial industrialization, since alternative
sources of funds are found in the financial markets of the
country.

Thus, we shall proceed just as we would when conducting
a statistical test for a numerical characteristic of a population
by assuming that the null hypothesis is true—the null in this
case being the hypothesis of limited impact, the hypothesis we
wish to reject on the basis of the historical and economic evidence presented here.

CHAPTER OUTLINE

Chapter 2 develops a theoretical framework from which to
assess the economic performance and impact of development
banks in the period of late-late industrialization.[7] In light of
the Latin American experience, particular attention is given to
the literature that investigates the promotional activities in
which these institutions are engaged—operations that, for
want of a better name, characterize them as entrepreneurs of
last resort. Also, the evolutionary nature of these entrepreneurial functions is analyzed in light of the different opportunities and structural rigidities the development bank faces at
each phase of industrial development. A simple model is developed to enable the reader to conceptualize the possible effects,
if any, of development banks upon the rate of capital formation.
Last, this chapter explores recent trends in development banking designed to meet the new opportunities and structural rigidities facing Latin America. Since the beginning of the 1960s,
there has been a rapid rise in the number and variety of

development banks providing specialized services to leading
sectors and/or regions in several nations of the region.

All in all, the purpose of this chapter is to suggest a
rationale for the intervention of financial intermediaries in a
specific development objective, whether it is in raising the
savings and investment rate or playing an active role in mobilizing resources to fields of prime importance to the economy.

The historical and institutional evolution of Nacional
Financiera and related agencies, such as development funds,
is examined in chapter 3. In the course of this review, it
becomes apparent that the reorientation of NAFIN's goals has
more or less coincided with changes in those of the federal
government. A case in point is the radical change in the
bank's objectives in relation to promotion of basic industry
that took place when Avila Camacho assumed the presidency of
Mexico during the early 1940s. A similar reorientation has taken
place in recent years, in the administration of President José
López Portillo, toward the promotion of the petrochemical and
capital goods industries. Finally, in light of Mexico's increasing
foreign indebtedness, a section of this chapter is devoted to
examining the important role played by NAFIN in securing foreign capital from multilateral agencies and private banks.

Chapter 4 analyzes the bank's promotional and financial
activities in the industrial sector during key periods in Mexico's
history since the industrialization drive of the 1940s. The
investigation is conducted along empirical lines by developing a
number of bank performance indicators and testing a reduced
form model. The latter relates the change in real industrial output during the current period to, among other variables,
lagged changes in real financing to industry by NAFIN. Also,
for comparison, the change in real financing by private *financieras* is incorporated into the analysis. Next, the chapter proceeds to analyze the mixed economic and social record of the
Echeverría and López Portillo administrations. By and large,
the central focus is upon the severe difficulties encountered by
these administrations in dealing with the socioeconomic problems
generated by the pursuit of an import-substitution industrialization strategy. This sets the stage for a detailed examination
of NAFIN's intense promotion of basic industry during these
administrations.

Chapter 5 examines the various ways in which NAFIN and
its related agencies have fostered the development of a capital
market in Mexico. During the period under review, and especially after the mid-1950s, the Mexican financial system experienced a remarkable growth and development rivaled only by

that of its real sector. In large measure, it is argued, this was the direct outcome of policies specifically aimed at increasing the participation of private credit institutions in the process of capital formation. The task of implementing these policies was, and is, one of the more compelling examples of collaboration between the public and private sectors in a developing economy.

The chapter begins by examining the evolution of a number of key financial variables, such as total real assets and liabilities, the distribution of assets between the public and private sectors, and certain developments in Mexico's capital market. Next, it delves into the specific nature of the policies pursued by the monetary authorities, as well as their implementation by the network of public and private development banks. The discussion closes with an empirical assessment of whether NAFIN and private *financieras* exerted a positive and significant influence on the rate of capital formation during key periods in Mexico's economic development. In addition, we estimate a supply-demand model that explicitly incorporates the financial and promotional activities of Nacional Financiera.

Chapter 6 summarizes the major results and discusses the future importance of research in this area for countries engaged in the process of industrialization.

SOURCES OF INFORMATION

The information used in this study has been obtained from a number of sources, ranging from bank reports and publications to interviews with Mexican economists and representatives of Nacional Financiera. In particular, special thanks are extended to Lic. Luis Arturo Nava Hernández, senior representative of NAFIN, who provided valuable information used throughout this book. For the most part, weekly publications such as *El mercado de valores* and *Informes anuales* (annual reports) from NAFIN and the Banco de México have been the primary source of factual data employed here (see the bibliography). These include data on aggregate growth of resource application since NAFIN's founding, changing sectoral distribution of such resources, and changing methods of inserting resources into the economy (for instance, equity vs. long-term lending, direct creation of enterprises). In addition, data on the changing role of NAFIN as a policy instrument have been obtained from government documents and, more important, through interviewing Mexican officials, policy makers, and businessmen. Finally, information concerning the theoretical aspects of development banking and its impact on the environment in which it functions has been obtained from the published literature. This includes journal articles, reports and publications of the World Bank, seminars, and a number of books, with William Diamond, Joseph A. Kane, and Leopoldo Solis M. among the major contributors.

NOTES

1. Joseph A. Kane, *Development Banking* (London: Lexington Books, 1975), p. 34.
2. For further detail, see Alexander Gerschenkron, *Economic Backwardness in Historical Perspective* (New York: Praeger, 1965), pp. 11-30.
3. Hugh T. Patrick, "Financial Development and Economic Growth in Underdeveloped Countries," *Economic Development and Cultural Change* 14, no. 2 (January 1966): 174-89.
4. Ibid., pp. 174-76.
5. For an excellent, if somewhat dated, interpretation of the relationship between financial and economic development in Mexico, see David H. Sheton, "The Banking System," in Raymond Vernon, ed., *Public Policy and Private Enterprise in Mexico* (Cambridge, Mass.: Harvard University Press, 1964).
6. He in fact calls it the "hypothesis of limited utility." In the author's opinion, this is an unfortunate choice of words, since the term "utility" has a rather restricted meaning in microeconomic theory. For further details, see Kane, op. cit.
7. Usually the term "late industrializers" is reserved for those countries in Europe that entered the process of industrialization on the heels of England. "Late-late industrializers" seems an appropriate term to use in characterizing those nations that embarked upon industrialization programs during and after World War II.

2
Theoretical Aspects
Of Development Banking

INTRODUCTION

The present chapter is concerned with developing a theoretical framework that will enable us to assess the economic performance and impact of development banks. In order to do this, the first part of the chapter investigates the nature and functions of development banks within the broader context of financial intermediation. Here, at the most abstract level, we shed light on certain theoretical aspects common to all financial entities, as well as their possible relationships to the pattern and growth of economic activity. We review the functions of financial intermediaries insofar as they create credit and permit the accumulation and diversification of assets within a private or mixed economy. Next, we examine the changing role of financial intermediation at different phases of economic development, with a general emphasis on the Latin American experience, especially that of Mexico. Finally, we proceed to make our analysis more concrete and complex by identifying the development bank as a financial intermediary with an express development objective (as opposed to, say, commercial and/or private investment corporations). In particular, we are interested in bringing to light certain outstanding features that make development banking ". . . neither so narrow in scope as to be limited to institutions financing profit-oriented private sector investment projects only, nor so broad as to be a general channel through which funds are directed to any development-oriented project or program."[1]

The second part of the chapter investigates, for the most part, the promotional and financial activities in which development banks are engaged, and how these functions evolve and adapt to the opportunities and structural rigidities the bank encounters at each phase of industrial development. Of particular importance will be the change in, or redistribution of, activities that takes place whenever economic expansion brings with it significant developments in the structure of industry. For instance, when the economy grows, both the size and the nature of the financial requirements of industry may change drastically. Last, this chapter will explore recent trends in development banking for Latin America in general and for Mexico in particular. Since the beginning of the 1960s, new forms of private and public financing have emerged in the financial sectors of several Latin American countries. These new institutions have, in some cases, provided specialized services that are in direct competition with those offered by development banks or corporations.

NATURE AND EVOLUTION OF
FINANCIAL INTERMEDIATION

To the extent that development banks participate in the creation of credit, the transmission of funds from surplus to deficit spending units, or the creation of financial instruments that permit the accumulation and diversification of assets, they can be said to perform the functions of financial intermediaries. This being the case, it will be worthwhile to review the basic functions of financial intermediation within the context of a rapidly growing capitalist economy. It might be objected that such an undertaking is irrelevant with regard to a number of Latin American countries whose socioeconomic conditions can in no way be characterized as "capitalistic" or, for that matter, as giving rise to a path of economic development along private lines. Insofar as this is the case, the objection stands and the reader may disregard certain of the arguments presented below. However, if the financial and economic landscape contains elements of exchange and production that are distinctively market-oriented, such as a commercial banking system and/or a nascent capital market, the remarks made here are fully applicable.

Direct Financing System

A simple set of social accounts that explicitly incorporates the financial sector begins by dividing the final buyers of output, or spending units, into three major groups.[2] Units that keep their spending in line with their income are called balanced units, regardless of whether their expenditures are on consumption, investment, and/or government goods and services. Put differently, ". . . if they save they invest a like amount, so that their financial assets do not change relative to outstanding debt including equity claims other than earned surplus."[3] Second, final buyers of output who are characterized by having an excess of income over spending on goods and services are—not surprisingly—called surplus spending units. If they save, their financial assets increase more or decrease relatively less than their liabilities, so that their net worth improves. This state of affairs enables them to be net suppliers of loanable funds to the final group of buyers, the so-called deficit spending units. The latter, as the name implies, spend in excess of their income by releasing or issuing debt, so that their financial position deteriorates.

Furthermore, the flow of funds is such that, ex post, loanable funds supplied are, in the aggregate, equal to loanable funds demanded; net financial assets and liabilities are, on balance, equal for surplus and deficit spending units, respectively. In other words, when budgets are unbalanced, accumulation of debt and financial assets is a natural concomitant of the rise in real income and wealth taking place in a profit-oriented economy.

Our discussion may be rendered more precise if we introduce the following definitions and relationships. Let ΔR be defined as the change in receipts, ΔE the change in expenditures, ΔD any increase in debt, and ΔA any rise in financial assets accruing to our spending unit. Hence, for any spending unit we have the following condition:

$$\Delta E - \Delta R = \Delta D - \Delta A \qquad (2.1)$$

or

$$\Delta E = (\Delta R - \Delta A) + \Delta D = \Delta F \qquad (2.1')$$

where

$$\Delta F = \text{change in total finance}$$
$$\Delta R - \Delta A = \text{change in internal finance}$$
$$\Delta D = \text{change in external finance}$$

That is, the total change in expenditures by our final buyers must be equal to any increase in their internal and/or external finance. Furthermore, if we let the subscripts b, s, and d stand for balanced, surplus, and deficit spending units, respectively, we may classify them in the following fashion:

Balanced-budget	$\Delta D_b = \Delta A_b$
Surplus-budget	$\Delta D_s < \Delta A_s$
Deficit-budget	$\Delta D_d > \Delta A_d$

Finally, the flow-of-funds condition for the economy at large may be written as

$$\sum_{i=1}^{n} \Delta A_{si} - \sum_{i=1}^{n} \Delta D_{si} = \sum_{i=1}^{n} \Delta Dd_i - \sum_{i=1}^{n} \Delta Ad_i \qquad (2.2)$$

In words, the net increment in financial assets by surplus spending units is just sufficient to absorb the net issue or release of liabilities by the deficit spending units.

So far, we have assumed that all external financing by deficit spending units is direct. In order to bridge its financial gap, a deficit spending unit must issue direct debt to surplus spending units that buy and accumulate these claims. To the extent that real capital formation is directly financed, debt tends to accumulate hand in hand with wealth. If all financing were of this type, the need for financial intermediaries such as commercial banks, savings and loan associations, insurance companies, investment companies, and development banks would be nonexistent. In the words of Gurley and Shaw, ". . . the saving-investment process would grind away without them."[4] A similar state of affairs could be imagined if all spending units were of the balanced type, for then ". . . each spending unit's saving would be precisely matched by its investment in tangible assets. In such a world, security issues by spending units would be zero, or very close to zero."[5]

Although these scenarios are, in principle, conceivable, they are hardly applicable to most, if not all, Latin American countries, where a significant division of labor between savers and investors is more or less present. In such a world financial intermediaries are likely to thrive, and it is their nature and functions that we take up next.

Functionally Neutral Financing System

We have seen that under a direct system of financing, deficit spending units borrow resources by releasing primary securities (shares, bonds) that are bought by surplus spending units either directly or via the securities market. Under an indirect financing system, financial intermediaries intervene in the flow of loanable funds by primarily attracting surplus funds through issuing their own liabilities (indirect debt), and allocating those savings to deficit spending units whose direct obligations they absorb. Their profit is generated by the difference between the interest rates at which they lend and the lower ones at which they borrow.

Thus, with the development of production along private lines, a more rapid growth in financial instruments than in national income or wealth begins to take place.[6] For instance, in the United States the ratio of financial assets to gross national product increased from about unity at the turn of the 20th century to something on the order of 2.5 in the early 1960s.[7] Similarly, Japan's ratio of financial assets to real wealth rose from approximately 10 percent in 1885 to over 150 percent in the early 1960s.[8] Developing countries such as Argentina, Brazil, and Mexico have a ratio that hovers between 30 and 60 percent—a figure that, though considerably lower than those of the United States and Japan, is not far from that of the Soviet Union. For the latter country the ratio moved from 10 percent in 1928 to approximately 35 percent during the mid- to late-1960s.[9]

Moreover, not only the magnitude but also the composition of total debt has changed in favor of the indirect debt issued by financial intermediaries. Originally the composition of debt may have been 20 percent indirect and 80 percent direct; later, with the development of private production, just the reverse may ensue. This progressive growth of the indirect part of debt relative to the direct component mirrors the diminishing importance of self-finance as well as of the direct issue of debt to surplus spending units by families and enterprises.

This financial outcome is of particular significance in the early stages of development, for in many cases families and enterprises have inventories in excess of their normal produc-

tion and consumption requirements that might lie idle were it
not for the possibility of placing them in a wide variety of
financial assets. Thus, freeing those inventories will make it
possible to use them to increase the country's productive
capacity and, ultimately, its long-term growth.[10] In the words
of Hugh Patrick:

> The ownership of productive fixed assets in
> underdeveloped countries usually entails entre-
> preneurial functions as well, especially since
> equities markets are not well developed. Not all
> wealth-holders are willing to engage in these
> functions. The opportunity to hold financial
> assets of superior characteristics to inventories
> and specie as a store of wealth enables holders
> of such tangible assets to give them up for
> financial assets, and for others to arrange the
> transformation of these freed, tangible assets
> into more productive form.[11]

With this growth in the magnitude and variety of nonmonetary indirect financial assets, the spread between the primary or
lending rate and the deposit rate narrows. This induces not only
a further increase in capital formation but also a greater
". . . layering of indirect debt upon primary debt and growth
in total financial assets of savers relative to national income
and wealth."[12]

On the whole, one may venture to say that the growth
and development of the credit system reconciles the pecuniary
interests of economic actors. First, it makes resources available
to deficit spending units so that they may finance their expenditures on investment, consumption, and/or government goods
and services. Second, it provides surplus spending units with
a variety of assets whose divisibility, liquidity, and profitability make them especially attractive. Finally, it stimulates
the growth of financial intermediaries that are able to reap the
benefits of making funds available at the lowest possible risk
and highest possible return. To the extent that this is the
case, one may characterize the system as functional in what may
be called a "neutral" sense. That is,

> . . . the sole purpose of a functionally neutral
> system is to permit and facilitate the accumula-
> tion of just the amount of investment actually
> required by economic agents, and to promote the

> channeling of funds to the most important sectors
> or activities from the point of view of their
> profitability and sure prospects of dynamic
> growth . . . .[13]

When it is viewed in this context, one can hardly expect
the financial sector to assume specific functions designed to
raise the real investment rate or, for that matter, to correct a
pattern of development characterized by a high concentration
of income and wealth among certain groups and regions of the
country.[14]

Nevertheless, many Latin American countries have found
it necessary—nay, imperative—to create financial institutions
such as development banks, public investment corporations,
and special funds that will channel resources in a direction
different from that in which they would flow if the intermediaries had solely a pecuniary objective. Put differently, financial intermediaries may be conceived to have a development
function that assigns them the responsibility of actively allocating scarce financial and human resources to sectors and/or
regions deemed of prime importance to the social and economic
development of the country.[15] The extreme version of this
developmental financing system is found in centrally planned
economies, where financial intermediaries are run by the state
so as to meet the requirements of the existing development
plan. This strict compliance by the credit system with the
directives and controls of the state is not, by any means, an
exclusive property of socialist and communist regimes; it has
also been a trademark of state fascism.

With this in mind, it can generally be said that among the
many forms that a financing system may take, we have, on the
one hand, a financially neutral arrangement and, on the other,
one that may be termed, for lack of a better name, a functionally planned financing order. Obviously there are many shades
of gray between these two model alternatives, among which we
can identify the supply- and demand-leading systems alluded
to in chapter 1. These, and other intermediary forms of finance, may be classified under the all-embracing appellation
"developmental financing systems." Figure 2.1 makes this
classification somewhat clearer by providing a schematic representation of the possible subdivisions of the financial hierarchy.

The demand-leading paradigm is classified under the
developmental financing heading, and is characterized by having development banks and the likely presence of a commercial
banking system as well as an emerging capital market. The

FIGURE 2.1

Financing Systems

	Financially neutral arrangement	Developmental financing system		Planned Financing system (Soviet Union)
	Demand-following system (England)	Supply-leading (Japan)	Demand-leading (Mexico)	
1) Established banking system	yes	no	no	
2) Developed capital market	yes	no	no	Not Applicable
3) Legal institutional apparatus conducive to business activity	yes	yes	yes	
4) Public development banks	no	yes	yes	
5) Role of the state	weakest → strongest			
6) Relative backwardness	increasing →			

Source: **Prepared by author.**

15

role of the state is typically greater in such a financial arrangement, as opposed, say, to a demand-following system. The increasing role of the state is indicated at the bottom of the figure by an arrow pointing to the right. It is no coincidence that those countries with a greater participation of the public are, more often than not, latecomers to industrialization (Japan, Mexico, and Brazil, for instance). In all of those countries the state has, in one form or another, stepped in to create ". . . special institutional factors designed to increase the supply of capital to the nascent industries and, in addition, to provide them . . . with better entrepreneurial guidance . . . ." Indeed, ". . . the more backward the country, the more pronounced was the coerciveness and comprehensiveness of those factors."[16]

Briefly, then, the more backward a country is on the eve of its industrialization or takeoff, the more institutions it will create to substitute for those factors that were preconditions for industrialization in the developed nations but are missing in its own case.

In this connection, it may be worthwhile to point out that the backwardness of a country is to be understood in Gerschenkron's sense: it is determined by the extent of industrialization relative to that in the more advanced industrial economies.[17] In other words, backwardness should be taken to mean relative backwardness (it, too, is shown at the bottom of Figure 2.1). Once again, these generalizations apply more or less to countries whose socioeconomic conditions can be characterized, to a certain or limited degree, as capitalistic or as giving rise to a path of economic development along private lines.

THE DEVELOPMENT BANK AS A SPECIAL KIND OF FINANCIAL INTERMEDIARY

General Introduction

The previous section reviewed a number of theoretical aspects common to all financial intermediaries, insofar as their institutional evolution has taken place within a mixed or private economy. Their impact upon the savings-investment process was considered, as was their contribution to the development of financial instruments for the reallocation and spreading of risk. These and other considerations led us to the conclusion that such a system is functional in what may

be termed a neutral sense, quite apart from the fact that
". . . it may achieve neither peak microeconomic efficiency
(minimum operating costs or optimal scale of the financing
unit) nor peak macroeconomic efficiency (optimum distribution
of real resources or maximum economic growth rate)."[18] Last,
but not least, we divided the financial system into three major
categories in which the role played by the state increased in
magnitude and scope as we moved from a functionally neutral
financing arrangement to one in which the flow of scarce financial resources conformed strictly to the directives and controls
of a central planning body.

In this section, we shall be concerned primarily with the
middle ground, which I have termed a developmental financing
system, in particular, the workings of a demand-leading financing order. Moreover, the focus of our attention with regard to
the latter will be, for the most part, confined to the special
intermediaries to which it gives rise: development banks with a
variety of entrepreneurial operations.

To begin with, we shall briefly review the historical and
institutional evolution of financial intermediation in Latin America, with special emphasis on the period since the mid-1950s—
years that have witnessed the rapid growth and diversification
of development banks. Second, the development bank will be
defined in terms of its structural components and of the operations in which it engages. Particular attention will be given to
classification of development banks according to ownership and
size of assets. Third, the potential conflict arising from the
dual nature of this special intermediary will be discussed;
". . . as a development institution it should deal with those
projects with the highest ranking on the development-impact
scale. As a banking institution, it should finance those projects with the highest ranking on the interest-rate scale."[19] As
we shall see, more often than not, these two goals are far from
being reconciled. Finally, the major sources of funds for
these institutions will be discussed.

Financial Intermediation in Latin America:
Its Evolution and Scope

The financial evolution of the relatively developed Latin
American countries can be divided into two well-defined economic stages. The first of these lasted until the 1930s and is,
by and large, associated with the export of primary goods,
agricultural and/or mineral. The second, which dates from

roughly World War II on, has been associated with a strategy
of inward-directed growth, and in particular with the financial
requirements arising out of import-substitution policies.

In the first scenario, financial intermediaries emerged,
by and large, in the form of international financing houses
and/or subsidiaries of major world banks. Their activities
were, for the most part, centered on the provision of finance
for the production and marketing requirements of the export-
import sector, and only indirectly to the process of internal
capital accumulation. For instance, in Mexico, until 1911 external demand was the determining factor in the growth and modernization of industry; it was financed to a considerable degree
by ". . . French capital which flowed into . . . industrial
activities, where it accounted for 55 percent of all foreign investment."[20] In fact, the commercial and banking community
was to a marked extent dominated by a ". . . small but ener-
getic French colony, including many families whose roots in
Mexico extended back to the early decades of the 1800s."[21] A
similar description could be applied to most Latin American
countries of this period, with the possible exception of
Argentina.

Briefly, then, until World War I most of these countries
did not have a central bank or savings associations—not to
mention a functioning capital market. Moreover, most of the
important banks, even the smaller ones, were of foreign origin.
Finally, practically all bank credit was short-term and obtain-
able only at very high real interest rates.[22]

The period between the two wars witnessed the creation
of a central bank in many, if not all, of the relatively advanced Latin American countries. The control of this institution
rested with the state, which owned it completely or in part.
More often than not, the structure and functions of this financial entity were patterned after those found in the more advanced countries, but it was soon realized that they could not
always be imitated, given the structural rigidities peculiar to
less-developed nations. So, in many cases, these banks assumed
responsibilities that went beyond the regulation of the money
supply and the release of indirect debt, as well as the provision of short-term capital. That is, they began to supply, to a
greater or lesser extent, local and foreign entrepreneurs with
medium- and/or long-term debt.[23] Once again, Mexico provides
an illuminating example of this general trend, for the country
". . . faced nearly total financial collapse following the revolution. Paper currency was worthless, most of the private
banks were in ruins, and the country's standing in international

financial circles had fallen so low that further credits were
unobtainable."[24] To remedy this situation, the Bank of Mexico
was created in 1925, not only to supervise the banking system
but also to use its complex system of reserve requirements to
". . . channel private investment into high priority sectors
and . . . also extract savings for public sector investment."[25]

A second major financial innovation during the interwar
period—and of direct import to this study—was the creation of
public and/or mixed institutions specifically assigned the task
of supplying various sectors of the economy with medium-to-
long-term loans. They emerged chiefly in response to the
pressing financial requirements that the various countries
faced as a consequence of the worldwide economic crisis of the
1930s. Among the more noteworthy examples are the creation of
Nacional Financiera, S.A., in Mexico (1934) and, some years
later, the establishment of the Chilean Development Corporation (CORFO).[26] These two institutions played key roles in the
economic and financial development of their respective economies, especially during and after the war. Raymond W. Goldsmith has called Nacional Financiera ". . . the most important
original contribution made by Mexico to the type of financial
institutions participating in financing economic development and
economic growth."[27]

In general, the economic stagnation of the 1930s and the
shortages of consumer and capital goods as a result of the war,
redirected the economic activities of most Latin American countries toward inward-directed growth via the strategy of import
substitution. Not surprisingly, the state began to play an
increasingly important role, not only in the creation of public
enterprises to produce what was formerly imported but also in
channeling domestic and, particularly, external financial resources into these emerging activities. In what follows, we
shall be concerned with the economic opportunities and problems created by this pattern of industrialization, insofar as
they affect, and are affected by, developments within the
financial sector.

The two decades or so following the end of World War II
were witness to a great expansion in the number and size of
financial intermediaries, especially those of public origin. This
phenomenon was, in many respects, the direct outcome of the
industrialization effort in which a number of the leading nations,
particularly Mexico and Brazil, were engaged. In Mexico, for
instance,

> Finance companies, both publicly and privately
> owned, were the group growing most rapidly in
> absolute and relative terms. . . . Thus Nacional
> Financiera and the private finance companies
> each accounted for over one sixth of the assets
> of all financial institutions in 1963 against shares
> of only 1 percent and 3 percent respectively in
> 1940 . . . . the increase was also very sharp in
> comparison to national product, the assets of
> both types of finance companies reaching 6 per-
> cent of national product in 1963.[28]

In Brazil, similar developments took place with the creation of
the Brazilian National Development Band (BNDE) in the early
1950s. Its principal purpose was ". . . to give long-term
loans to government and private companies engaged in infrastructure investment or basic industry investment."[29] Table 2.1
gives an indication of the relative importance of the bank's
operations during the 1950s.

It can be readily seen that beginning in ". . . the second half of the decade the bank's activities measured in terms
of local currency loans as percentage of gross capital formation
was large enough to have an influence on the direction of
national capital formation . . . ."[30] The bank's importance is

TABLE 2.1

Relative Importance of Development Bank Financing, 1952–60
(percent)

	1952	1953	1954	1955	1956	1957	1958	1959	1960
Domestic currency loans as a percent of gross fixed capital formation	—	1.7	—	—	3.3	7.3	5.5	7.4	6.2
Foreign currency loans as a percent of autonomous capital inflow	—	1.9	30.9	50.2	23.9	38.7	86.6	69.9	78.4

Source: Reproduced from Werner Baer, *Industrialization
and Economic Development in Brazil* (Homewood, Ill.: Yale University-Economic Growth Center, 1965), p. 108.

further revealed when we measure its foreign currency loans
as a percentage of total capital inflow, a figure that increased
by almost 154 percent between 1954 and 1960. The majority of
these loans were taken out to meet the financial requirements
of basic industry and infrastructure. In fact, during 1952-62
infrastructure absorbed practically 60 percent of the long-
term credit granted by the bank, and 75 percent of that
amount went to finance the expansion of electric energy.[31]

Not only did the newly created financial institutions engage in the provision of long-term capital, they also began to
undertake various promotional and innovative activities, such
as equity financing, the creation of new enterprises, provision
of technical assistance, and the transfer of technology. In
this respect, Mexico was a leader. (We shall have more to say
on this score when we review, in chapter 3, the historical and
institutional evolution of Nacional Financiera and related
agencies.)

Once they had been established in the more advanced
countries of Latin America, development banks began to appear
in the rest of the hemisphere. For example, until 1955 only 29
such institutions had been established, while during 1956-73,
43 were created.[32] Moreover, those development banks established after 1955 apparently were more specifically oriented in
their operations; only 19.8 percent of them participated in at
least 5 industrial branches, as opposed to 39.4 percent for
those founded before that date.[33] Still, the participation of the
state in the social capital of these institutions was quite high;
25 of the 43 institutions (approximately 58 percent) created
during this period had a state participation of at least 50.1
percent. Furthermore, 19 of those 25 banks (76 percent) had
a participation exceeding 95 percent.[34]

Other developments were the creation of regional banks,
such as the Central American Bank for Economic Integration
(1961) and the Andean Development Corporation (1970). However, any detailed investigation of these institutions, as well as
other questions touched upon but left open for discussion, are
best taken up in the last section of this chapter.

To summarize, the evolution of financial intermediation in
Latin America may be viewed as a process in which important
structural changes are the result of what I call adaptive modification. That is, not only are new institutions created, but
existing financial entities reorient their activities in order to
adapt more successfully to the underlying economic realities
facing late-late industrializers. Second, it may be maintained
that during early industrialization, financial intermediaries

usually share many common characteristics, yet as industrialization proceeds, they begin to develop a number of special
traits that can be explained only in terms of their unique history. In this respect, it is worthwhile recalling the post-1955
emergence of a number of development banks with specific functions. This increasing specialization, as we shall see in chapter 3, has not been confined to the more recent institutions;
it has also affected the older development banks, such as
Nacional Financiera and BNDE. They too have found it necessary to delegate responsibility to special agencies and funds.
Finally, the participation of the state in the creation and supervision of these developmental financing institutions has not
declined—for many countries it has increased substantially.
Moreover, this trend is not likely to be reversed in the near
future, in light of the sizable foreign debt of many of these
countries, much of which has been contracted to meet the financial requirements of government-sponsored projects. A case in
point is the important role played by Nacional Financiera in
obtaining long-term foreign capital for the industrial projects
of the Mexican government. We shall have more to say in this
connection when we review the history of NAFIN.

The Development Bank Defined

So far, our discussion has been concerned primarily with
the development and growth of financial intermediaries in a theoretical and historical framework. We have witnessed the
emergence of a special intermediary whose dual purposes of
banking and development have transformed it, more often than
not, into ". . . an activist institution, interested in development and unafraid of change, and fully aware that there can
be no development without new ideas . . . ."[35] It is to the
problem of defining this financial entity that we now turn.

As indicated in the previous section, a great variety of
development banks have come into existence since the end of
World War II. This makes it especially difficult to give a
standard or universal definition to which development banks
conform, for ". . . each bank is structured with the political,
social, and economic fabric of the country in mind. And each
in its own way is a unique institution."[36] Still, in spite of the
great diversity, it is possible to discern a number of structural components and functions that are, to a greater or lesser
extent, present among the majority of these institutions. For
instance, all 340 development banks surveyed in Nyhart and

Janssens' comprehensive directory are engaged in at least one of the following operations:[37]

1. To help mobilize and/or direct domestic resources to investments whose social marginal cost is less than, or whose marginal benefit is greater than, its private marginal cost or benefit, respectively (or if the following conditions hold):

$$MSC < MPC => MEC < 0, \text{ since } MSC = MPC + MEC$$

or

$$MSB > MPB => MEB > 0, \text{ since } MSB = MPB + MEB$$

where

MSC = marginal social cost
MSB = marginal social benefit
MPC = marginal private cost
MPB = marginal private benefit
MEC = marginal external cost
MEB = marginal external benefit

2. To assume a demand-leading role, whether in the creation of new enterprises and/or the provision of equity financing

3. To attract long-term financing from the international sector and channel it to high-priority investment projects as defined in (1) above

4. To be able to expand, through efficient management of its resources, in order to meet the varied needs of a developing economy

5. To act as fiduciary for the national government with regard to the management and supervision of certain agencies and trust funds

6. To provide technical and managerial assistance to ensure the successful implementation of projects financed by the bank

7. To work closely with the government and the private sector, in order to eliminate the overlapping of activities; this will ensure that its operations conform to publicly established and generally agreed upon development goals and priorities[38]

8. To foster the development of a capital market with all that this implies

9. To help transfer and diffuse technology from the developed countries, so as to improve the human-resource base of the country.

Other activities could be cited, but they are for the most part reducible to one or a combination of those listed above.

Given that this is the case, we may offer the following definition of development banking: "A development bank is a financial intermediary providing productive financing and related services to a developing economy." By "productive financing" we mean the summation of the real value of medium-to-long-term loans plus equity investments granted to high-priority investment projects. Second, under the general heading "related services" we include all other innovative activities in which the bank typically engages. Although this definition is somewhat broad, it is sufficiently narrow to exclude ". . . central banks, short-term credit institutions, and a number of very specialized institutions (i.e., marketing boards, mortgage banks, and land reform authorities)."[39]

With this definition in hand, let us proceed to examine a number of criteria used in the classification of these institutions.

Classification of Development Banks

Development banks may be classified under several categories, including ownership, nature of functions, size of assets, regional distribution, and age. Although this list is by no means exhaustive, it does provide a benchmark for further subdivision and analysis. In what follows, we shall be concerned primarily with ownership, since it is typically employed in the classification of development banks. The other categories will be brought into play insofar as they are relevant to our discussion of ownership.

To begin with, we may think of ownership in terms of a continuum with complete private ownership at one extreme and complete public control and ownership at the other. Private development banks are those whose entire capital stock is provided by individuals or institutions operating in the private sector of the economy. A good example of such an institution is the Corporación Financiera de Caldas in Colombia, whose immediate objective ". . . is to assist in the development of private industry mining, agriculture and livestock by providing medium- and long-term capital, by strengthening Colombia's

capital market and by channeling private foreign capital into
Colombia."[40] Public development banks are those whose equity
capital is entirely in the hands of the government and affiliated
institutions. This is the case with CORFO in Chile, whose purpose is primarily ". . . to formulate and implement the general
development plan for national production."[41]

Between these two extremes are the mixed banks, which
include private- and public-leaning institutions. We would
classify a mixed bank as public-leaning if at least 51 percent
of the capital stock is owned within the public sector and/or
the operating policy of the institution is generally dominated
by what Joseph Kane calls ". . . public sector weighting of
project selection criteria."[42] Nacional Financiera, S.A., of
Mexico is an excellent example of such an institution, for "priority is given to projects in the national interest."[43] A mixed
bank would be characterized as private-leaning to the extent
that the above conditions were reversed.

The relative importance of the different types of development banks in Latin America can be seen in Table 2.2. Public
banks by far outnumber private ones, and the latter are
slightly more numerous than mixed institutions. Also, public
development banks typically are older, and the size of their
assets is greater than those of their private counterparts.
(See Appendix A for further details.) A similar, though less
striking, result is obtained when we compare public development banks with mixed ones. No clear-cut inferences can be
drawn when private and mixed institutions are compared.

Having made this observation, it is worthwhile to recall
that many of the more recent banks are specific in function,

TABLE 2.2

Latin American Development Banks, Classified by Ownership

Type of Bank	No. of Banks	Percent Distribution
Private	19	26
Public	40	55
Mixed	14	19
Total	73	100

Source: Computed from J. D. Nyhart and E. J. Janssens,
Global Directory of Development Finance Institutions 1.1.1.
(Paris: OECD, 1967).

providing long-term capital to specific industries and/or sectors, such as steel, mining, and agriculture. Consequently, a significant proportion of them tend to be private and/or mixed, although public development banks are by no means excluded. Still, evidence seems to indicate that—at least in Latin America—the public banks are more likely to be both multipurpose and older. This general observation also applies to mixed banks, insofar as they are of the public-leaning type, a prime example being NAFIN in Mexico.

These observations and hypotheses seem to support the Gerschenkronian thesis, in the sense that in the early phases of industrialization, the state will create public institutions to function as substitutes in ". . . stimulating the growth of the factors which evolved somewhat spontaneously over a longer time span in the experience of the developed countries."[44] Moreover, these institutions will typically be multipurpose, since, in the early stages of industrialization, the total economic activity is relatively small and there is no advantage in setting up more than one development bank. More research is needed to settle this important question, for its ramifications will be of considerable interest to countries in the process of industrialization.

The Dual Aspect of Development Banking

Development banks are peculiar institutions, for, unlike other intermediaries, they must ". . . seek to achieve their purpose as a development institution simultaneously with achieving their purpose as a banking institution."[45] They often find themselves having to choose between projects that have a high monetary return but marginal social impact, and those whose development impact far outweighs their pecuniary return. Our classification of development banks sheds some light on this difficult problem.

To begin with, the development objective is, more often than not, stressed in public development banks, as well as in mixed banks with a public orientation. CORFO and NAFIN provide two excellent examples. Private development banks, on the other hand, emphasize the rate of return to a far greater extent. In other words, private-oriented banks "tend to support projects which yield a high marginal monetary return whether or not they have a low marginal social benefit."[46] This characterization applies, mutatis mutandis, to private-leaning banks. Obviously, all types of banks are willing, in principle, to fund

TABLE 2.3

Projects Ordinarily Financed by Different Types
of Development Banks

Rate of Return

	High	Low
High	All banks	Public and public-leaning banks
Low	Private and private-leaning banks	No banks

Social Benefit

Source: Prepared by author.

projects that are rated high on both sets of criteria and vice
versa. Table 2.3, in the form of a contingency table, lists
projects that would ordinarily be financed by different types
of banks.

Although perhaps useful from a pedagogical standpoint,
this distinction on the basis of ownership leaves much to be
desired when we are confronted with more concrete and complex
economic realities. In many cases, it is not the structure of
ownership that is decisive in determining which investment
projects are financed, but the sources, terms, and cost of the
funds obtained. For instance, private development banks have
at their disposal not only profit-generated funds but also funds
obtained from their governments and international institutions
such as the World Bank and IMF. To the extent that this is
the case, it is not surprising to find a private development
bank like Financiera Metropolitana, S.A., of Mexico financing
investment projects with a relatively high marginal social benefit but a comparably low monetary return.[47]

However, it is generally the case that factors besides the
structure of ownership are most important among mixed banks,
yet less influential in the case of well-defined banks, when it
comes to the question of which projects to undertake.

Sources of Funds

In light of the importance of the sources, terms, and cost
of funds to the general operations of development banks, it
will be expedient to consider the question of sources in more
detail. First, one can identify three major sources of funds for
development banks: the government, the private sector, and
international organizations both private and public. Second,
there is, generally speaking, a direct relationship between the
role of government as a net creditor and the type of bank.
Thus, it is not surprising to find that CORFO obtains most of
its funds from the state, be it from taxes earmarked for that
purpose and/or the absorption by the state of the bank's
equity and bond issues.[48] Third, given that this is the case,
private and private-leaning mixed banks typically pay more
attention to their leverage ratios. That is, they are concerned
with maintaining a total-debt-to-total-assets ratio that is accept-
able to potential lenders in both the domestic and the international private sectors. Similarly, the cost of obtaining funds,
exceptions notwithstanding, is more of a concern to private-
oriented and mixed banks. Finally, to the extent that these
banks contract debt from abroad, they must guard against
exchange-rate fluctuations that, unless the debt is payable in
domestic currency, may increase their costs prohibitively.

In general, then, most banks obtain their funds via the
release of bonds and equity issues to the government, private
sector, and/or international sector. Thus, for the remainder of
this subsection, we will examine more closely the financial
structure and cost of funds facing development banks.

To begin with, the debt-equity ratio,* generally called
the debt ratio, measures the proportion of total funds supplied

---

*The debt-to-assets (D/A) and debt-to-equity (D/E)
ratios are transformations of each other:

$$D/A = \frac{D/E}{1 + D/E} \quad \text{and} \quad D/E = \frac{D/A}{1 - D/A}$$

Both ratios increase as a bank of a given size (total assets)

by creditors. Debt includes current liabilities and all outstanding bonds issued by the bank. By and large, creditors (especially from the private sector) prefer moderate debt ratios,
since the lower the ratio, the less likely they are to incur substantial losses in the event of liquidation. On the other hand,
equity owners may prefer to have a somewhat higher debt ratio
because it magnifies earnings per unit of equity capital invested and/or because raising new equity means giving up
some degree of control.[49] Thus, one would expect the debt
ratio to be higher, on average, for private banks, since the
profit motive is stressed somewhat more than in public banks.
This is exactly what Geraldo L. Salgado found when examining
the long-term debt-equity ratio of 189 development banks iden-
tified in Nyhart and Janssens. The median value of the debt
ratio for this sample was 46 percent, compared with 53 and 45
percent for private and public banks, respectively.[50]

Debt and equity may now be combined to determine the
average cost of funds for our model bank. This weighted cost
of funds can then be related to the leverage or debt ratio in
order to determine the optimal cost of funds. A generalized
equation can be used to calculate the cost of funds:

$$K = \sum_{i=1}^{n} w_i^D k_i^D + e \left[\sum_{i=1}^{n} w_i^F k_i^F \right] \qquad (2.3)$$

where

k_i = cost of the i-th component (percent)

w = weight of i-th type of funds

e = domestic price of a unit of foreign exchange

and the superscripts D and F designate the domestic and foreign origin, respectively, of the funds obtained by the development bank.

Hence, if the bank acquired funds through the issue of
long-term bonds (B), preferred stock (PS), and equity issues
(E), whether their origin be domestic or foreign, the total
cost of funds would be

---

uses a greater percent of debt; however, D/A rises linearly
and approaches a limit of 100 percent, while D/E rises exponen-
tially and $\rightarrow \infty$.

$$K = w_B^D k_B^D + w_{PS}^D k_{PS}^D + w_E^D k_E^D + e[w_B^F k_B^F + w_{PS}^F k_{PS}^F \; w_E^F k_E^F] \quad (2.3')$$

Furthermore, as the leverage ratio increases, the average or composite cost of funds at first decreases, then beyond some point begins to increase. Figure 2.2 plots the average cost, together with the component costs of debt and equity, against the debt ratio expressed in percentage terms. (See Appendix B for calculation of this example.)

It is readily apparent from Figure 2.2 that this hypothetical bank should choose a leverage ratio of 35 percent if it is going to minimize its costs of funds, ceteris paribus. The marginal cost of funds is just equal to the average cost of funds at this level of leverage.

FIGURE 2.2

Cost-of-Capital Curves

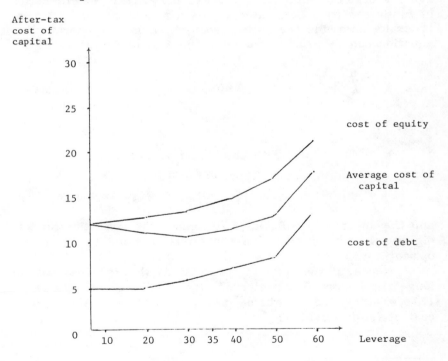

Source: J. Fred Weston and Eugene F. Brigham, *Managerial Finance*, 6th ed. (Hinsdale, Ill.: Dryden Press, 1977), p. 711.

DEVELOPMENT BANKING AT SIGNIFICANT STAGES
IN INDUSTRIAL DEVELOPMENT

Introduction

In the last section we focused our investigation, for the most part, on those structural components that set development banks apart from other financial intermediaries. We briefly reviewed the historical and institutional evolution of this special intermediary for Latin America. Second, we provided a definition for development banks that, although somewhat vague, was sufficiently narrow to be of operational use. Next, we proceeded to tackle the difficult question of a conflict of purposes in the operations of these institutions. Here the classification of banks into types helped us, if not to resolve the issue, at least to visualize the problem more clearly. Finally, it was pointed out that in private and mixed banks it is not so much the structure of ownership that determines which investment projects are financed, as it is factors such as the origin and cost of funds. These were examined in some detail for a representative development bank.

In this section, we shall develop a theoretical framework that allows us to conceptualize the possible effect that the development bank has over time upon the shape and location of the aggregate demand curve for long-term capital. Similarly, the effect of the development bank upon the aggregate supply of long-term capital will be investigated. The role played by the development bank is analyzed for two related, but conceptually distinct, periods: initial industrialization and sustained industrialization.

It will become apparent, particularly with regard to the first stage, that distributional rigidities in the form of discontinuities, inelasticities, and nonprice determinants define the manner in which the development bank affects the long-term capital market. The analysis is also conducted from the vantage point of the representative bank.

Initial Industrialization and the Development Bank

During initial industrialization, developing countries are characterized, to a marked degree, by wealth holdings that consist, for the most part, of

> . . . land and land improvements, simple agricul-
> ture and handicrafts tools, livestock, inventories
> (notably foodstuffs), and durable consumer goods
> (especially housing, but in some countries metals
> and jewelry as well).[51]

Thus, a sizable portion of their wealth is held in forms
that are not conducive to economic growth and development
along private lines, although in many instances these assets
can be transformed without much difficulty into productive
capital goods. Such is the case with precious metals, excess
inventories, foreign exchange, and other foreign and domestic
liquid assets, such as short-term securities. Moreover, the
magnitudes involved are not, by any means, negligible, as can
be attested by the fact that for many countries

> It is not unreasonable to think of ratios of tan-
> gible wealth to GNP, even excluding land, of 2
> or 3. A re-allocation of as much as 10 percent of
> this wealth to more productive forms would be
> equivalent to 20 or 30 percent of GNP and would
> raise the level of output by about 10 percent.[52]

In this regard, Japan provides an excellent example of a
country that had a considerable portion of its wealth in unpro-
ductive forms:

> . . . between 1872 and 1881, the net outflow of
> specie amounted to 71 million yen, 24 percent of
> total imports during this period. For the entire
> period (1853-1881), the outflow was of the order
> of 220 million yen. This was equivalent perhaps
> to half of her national income for an average
> year during this period.[53]

It may therefore be maintained that it is not so much the
lack of a sizable flow of investable funds that acts as a fetter
upon the industrial growth of these countries, as it is the
lack of effective use of what is already there. As a result of
the presence of considerable structural rigidities, viable investment projects are not found outside of commerce and agriculture
in many late-late industrializers. And, if they are present, it
is unlikely that "entrepreneurs" in commerce and agriculture
could transfer their know-how and capital to them. During
this early phase, investments in the industrial sector do not

provide the highest possible expected return for any degree of risk, or the lowest possible risk for any expected return. In Figure 2.3, the boundary BCDE defines the efficient set of investments available to entrepreneurs in the initial phase of

FIGURE 2.3

The Efficient Set of Investments

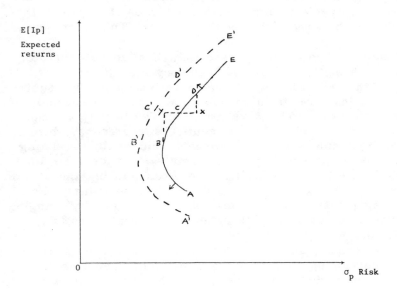

where

$$E[Ip] = \sum_{j=1}^{n} w_j i_j = \text{expected returns on an} \qquad (2.4)$$
$$\text{n-investment portfolio}$$

$$\sigma_p = \sqrt{\sum_{s=1}^{n} (i_{p_s} - \bar{i}_p)^2 P_s} = \text{standard deviation} \qquad (2.5)$$
$$\text{of the portfolio's}$$
$$\text{expected returns}$$

and

$$\sum_{j=1}^{n} w_j = 1.0 \qquad (2.6)$$

Source: J. Fred Weston and Eugene F. Brigham, *Managerial Finance*, 6th ed. (Hinsdale, Ill.: Dryden Press, 1977), p. 358.

industrialization.[54] Investments to the left of the efficient set
are not possible, because they lie outside the attainable set.

Investments outside the attainable set would correspond
to those industrial, commercial, and/or agricultural activities
that, although desirable, are not possible, given the relative
backwardness of the economy. Such an investment portfolio
would be given by point y, which offers a higher expected
return than B at the same amount of risk. Investment projects
to the right of the boundary would be inefficient, in the sense
that some other project could provide a higher return with the
same risk, or the same return with less risk. This is the case
for point X.

However, it is often the case that these investment projects, although inefficient from a pecuniary standpoint, are
crucial for the economic growth and development of the country—
for instance, investments in roads, canals, ports, basic industry, and agriculture. The development bank can play an important role by ". . . identifying potential entrepreneurs, helping
them identify viable investment projects, and finally, assisting
them with back-up services during their early efforts."[55] In
terms of Figure 2.3, it would not only mean pushing the boundary outward to B'C'D'E' but also, for a given investment fron-
tier, moving points such as X toward the boundary by bringing
marginal private costs/benefits in line with marginal social
costs/benefits.*

This process, already a slow one, becomes even more so
when the developing country lacks a substantial nucleus of
entrepreneurs in such traditional economic activities as commerce and small-scale manufacturing. In this case,

> The opportunity for or the availability of special
> financial incentives does not create entrepreneurs.

---

*In this context, risk can be thought of as being a cost,
and expected return a benefit. The development bank, by
borrowing any amount of capital offered to it at home and
abroad and lending it to private investors, helps reduce the
risk to the savers. Development bank borrowing provides
savers with a relatively low-risk investment medium, the bank's
securities. This stimulates saving at any level of income and
interest rates, which makes it possible to increase the rate of
capital formation.[56]

Development banks usually have to demonstrate that
it pays to set up an industrial unit and show it can
be successfully done.[57]

As we shall see in chapter 3, this scenario is, in many
respects, applicable to the role played by Nacional Financiera
in the industrialization drive of the 1940s.[58]

However, once this process gets under way,

. . . it becomes more apparent to more people how a
business enterprise is conducted. . . . Entrepreneurs tend to come of their own volition and in larger
numbers have a pari passu increasing demand for
capital. Well placed industrial units tend to set up
linkage relations that in effect provide potential
projects for the emerging entrepreneurial group.[59]

Eventually, the relative shortage of an effective demand for
long-term capital becomes less of a constraint as we enter the
stage of sustained industrialization. However, before proceeding
to a more detailed analysis of the latter, let us depict the impact of the development bank on the short-term market demand
and supply curves for long-term capital.

To begin with, during initial industrialization many
imperfections—inelasticities, discontinuities, nonprice determinants, and relatively high and varied real interest rates—
characterize the long-term capital market, if one exists. Often
these imperfections, to the extent that they are present, make
it very difficult, and at times well-nigh impossible, to derive
market supply and demand schedules. This is the case for even
the best of markets. Thus, our analysis in terms of demand and
supply functions for long-term capital should be taken in the
spirit of a simple and abstract depiction of those relationships
on which we wish to focus—in no way a substitute for the
more concrete and complex empirical/historical investigation in
the ensuing chapters.

The aggregate supply and demand functions for long-
term capital can be represented by the following functions.

$$\tilde{Q}_L^S = \delta_1 + \gamma_1 r_L + \gamma_1^*(r_o^S - r_L)X_1 + \beta_1 D_o^F + \varepsilon^S \qquad (2.7)$$

and

$$X_1 = \begin{cases} 1 & \text{if } r_L > r_o^s \\ 0 & \text{otherwise} \end{cases}$$

also

$$\gamma_1^* < 0 \quad \text{and} \quad |\gamma_1^*| < \gamma_1$$

$$\tilde{Q}_L^D = \delta_2 + \gamma_2 r_L + \gamma_2^*(r_L - r_o^D)X_2 + \beta_2 D_o^P + \varepsilon^D \qquad (2.8)$$

and

$$X_2 = \begin{cases} 1 & \text{if } r_L < r_o^D \\ 0 & \text{otherwise} \end{cases}$$

also

$$\gamma_2^* > 0 \quad \text{and} \quad |\gamma_2| > \gamma_2^*$$

where

$\tilde{Q}_L^S$ = random aggregate supply function of long-term capital

$\tilde{Q}_L^D$ = random aggregate demand function of long-term capital

r_L = real rate of interest for long-term capital

D^F = development bank's provision of real finance (long-term loans)

D^P = development bank's provision of entrepreneurial services (equity capital and enterprise creation)

ε^S = stochastic error in the supply function

ε^D = stochastic error in the demand function

Also, γ_1, γ_1^*, $\beta_1 > 0$, while γ_2, $\gamma_2^* < 0$, and $\beta_2 > 0$. Finally, we assume that $E[\varepsilon^S] = E[\varepsilon^D] = 0$.

Our model would not be complete without an equilibrium condition:

$$Q_L^S = Q_L^D = Q_L \qquad (2.9)$$

These functions and the equilibrium conditions above are illustrated in Figure 2.4. The demand and supply curves exhibit breaks at r_o^D and r_o^S, respectively. These curves are designed to capture the imperfections that afflict the long-term

FIGURE 2.4

Initial Industrialization

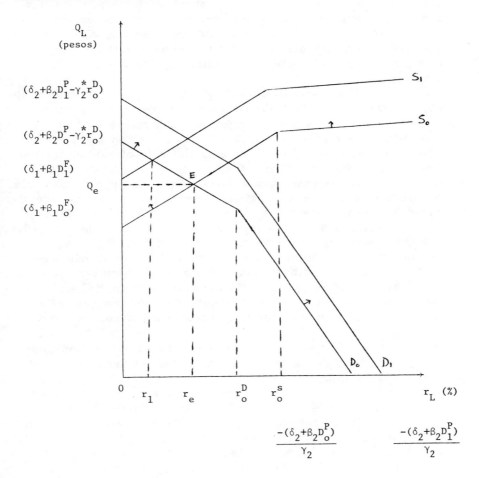

Source: Prepared by author.

capital market of a developing economy during initial industrialization. For instance, as the real rate of interest is lowered,
the demand for long-term capital increases accordingly. However, beyond some point that we designate as r_0^D, the effective
demand curve for capital funds becomes quite inelastic. This
lost interest elasticity of demand is ". . . attributable to the
fact that in an underdeveloped economy the number of viable
investment opportunities is quite limited."[60]

Similarly, the supply of long-term capital funds becomes very inelastic beyond point r_O^s. This may be due to the fact that the distributional rigidities discussed above prevent savings from moving out of agriculture and/or commerce and into the industrial sector.[61] Indeed, the more traditionally oriented the socioeconomic fabric of society, the more pronounced the structural and distributional rigidities on the eve of industrialization.

Also, the demand curve (D_O) becomes inelastic before the supply curve (S_O) does. This outcome is particularly relevant to our hypothesis of limited impact, which claims that during the initial phase of industrialization, it is not so much the supply of capital funds that constrains the rate of capital formation as it is the lack of an effective demand. Thus, to the extent that the development bank acts on the supply side only, it will have a minimal impact on economic growth. This potential scenario can be illustrated via Figure 2.4, for if the development bank increases the supply of capital funds from D_O^F to D_I^F, the aggregate supply curve shifts upward from S_O to S_1, driving the real interest rate downward from equilibrium rate r_e to r_1, ceteris paribus. This development, however, has had a minimal impact on the demand for long-term capital and, to the extent that the latter is a rough index of the rate of capital formation, a correspondingly minimal impact on industrialization.

Yet this is not the end of the story, for the development bank (especially a multipurpose and/or mixed bank) acts not only on the supply side but on the demand side as well; and to the extent that this is the case, the hypothesis of limited impact is not supported. This is shown in Figure 2.4 by a shift in the demand curve from D_O to D_1 as a result of an increase in the promotional operations of the bank from D_O^P to D_1^P. In this connection, it may be objected that even though the bank engaged in financial and promotional activities, those activities are not large enough in magnitude and/or scope to have a significant effect on the market supply and demand schedules for capital funds. This may be true with regard to the smaller private and private-leaning mixed banks, which typically appear at a later stage in the industrialization process. However, for the larger multipurpose banks like CORFO and NAFIN it is less likely. In fact, we shall see in chapter 3 that this criticism can hardly be levied against NAFIN, especially during the industrialization drive of Mexico.

Mathematical Digression

The comparative statics of the prototype financial model can be derived from the equilibrium condition given in equation (2.9). The latter does not entail a stochastic term, and equilibrium values r_e and Q_e are shown in Figure 2.4 at point E. In this range of values the demand curve* is given by

$$E[\tilde{Q}_L^D] = (\delta_2 - \gamma_2^* r_o^D) + (\gamma_2 + \gamma_2^*) r_L + \beta_2 D_o^P \tag{2.10}$$

and the supply curve by**

$$E[\tilde{Q}_L^S] = \delta_1 + \gamma_1 r_L + \beta_1 D_o^F \tag{2.11}$$

At equilibrium point E we can write equations letting Q_L represent the equilibrium quantity—the common value of Q_L^S and Q_L^D—as follows:[62]

$$Q_L = (\delta_2 + \beta_2 D_o^P - \gamma_2^* r_o^D) + (\gamma_2 + \gamma_2^*) r_L + \varepsilon^D \tag{2.12}$$

$$Q_L = (\delta_1 + \beta_1 D_o^F) + \gamma_{1r} + \varepsilon^S \tag{2.13}$$

The prototype financial model, then, consists of these structural equations that determine values of the endogenous variables Q and r in terms of the exogenous variables D_o^P and D_o^F. The two equations can be solved simultaneously by equating one to the other. Solving for r_L and Q_L yields

$$r_L = \frac{(\delta_2 - \delta_1) - \gamma_2^* r_o^D + \beta_2 D_o^P - \beta_1 D_o^F + (\varepsilon^D - \varepsilon^S)}{\gamma_1 - (\gamma_2 + \gamma_2^*)} \tag{2.14}$$

$$Q_L = \frac{\gamma_1 \delta_2 - \delta_1 (\gamma_2 + \gamma_2^*) - \gamma_1 \gamma_2^* r_o^D + \gamma_1 \beta_2 D_o^P - (\gamma_2 + \gamma_2^*) D_o^F + \gamma_1 \varepsilon^D - \varepsilon^S (\gamma_2 + \gamma_2^*)}{\gamma_1 - (\gamma_2 + \gamma_2^*)}$$

$$\tag{2.15}$$

---

*Before and including the break, $X_2 = 0$, it is given by $E[\tilde{Q}_L^D] = \delta_2 + \gamma_2 r + \beta_2 D_o^P$.

**Beyond r_o^S, $X_1 = 1$, so that $E[\tilde{Q}_L^S] = \delta_1 - \gamma_1^* r_o^S + (\gamma_1 + \gamma_1^*) r_L + \beta_1 D_o^F$.

In vector-matrix notation it could be written as

$$
\begin{bmatrix} r_L \\ \\ \\ Q_L \end{bmatrix} = \begin{bmatrix} \dfrac{\beta_2}{\gamma_1-(\gamma_2+\gamma_2^*)} & \dfrac{-\beta_1}{\gamma_1-(\gamma_2+\gamma_2^*)} & \dfrac{(\delta_2-\delta_1)-\gamma_2^* r_o^D}{\gamma_1-(\gamma_2+\gamma_2^*)} \\ \\ \dfrac{\gamma_1\beta_2}{\gamma_1-(\gamma_2+\gamma_2^*)} & \dfrac{-(\gamma_2+\gamma_2^*)\beta_1}{\gamma_1-(\gamma_2+\gamma_2^*)} & \dfrac{\gamma_1\delta_2-\delta_2(\gamma_2+\gamma_2^*)-\gamma_1\gamma_2^* r_o^D}{\gamma_1-(\gamma_2+\gamma_2^*)} \end{bmatrix} \begin{bmatrix} D_o^P \\ \\ D_o^F \\ \\ 1 \end{bmatrix}
$$

$$
+ \begin{bmatrix} \dfrac{(\epsilon^D-\epsilon^S)}{\gamma_1-(\gamma_2+\gamma_2^*)} \\ \\ \\ \dfrac{\gamma_1\epsilon^D-\epsilon^S(\gamma_2+\gamma_2^*)}{\gamma_1-(\gamma_2+\gamma_2^*)} \end{bmatrix} \qquad\qquad (2.16)
$$

The coefficients of the reduced-form equations summarize the comparative statics results of this simple model. Thus, from (2.14) or (2.16),

$$
\left.\frac{\partial Q_L}{\partial D_o^P}\right|_{dD^F=0} = \frac{\gamma_1\beta_2}{\gamma_1-(\gamma_2+\gamma_2^*)} > 0 \qquad\qquad (2.17)
$$

Since the denominator is positive ($\gamma_1 > 0$ being the slope of the supply curve and ($\gamma_2+\gamma_2^*) < 0$ being the slope of the demand curve, provided $|\gamma_1| > \gamma_2^*$), and to the extent that $\beta_2 > 0$ (the development bank has a positive impact on the demand for long-term capital funds), the partial derivative is positive. Hence, an increase in promotional activity, ceteris paribus, whether it be equity financing or the provision of technical know-how, would tend to increase the effective demand for capital funds.

Table 2.4 conveniently summarizes the comparative statics of the prototype financial model. A major objection to the procedure outlined above is that, in the absence of an equilibrium condition, the observed quantity of long-term capital transacted in the market may not satisfy both the demand and the supply schedules. Hence, unless one possesses

TABLE 2.4

Comparative Statics

| Exogenous Variables | Endogenous Variables | |
	r_L	Q_L
D_o^P	$\dfrac{\beta_2}{\gamma_1 - (\gamma_2 + \gamma_2^*)} > 0$	$\dfrac{\gamma_1 \beta_2}{\gamma_1 - (\gamma_2 + \gamma_2^*)} > 0$
D_o^F	$\dfrac{-\beta_2}{\gamma_1 - (\gamma_2 + \gamma_2^*)} < 0$	$\dfrac{-(\gamma_2 + \gamma_2^*)\beta_1}{\gamma_1 - (\gamma_2 + \gamma_2^*)} > 0$
1	$\dfrac{(\delta_2 - \delta_1) - \gamma_2^* r_o^D}{\gamma_1 - (\gamma_2 + \gamma_2^*)} \gtreqless 0$	$\dfrac{\gamma_1 \delta_2 - \delta_2(\gamma_2 + \gamma_2^*) - \gamma_1 \gamma_2^* r_o^D}{\gamma_1 - (\gamma_2 + \gamma_2^*)} \gtreqless 0$

Source: Derived from equations (2.14) and (2.15).

individual data pertaining to demand and supply regimes, it is not possible for structural coefficients to be uniquely determined from the reduced-form coefficients.

One way of dealing with this problem, according to Fair and Jaffee, is to make use ". . . of price-setting information to reduce computational difficulties and to make more use of the available data."[63]In particular, the method postulates that the change in the long-term real rate of interest is a positive function of the excess demand in the loanable-funds market. More precisely,

$$\frac{dr_L}{dt} = \phi(Q_L^D - Q_L^S), \quad \phi > 0 \tag{2.18}$$

and

$$\frac{dr_L}{dt} \gtreqless 0 \quad \text{as} \quad Q_L^D \gtreqless Q_L^S$$

In addition, if the actual quantity transacted in the market is constrained by the quantity demanded or supplied, it will be equal to the minimum of these two quantities:

$$Q_L = \min(Q_L^D, \ Q_L^s) \tag{2.19}$$

Thus, in periods of falling rates, we know from (2.18) that there is excess supply, and from (2.19) that the observed quantity will equal ex ante demand. It is a simple matter to implement this method, for one only needs to separate the sample data into periods of excess demand and excess supply on the basis of the observed price change. The demand function can be estimated over periods of excess supply, and the supply function over periods of excess demand.

The Development Bank
and Sustained Industrialization

As the economy expands, the development bank is faced with different opportunities and structural rigidities. These may be brought about by the changing size and nature of the financial requirements of the emerging industrial sector and/or the emergence of new financial intermediaries to provide specific services, such as development banks with a specific function. Moreover, the change in the bank's orientation may result from the enactment of new government regulations that alter the distinction between different types of financial intermediaries. For instance, the development bank is allowed to assume certain functions—say, short-term lending—that were the exclusive prerogative of commercial banks.

In general, though, as the developing country enters the stage of sustained industrialization, the promotional activities of the bank diminish in importance relative to its financial function. The more developed a country is during this late–late industrialization period, the less of a constraint demand becomes on the rate of capital formation.[64] In terms of Figure 2.5, demand no longer becomes inelastic before supply does. The point at which the break occurs is farther to the left of the original one. Furthermore, not only is the break encountered at a lower rate of interest, but once it occurs, it is not as insensitive to movements in the interest rate as it was during initial industrialization. This development reflects the existence of a greater number of viable investment projects and an emerging entrepreneurial class.

In a similar vein, with the increasing size and complexity of the economy, capital funds become more readily available to domestic and foreign entrepreneurs. This is a reflection

FIGURE 2.5

Sustained Industrialization

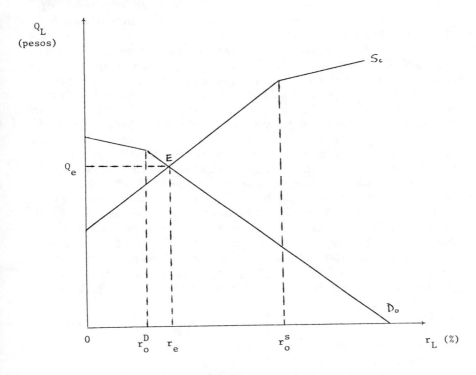

Source: Prepared by author.

of the increasing variety of financial institutions that begin to appear at a given point in the economic growth of a country:

> Among them are savings banks, commercial banks, long-term credit institutions, venture capital companies, institutions providing advisory financial services . . . all of them involved in mobilizing resources from some individuals and entities and transferring them to others.[65]

Ever since the early 1960s, many Latin American countries have gradually entered this phase, as evidenced by the growth and development of their financial sectors. For instance, the region's real financial assets of commercial banks rose from U.S. $18.7 billion in 1960 to U.S. $65.2 billion in

1975 (constant 1973 dollars). In relative terms, this amounted
to an average annual real growth rate of 9.3 percent for
1961-75.[66] A more precise measure of the rapid expansion of
the financial superstructure is given by the regional coefficient of mobilization of financial resources, shown in Table 2.5.

The regional coefficient increased continuously throughout 1960-73, declined to 19.8 in 1974, and rose to over 28 percent in 1975. Of the countries selected, Argentina registered
an impressive increase in its coefficient, while Mexico exhibited a sharp decline in its coefficient during 1972—the year in
which it abandoned the policies of "stabilizing development."[67]

A final indication of the relaxation of supply and demand
constraints on the rate of capital formation is reflected in the
increasing number and variety of financial institutions. For
example, in 1960 the region had 502 financial institutions, of
which 465 were commercial banks, 22 were official monetary
institutions, and 15 were public development banks. Among the
commercial banks, Mario Rietti notes, 24 were classified as
development banks (mostly private).[68] By 1975, there were
1,291 financial intermediaries, of which 720 were commercial
banks, 24 were official monetary institutions, and 547 were
public development banks, specialized banks, savings banks,

TABLE 2.5

Coefficient of Mobilization of Financial
Resources by the Commercial Banking
System: Selected Countries, 1960-75*

Country	1960-63	1964-67	1968-71	1972	1973	1974	1975
Argentina	15.6	23.4	24.5	34.3	45.3	33.5	61.7
Brazil	21.3	20.6	21.2	26.5	26.1	26.2	24.3
Colombia	14.8	10.4	13.2	12.3	13.4	28.2	16.9
Ecuador	5.1	10.4	10.8	7.9	9.8	12.1	7.8
Mexico	5.1	6.3	4.9	-4.1	2.3	3.9	5.3
Peru	9.4	7.7	14.4	21.9	23.0	5.7	12.6
Venezuela	3.2	6.6	8.1	11.5	17.4	24.1	27.1
Latin America	13.0	14.7	15.7	19.1	21.9	19.8	28.2

*Annual increases in commercial bank credit to the public
and private sectors as a percentage of gross domestic investment.

Source: Derived from Mario Rietti, *Money and Banking in
Latin America* (New York: Praeger, 1979), Table 2.3, pp. 33-
34.

or mortgage banks—all of which specialized in long-term lending.[69] Among the commercial banks 165 were classified as development banks, existing ". . . primarily in Brazil, Costa Rica,
Dominican Republic, Ecuador, Honduras, Mexico, Uruguay and
Venezuela."[70]
newly created development banks are highly specialized; they
provide financial services to specific industries and/or sectors,
such as steel, mining, agriculture, and commerce. Also, a
significant proportion of them tend to be of a private or
mixed nature, although public development banks are by no
means excluded. Evidence seems to indicate that—at least in
Latin America—the latter are more likely to be multipurpose
and to appear earlier in their countries' histories. This general observation applies to public development banks such as
NAFIN, CORFO, and BNDE.

RECENT TRENDS IN
DEVELOPMENT BANKING

Whatever strategies the development bank may choose
during initial industrialization, the economic landscape sooner
or later changes, requiring the bank to reorient its activities
significantly. In particular, it has been argued that during
the early days of industrialization, the development bank tends
to be public or mixed, as well as heavily involved in promotional activities concerned with equity provision and/or enterprise creation. They are also involved in the provision of
technical assistance and related services, such as project
appraisal and follow-up.[71]
In this regard, public and mixed banks seem to enjoy a
comparative advantage, since technical assistance is relatively
expensive for many development banks. In fact,

> Unless an industrial development bank is subsidized
> by the government or is able to make technical
> assistance and advisory functions self-supporting
> through the charging of fees . . . the development
> bank, especially a private bank which is expected
> to show a profit to the owners on its operations,
> cannot as a rule provide them.[72]

The figures do not belie this observation, for out of
189 development banks studied by Geraldo L. Salgado, "the
proportion of public development banks which provide technical

assistance is 70 percent. This proportion is higher than that
of mixed development banks (60%) or private banks (53%)."[73]
Moreover, Salgado found that the provision of technical assistance is directly proportional to the size of the bank. This is
not surprising, for many of the public and mixed banks, such
as CORFO and NAFIN, are large by virtue of their multipurpose
nature—a feature that is peculiar to initial industrialization.

However, with the advent of sustained industrialization,
circumstances not only change in the real sector of the economy but also bring about substantive developments in the
financial sector. Hence, for many of the Latin American countries, the growth of the financial system in general, and of
development banks in particular, cannot be understood without
reference to the inflationary pressures, stabilization policies,
and, more important, the monetary policies implemented since
the 1960s.

Broadly speaking, ever since the 1960s new and specialized
development banks have been established where they did not
already exist, ". . . partly because of the lack of modernization and diversification characterizing the traditional development agencies and partly because of the specialized nature of
the external loans obtained from some international credit institutions."[74] For instance, in Argentina, Chile, Brazil, Peru,
and Colombia, ". . . official external resources intended for
specific sources (in industry, agriculture, energy, etc.) are
no longer transmitted through public institutions but directly
to specialized and private agencies and even to the investor
enterprises themselves."[75] In conjunction with this trend, a
considerable amount of foreign infiltration has taken place, in
some cases leading to the takeover of enterprises in the manufacturing sector. This has led countries like Mexico to implement policies designed to regulate and control the activities of
foreign institutions, particularly transnational corporations.
Mexicanization became the preferred strategy and, as we shall
see, NAFIN has played a key role in its implementation.[76]

Another noteworthy development is the appearance of
development banks to meet the financial requirements of a market characterized by the concentration of income and wealth in
small segments of the population. In this regard, Colombia and
Peru are good examples of countries where private development banks have been created to meet the economic interests
of certain segments of the population and/or regions of the
country. For instance, in Colombia, the Corporación Financiera
de Caldes was established in late 1961 ". . . to help diversify

the economy of the main coffee belt . . .,"[77] and the Corporación Financiera del Norte was created in early 1964

> . . . to promote, organize, develop, provide with
> technical assistance and modernize every type of
> manufacturing, agricultural, stockfarming . . .
> enterprise which furthers the integration and devel-
> opment of Northern Colombia.[78]

In Peru, Peruinvest Compañía de Fomento e Inversiones, S.A., was established to promote the nation's industrial development by encouraging the establishment of new private enterprises.[79] These, in practice, number four: a metalworking plant (in which the development bank holds 41 percent of the shares); an office furniture, and television and radio, manufacturer (31 percent); a firm manufacturing plywood (10 percent); and a general storage enterprise (25 percent). Approximately 81 percent of the development bank's capital is held by shareholders in the United States, Germany, and Switzerland.[80]

    As a result of the high rates of inflation and the institutional weakness of the capital markets of many Latin American countries, new mechanisms were introduced to bridge the gap between savers and investors. In Mexico, under the impetus of the state, private *financieras* (development banks) were able to increase the mobilization of financial resources by offering surplus spending units the opportunity to hold less risky and more diverse financial instruments. Table 2.6 shows the volume of real domestic resources captured by private *financieras* in 1950-75. Between 1960 and 1972 these financial intermediaries had an average annual growth rate of 24.7 percent in real domestic obligations. In absolute terms, the real resources captured by these institutions increased from 5,543.2 to 61,442.0 million pesos. This remarkable increase in the mobilization of domestic resources was the direct outcome of the stabilization policies pursued by the Mexican government throughout the 1960s and early 1970s.[81] The captured funds were channeled to a variety of investments of critical importance to the nation's industrialization drive. In chapters 4 and 5 we shall see that this was accomplished, in large measure, by altering the complex system of marginal reserve requirements demanded of private *financieras*.

    Turning to Table 2.6 once again, there was a sharp drop in the real value and attractiveness of the securities issued by these institutions with the abandonment of the stabilization

TABLE 2.6

Real Domestic Resources Captured by
Private *Financieras* in Mexico, 1950–75
(millions of 1960 pesos)

Year	Total	Increase (percent)
1950	925.2	—
1951	1,190.2	28.6
1952	1,354.4	13.8
1953	935.2	−31.0
1954	1,039.2	11.1
1955	1,077.2	3.7
1956	1,559.8	44.8
1957	1,960.8	25.7
1958	1,943.6	−17.2
1959	3,724.2	91.6
1960	5,543.2	48.8
1961	5,528.8	−0.3
1962	7,167.4	29.6
1963	8,815.8	23.0
1964	10,902.1	23.7
1965	14,015.4	28.6
1966	19,330.8	37.9
1967	25,661.2	32.7
1968	30,557.1	19.1
1969	39,361.5	28.8
1970	47,789.9	21.4
1971	54,351.3	13.7
1972	61,442.0	13.1
1973	56,051.2	−8.8
1974	53,739.9	−4.1
1975	55,923.9	4.1

Sources: Computed from Mario
Rietti, *Money and Banking in Latin
America* (New York: Praeger, 1979),
Table 4.1, p. 68; and NAFIN, *La
economía mexicana en cifras* (México,
D.F.: NAFIN, 1978).

program in late 1972. Similar but less dramatic financial developments have taken place in Brazil, Colombia, and Venezuela.

In summary, with the development and growth of an economy along private lines in this late-late industrialization period, development banks are likely to become part of a group of specialized institutions providing financial services to leading foreign and domestic economic interests. This pattern of development is a trademark of the more recent institutions, and it has also affected the activities of older public and/or mixed institutions, such as NAFIN. In fact, it seems that for many development banks the evolutionary sequence has been from term finance to industrial promotion and management in the early days of industrialization. This scenario led the managing director of the Industrial and Mining Development Banks of Iran to remark in 1975:

> Looking to the more distant future, it is perhaps
> a moot point when the development function of a
> financial institution might take a less dominant
> place as against its investment and merchant func-
> tions. We have to be ready for the day when this
> happens, as it happened perhaps to the Industrial
> Bank of Japan or some of the French banks. We
> feel that in the long run we should be working
> towards a fully integrated banking function, pro-
> viding a full range of services with a number of
> closely affiliated banking institutions.[82]

SUMMARY AND CONCLUSIONS

This chapter has reviewed a number of leading issues in the theory of financial intermediation, so as to better understand the role played by development banks in the period of late-late industrialization. The discussion began with an inquiry into the theoretical underpinnings of a financial system that was functionally neutral. By this we meant a system that came into existence in order to passively meet the financial requirements of the essentially private, profit-oriented real sector of the economy. This model provided a frame of reference from which we could analyze and compare other types of financial systems. The distinction was made between financial systems that are essentially passive, such as the demand-following type, and the more active ones, placed under the general heading of developmental financing systems.

In particular, we were interested in the nature and evolution of supply- and demand-leading financing arrangements insofar as they gave rise to what I call special intermediaries: development banks. The emergence of the latter was reviewed within the historical and institutional evolution of the financial sector in Latin America, with particular emphasis on the relatively more advanced countries. A number of interesting observations were made with regard to the fact that not only are new institutions created, but older ones reorient their activities as a result of what I call adaptive modification.

The discussion then became simpler and more abstract as we proceeded to analyze the structural components and functions of a representative development bank. Its definition, possible classification, conflict of purposes, and sources of funds were discussed from both a theoretical and an empirical viewpoint. Of importance was the fact that the classification by ownership, although useful from a pedagogical standpoint, was found to be wanting in explaining the behavior of mixed banks. Other factors, such as the sources and costs of funds, might lead to a better understanding of their behavior.

The next section focused on the question of whether the development bank has a positive impact on the rate of capital formation; the hypothesis of limited impact was revisited. With the aid of a prototype financial model it was shown that, to the extent that initial industrialization is constrained by a shortage of an effective demand for long-term capital, the development bank may play a significant role in mobilizing the productive use of the idle savings in many developing nations during this phase. Finally, we briefly reviewed recent trends in the continuing evolution of development banking, with special emphasis on the Latin American experience. It was found that the more recent institutions have become quite specialized in the financial services they provide, perhaps indicating a lesser role for the development bank in the not too distant future.

NOTES

1. Joseph A. Kane, *Development Banking* (London: Lexington Books, 1975), p. 14.
2. John G. Gurley and Edward S. Shaw, "Financial Aspects of Economic Development," *American Economic Review* 45, no. 1 (September 1955): 516-17.
3. Ibid., p. 516.

4. John G. Gurley and Edward S. Shaw, "Financial Inter-mediaries and the Saving-Investment Process," *Journal of Finance* 11 (May 1956): 258.

5. Ibid., p. 257.

6. Gurley and Shaw, "Financial Aspects," p. 519.

7. John G. Gurley and Edward S. Shaw, "Financial Structure and Economic Growth," *Economic Development and Cultural Change* 15, no. 3 (April 1967): 257-68.

8. Ibid., p. 257.

9. Gurley and Shaw, "Financial Structure."

10. *Economic Bulletin for Latin America* (United Nations) 16 (1971): 1-56.

11. Hugh T. Patrick, "Financial Development and Economic Growth in Underdeveloped Countries," *Economic Development and Cultural Change* 14, no. 2 (January 1966): 81.

12. Gurley and Shaw, "Financial Structure," pp. 257-65.

13. *EBLA*, p. 4.

14. See John G. Gurley, "Hacia una teoría de las estructuras financieras y el desarrollo económico," in *Estructura financiera y desarrollo económico* (Buenos Aires: Editorial del Instituto Torcuato di Tella, 1968), p. 89.

15. *EBLA*, pp. 4-5.

16. Alexander Gerschenkron, *Economic Backwardness in Historical Perspective* (Cambridge, Mass.: Harvard University Press, 1966), p. 46.

17. Kane, op. cit., p. 6.

18. *EBLA*, pp. 1-5.

19. Kane, op. cit., p. 20.

20. Roger D. Hansen, *Mexican Economic Development: The Roots of Rapid Growth* (Washington, D.C.: National Planning Association, 1971), p. 16.

21. Ibid., pp. 16-17.

22. Raymond W. Goldsmith, *La estructura financiera y el crecimiento económico* (México, D.F. Centro de Estudios Monetarios Latinoamericanos, 1963), p. 111.

23. Ibid., p. 112.

24. Douglas Bennett and Kenneth Sharpe, "The State as Banker and Entrepreneur: The Last Resort Character of the Mexican State's Economic Intervention, 1917-1970," in Sylvia A. Hewlett and Richard S. Weinert, eds., *Brazil and Mexico: Patterns in Late Development* (Philadelphia: ISHI, 1982), p. 178.

25. Ibid., p. 179.

26. *EBLA*, p. 13.

27. 27. Raymond W. Goldsmith, *The Financial Development of Mexico* (Paris: OECD, 1961), p. 12.

28. Ibid., p. 30.

29. Werner Baer, *Industrialization and Economic Development in Brazil* (Homewood, Ill.: Yale University-Economic Growth Center, 1965), p. 90.

30. Ibid., p. 110.

31. Ibid., p. 108.

32. Jorge Mustaffa and Alberto Varillas, *Capacitación de personal en el banco de desarrollo de América Latina*, I (Lima: ALIDE, 1976), p. 51.

33. Ibid., p. 51.

34. Ibid., p. 48.

35. E. T. Kuiper, "The Promotional Role of a Development Finance Company," in William Diamond, ed., *Development Finance Companies* (Baltimore: Johns Hopkins University Press, 1968), p. 5.

36. Kane, op. cit., p. 13.

37. J. D. Nyhart and E. F. Janssens, *Global Directory of Development Finance Institutions in Developing Countries* (Paris: OECD, 1967), p. 5.

38. See chapter 4, section "NAFIN's Promotion of Basic Industry during the Portillo Administration."

39. Nyhart and Janssens, op. cit., p. 2.

40. Ibid., p. 65.

41. See ibid., p. 57.

42. Kane, op. cit., p. 24.

43. Nyhart and Janssens, op. cit., p. 253.

44. Shirley Boskey, *Problems and Practices of Development Banks* (Baltimore: Johns Hopkins University Press, 1959), pp. 3-4.

45. Kane, op. cit., p. 20.

46. Ibid., p. 24.

47. Nyhart and Janssens, op. cit., pp. 246-47.

48. An informative review of CORFO's activities is provided by Markos Mamalakis in "An Analysis of the Financial and Investment Activities of the Chilean Development Corporration: 1939-1964," *Journal of Development Studies* 5, no. 2 (January 1969): 118-37.

49. J. F. Weston and E. F. Brigham, *Managerial Finance*, 6th ed. (Hinsdale, Ill.: Dryden Press, 1977), p. 30.

50. Geraldo L. Salgado, "Performance of Public, Private and Mixed Development Banks" (master's thesis in finance, University of Illinois, Urbana, 1974), p. 33.

51. Hugh T. Patrick, "The Mobilization of Private Gold Holdings," *Indian Economic Journal* 11, no. 2 (October–December 1963).

52. Ibid., p. 179.

53. Hugh T. Patrick, "Japan," in Rondo Cameron, ed., *Banking in the Early Stages of Industrialization* (New York: Oxford University Press, 1967).

54. Harry Markowitz, "Portfolio Selection," *Journal of Finance* 7, no. 1 (March 1952): 77–91.

55. Kane, op. cit., p. 34.

56. Haim Ben-Shahar, "Capital Formation and Government Policy in Developing Countries," *Journal of Development Studies* 4, no. 1 (October 1967): 86–96.

57. Kane, op. cit., p. 34.

58. S. S. Nadkami, "Development Banks and Project Promotion," in *Development Banking in the 1980s* (New York: United Nations, 1980).

59. Kane, op. cit., p. 34.

60. Ibid., p. 36.

61. Ibid., p. 35.

62. See Michael D. Intriligator, *Econometric Models, Techniques, and Applications* (Englewood Cliffs, N.J.: Prentice-Hall, 1978), pp. 28–51.

63. Ray C. Fair and Dwight M. Jaffee, "Methods of Estimation for Markets in Disequilibrium," *Econometrica* 40, no. 3 (May 1972): 497–514.

64. William Diamond, "Notes on Purposes and Strategies," in William Diamond and V. S. Raghavan, eds., *Aspects of Development Bank Management* (Baltimore: Johns Hopkins University Press, 1982), pp. 52–55.

65. Ibid., p. 54.

66. For a comprehensive analysis, see Mario Rietti, *Money and Banking in Latin America* (New York: Praeger, 1979).

67. Throughout 1955–72, the Mexican monetary authorities induced privately owned deposit banks (and subsequently *financieras*) to meet their marginal reserve requirement ratio by acquiring bonds and issues of public enterprises. Failure to do so meant that any additional funds acquired by these institutions had to be held as nonearning cash in the vaults of the Banco de México. (See chapters 4 and 5.)

68. Rietti, op. cit., p. 39.

69. Ibid., p. 42.

70. Ibid.

71. For further detail see *La banca de fomento* (Santiago, Chile: ALIDE, 1977).

72. See Robert Adler, *Public External Financing of Development Banks in Developing Countries* (Eugene, Ore.: Bureau of Business and Economic Research, 1966), p. 20.

73. Salgado, op. cit., pp. 62–63.

74. *EBLA*, p. 62.

75. Ibid.

76. See chapter 3, pp. 76–78.

77. *EBLA*, p. 18.

78. Nyhart and Janssens, op. cit., p. 65.

79. Ibid., p. 66.

80. Ibid., p. 309.

81. See chapter 5, "Structure and Organization of the Financial Sector."

82. Diamond, op. cit., p. 44.

3
Historical And Institutional Evolution Of Nacional Financiera, S.A.

INTRODUCTION

This chapter will investigate the historical and institutional development of Nacional Financiera (NAFIN) since its creation in 1934. During this period, the Mexican economy has experienced a number of significant developments in the structure of its basic industry and infrastructure—all of which have altered, in one form or another, the policies and operations of NAFIN and related agencies. This reorientation of the bank's basic goals and activities, in the face of the changing size and nature of the financial requirements of industry, is at the heart of the discussion that follows.

The first section will sketch the economic, social, and political landscape that emerged after the revolution. It was in many respects dismal, as attested by the available figures on population, real national product, agricultural production, and industrial output.* Yet it will be argued that "From the long range point of view the effects of the Revolution on the Mexican economy . . . were far from entirely, or even predominantly negative."[1] The reason for this is that between the mid-1920s and the beginning of World War II, a number of institutional developments took place that might not have occurred, or would have been delayed indefinitely, had the revolution not taken place. By and large, these developments

---

*The exception was oil production, which grew continuously during the revolution and after.

have been responsible for the economic growth and political
stability that the country enjoyed until recently. To put it
bluntly, the Mexican state created a legal-institutional appara-
tus conducive to business activity during this period.

The historical presentation outlined above sets the stage
for a detailed investigation of NAFIN's financial evolution. The
investigation will be divided into four distinct but related
periods corresponding to the next four sections of this chapter.

First, the formative years under the Cárdenas administration (1934-40) will be reviewed. In that period the bank
delved into a variety of activities in search of its proper role
and identity in the emerging financial system. Second, the
bank's crucial participation in the industrialization drive of
the 1940s will be analyzed. Particular attention will be devoted
to NAFIN's entrepreneurial functions, its provision of risk
capital as well as its participation in the creation of key enterprises. In the process, the special relationship between the
private and public sectors of the Mexican economy will be
partially revealed.

Next, we consider the reorientation of NAFIN's basic
policies and operations as it entered the stage of sustained
industrialization which may be roughly dated to the early or
mid-1950s. In particular, we will be interested in determining
whether the promotional activities of the bank diminished in
importance relative to its purely financial functions. Put differently, does demand for capital become less of a constraint on
the rate of capital formation as a country reaches the late-late
industrialization period? Also, we will examine the role that
NAFIN played in the "mexicanization" strategy begun during
the administration of Adolfo López Mateos (1958-63).

The final section is devoted to analyzing the operations
of Nacional Financiera under the administration of President
José López Portillo (1976-82). The interest in this period is
twofold: a renewed emphasis on the promotion of basic industry,
especially undertakings requiring large commitments of capital
and specialized manpower, took place; and the ratio of external
loan capital to direct foreign investment increased dramatically.
Needless to say, Nacional Financiera was an integral component not only through securing medium- and long-term loans
from international agencies, but also by virtue of its participation in a number of joint ventures with foreign multinational
corporations.

HISTORICAL AND ECONOMIC BACKGROUND

Mexican economic growth and political stability during the twentieth century have been largely the result of active state participation and the expansion of centralized political power. These features, by no means unique to the events that have transpired since the revolution of 1910-17, can be traced to the "Porfiriato"—the period of the dictatorship of Porfirio Díaz (1876-1911). Under his iron rule political stability was achieved, in large measure, by the creation of a political machine that ". . . went through the motion of 're-electing' the dictator every four years."[2] Those who dared oppose Díaz and the economic and political policies of his "científicos"* were dealt with harshly, being imprisoned, sent out of the country, or killed. In fact,

> Díaz, with the backing of generals, clergy, hacendados and merchants assumed all powers of government. Congress was only a showcase which Díaz referred to as "my herd of horses." Those with the strength to threaten his power were bought off with government contracts, a governorship, or an army command—all means for great personal profit.[4]

Be that as it may, the political stability and apparent peace of the Díaz regime did pave the way for a development strategy that called for strong state participation. This strategy demanded that the state take ". . . all measures necessary to encourage large amounts of foreign investment to come to Mexico."[5] Given this outlook, it is not surprising that between 1884 and 1911 foreign direct investment rose from 100 million pesos to 33.4 billion.[6] In this connection, Alfredo Navarrete notes that for the 1900-1910 decade, foreign direct investment constituted 66 cents of every dollar invested in Mexico.[7] Much of this investment originated in the United States, Great Britain, and France. In fact, as of 1911, for every dollar of foreign investment, the United States and Great Britain accounted for a little over 67 cents.[8] The bulk of this was

---

*A small group of advisers who helped formulate and implement the economic and social policies of the Díaz regime. Many of them used their privileged position to amass great fortunes, whether by fair means or foul.[3]

concentrated in railroads, mining, petroleum, and real estate.
French capital flowed into industry and banking, where it
constituted 55 and 60 percent of all foreign investment, respectively.[9]

The only sector of the economy that escaped foreign
domination and control was the hacienda, which pervaded agriculture. The hacendados, who formed the backbone of the
Díaz regime, benefited greatly from the expropriation of Indian
and church lands made possible by state action in the form of
laws, policies, and military support. For instance, the law of
1894 dropped all limitations on what lands could be appropri-
ated and on how large landholdings could be.[10] Moreover, it
placed the burden of proof of title on those who occupied the
lands—the latter were, in many instances, ignorant of the
"legal" system or too poor to pay court fees. When these legal
avenues did not produce the desired effect, the Mexican army
was called in to crush the "insurgents." A case in point was
the genocidal wars against the Yaqui Indians in the state of
Sonora; this proud and courageous people fought the Mexican
army for decades rather than hand over their fertile lands to
rich commercial farmers and land companies.

Some understanding of the dimensions of land concentration may be gained by noting that by the end of the Díaz
regime,

> . . . close to 90 percent of Mexico's rural families
> held no land, and many of them were tied to haci-
> endas through the debt bondage system. . . . At
> no time in history had more Mexicans been landless.
> . . . And, at the other extreme, were several thou-
> sand haciendas, some of them millions of acres in
> size, or larger than several American states.* Close
> to 50 percent of Mexico's rural population lived on
> these haciendas. Together, the land companies and
> the hacendados owned over half the nation's terri-
> tory.[12]

The excesses of the Porfiriato, however, did not endure,
for by the end of the decade 1900-10 widespread discontent
had set in, not only among the peasants and workers, but

---

*One individual owned 17 million acres in the state of
Chihuahua, a tract larger than the state of West Virginia.[11]

also among intellectuals, small businessmen, and progressive
landowners. It became even stronger as a result of the violent
suppression of the 1906 strike by workers at the U.S.-owned
copper mines in Cananea, Sonora, and the world depression of
1907.[13] Eventually Díaz lost even the support of the wealthy,
who feared that he couldn't stop the forces of Francisco Madero,
and was forced to resign and go into exile. By then the revolution had cast an imposing shadow upon Mexican society, and
the twin issues of foreign domination and concentration of land
ownership could no longer be ignored.

The end of major combats by 1916 and the writing of a
new constitution on February 5, 1917, under the leadership of
Venustiano Carranza, brought the revolution to a close. If
under the rule of Díaz the role of the state in economic matters
increased, its powers were vastly expanded by the reformist
articles of the 1917 constitution. In particular, articles 27
(agrarian reform), 28 (regulating monopolies), and 123 (labor
legislation) served ". . . to guarantee the implementation of
social reforms proclaimed during the revolution and to estab-
lish the political stability needed for national economic development."[14] This reaffirmation of the public's interventionist role
was in response to the demands of newly mobilized peasants
and workers who believed that their will had ". . . been
passed to the state in such a manner that the will of the state
was at the same time the will of the people."[15]

Still, the implementation of progressive measures included
in the constitution proved to be a slow and arduous process
that spanned the 1020s and 1930s. The revolution had taken
a heavy toll, in terms not only of human lives but also of
sharp production declines in manufacturing, mining, and agriculture, and the destruction of railways. Some indication of
the violence and economic disruption may be obtained by
noting that "Deaths caused by the Revolution probably ran well
above one million, close to 1 out of every 15 persons in the
country."[16] The growth of real national product declined from
an annual rate of approximately 3 percent during 1895-1910 to
a dismal 0.7 percent in 1910-20; it rose only to an average of
1.7 percent (-0.2 percent per capita) per year between 1922
and 1929.[17] Moreover, the depression of the 1930s did not
help matters:

> By 1932 real gross national product had fallen below
> that of 1910. The mining industry, which accounted
> for 10 percent of total output in 1929 was again
> particularly hard hit. Over the next five years,

mineral production fell by 32 percent. In addition,
agricultural output fell by 2 percent. Manufacturing held to its pre-depression proportion of
13 percent of total real product.[18]

In spite of the sluggish performance of the Mexican economy from the early 1920s to 1940, a number of institutional
developments took place that would prove to be extremely important for the post-1940 industrialization drive—not the least
of them was the creation of a national party, the PNR (Partido
Nacional Revolucionario). The latter enabled General Calles to
maintain personal power and, more important, created peaceful
avenues for the resolution of potentially violent disputes between the powerful figures (caudillos) who emerged from the
revolution. The political and social stability that prevailed
under the leadership of Calles (1925-34) permitted the state
to embark upon a number of undertakings whose immediate
objective was the reorganization and reconstruction of a financial system on the verge of collapse. The Bank of Mexico was
created in 1925 to help channel private funds into high-priority
sectors, as well as to attract savings to finance public investment projects. This was followed by the creation of the Agrarian Credit Bank (1926), the National Bank for Urban and Public Works Mortgages (1933), and, of particular importance for
this study, the Nacional Financiera in April 1934. Notwithstanding these accomplishments, perhaps the most significant
development of the period was the formation of a general orientation toward the emerging private sector: "Primary reliance
was placed on the private sector, but the state stood prepared
to do what the private sector was unable or unwilling to
do. . . ."[19] The men responsible for this "common outlook"
were referred to as Calles's "técnicos" (technocrats) and came
to occupy a number of key positions at the Ministry of Treasury. In fact, the ministry and the umbrella of financial institutions around it (the Bank of Mexico and, later, Nacional
Financiera) became the most important institutional complex in
the Mexican state, and until recently constituted ". . . the
sole source of well-trained economists in Mexico."[20] (This "in-
house" training was largely the work of Gonzalo Robles, who
as a young man studied engineering in the United States. He
also played a prominent role in the reconstruction and reorganization of the Mexican banking system.[21]) This led Mexican
economist Leopoldo Solis to remark:

There seems to exist little doubt that the essential
aspects of the present Mexican state—and of its

political economy—were formed during the ten years
in which Plutarco Elias Calles dominated the public
life of the country.[22]

The political influence of Calles began to wane as the 1934
elections approached, for Mexico was going through a profound
economic and social crisis. This was partly the result of the
world depression but, more importantly, a broad coalition ranging from peasants to small businessmen believed that the Calles
government was becoming increasingly conservative. Moreover,
the revolutionary rhetoric aside, ". . . it was apparent to all
that corruption was rampant and that many were becoming increasingly rich at the revolution's expense."[23] An outlet for
the growing dissatisfaction of the Mexican people was provided
by the liberal faction of the official party. Its members, who
were mostly of middle-class origins, felt alienated from the
ruling faction and, under the leadership of a humble general
named Lázaro Cárdenas, mounted a successful campaign against
Calles. The latter was practically forced to nominate Cárdenas
for the presidency, since the nomination of his favorite ". . .
would have risked rebellion by peasants and workers whose
salaries were decreasing."[24]

Once Cárdenas assumed the presidency, he began to
implement a number of far-reaching reforms whose economic
and social impact are felt to this day. Mexicans are fond of
saying that Cárdenas "reaffirmed the Revolution." Among the
more striking accomplishments of his administration (1934-40)
were the nationalization of the petroleum industry (1938) and
of many of the railways; the rapid transfer of 45 million-plus
acres of hacienda land to peasants under his far-reaching
agrarian reform program;* a massive public works push; and
the reorganization of the official party into the Partido Revolucionario Mexicano (PRM). The latter was designed to give
peasants and workers a greater degree of participation in the
political process, so that they could be effectively mobilized
against the entrenched interests of hacendados and foreign
monopolies. Needless to say, the role of the state in economic
development expanded still further under the Cárdenas administration; but, as under Calles, ". . . primary reliance was
placed on the private sector, with the state complementing but
not supplanting the role of private capital . . . ."[26] This

---

*The land distributed during the Cárdenas regime was
more than three times the amount distributed by the previous
revolutionary presidents.[25]

pattern was also seen in the behavior of the newly created financial institutions. It is to the detailed investigation of one of the more prominent of these that we now turn.

A PERIOD OF FORMATION: 1934-40

Nacional Financiera (NAFIN) was established by decree on April 24, 1934, to function as "a financial society with the character of a public institution."[27] (Using the typology developed in chapter 2, we may define NAFIN as a public-leaning mixed bank.) The development bank's capital was set at 50 million pesos (nominal), of which 50 percent had to be subscribed by the federal government in the form of series "A" common stock. The remainder was offered to private individuals and credit institutions of a public or private nature through the sale of series "B" stock.* Immediately the federal government contributed 20 million pesos, more than half of it in the form of real estate claims.[28] The reason for this lay in the fact that the Rodríguez administration (1932-34) sought to restore liquidity to a financial system that, as a result of the revolution and the great depression, "had left credit institutions holding unusual amounts of mortgage paper forfeited for nonpayment of loans."[29] There was therefore the need for an institution to which banks could hand over real estate and mortgage paper they were unable or unwilling to hold. NAFIN became that institution and was called upon to ". . . administer, subdivide, colonize, and sell real properties; collect mortgage loans, and organize credit unions and other enterprises which might be needed to liquidate properties and credits."[30] This first phase in the bank's operations was short-lived, however, for by the end of 1935 ". . . the law of Agricultural Credit transferred the function of managing real estate to the exclusive domain of the Banco Nacional de Crédito Agrícola."[31]

NAFIN could now begin to devote its financial resources to fostering the development of what was at the time an almost

---

*In addition, private stockholders elect four of the seven members of the board of directors and the three others are named by the federal government. In the past these three usually have been the finance minister, the minister of industry and commerce, and the minister of national properties.

nonexistent capital market. In 1937 NAFIN issued its own securities with a total value of over 2 million real pesos. According to Calvin Blair, these new securities, or "títulos financieros," were issued with the express purpose of encouraging widespread ownership, so much so that NAFIN rejected numerous offers by credit institutions to purchase the whole amount.[32] Not only did the development bank float securities, but by the end of 1937 it had purchased 7 million pesos' (nominal) worth of stocks and bonds—a figure that represented more than half of its total assets.[33] During this period NAFIN also experimented with its promotional role by buying and selling the stocks of a bank and a major brewery, and underwriting "an issue of bonds to finance a public hospital for children."[34] During 1938 and 1939 the bank was called upon to intervene in the capital market in order to minimize the fluctuations in the prices of public securities. The instability of those prices was largely the result of the uncertainty created by the nationalization of the petroleum industry in March 1938. Despite these events, or perhaps because of them, by 1940 NAFIN was clearly the most influential institution in the Mexican capital market, with purchases and sales worth over 300 million pesos, compared with a mere 11 million pesos in 1935.[35]

These and other developments support the characterization of this period as one in which the bank dedicated itself to consolidating a viable banking system and fostering the emergence of a capital market. However, students of the bank's history would quickly point out that what is conspicuously absent from this period, in light of the institution's subsequent development, is any major attention to industrial promotion. In fact, some would go as far as to say that the 1934-40 period of NAFIN's history is one of "indefiniteness of functions and paucity of activity."[36] This is an unfair depiction of the initial years, for Nacional Financiera came into existence during a time in which most major policies were concentrated on agriculture. The Cárdenas regime regarded the distribution of hacendado land as essential for the economic and social development of the country. The resolution of this problem became even more pressing in view of the hacendados' violent response, which plunged the country into a veritable civil war. To gain some idea of the gravity of the situation, it is sufficient to note that "In a three-month period in 1936 more than 500 were killed in land disputes; in the first years of the Cárdenas administration 2,000 were killed in the state of Veracruz alone."[37]

It is not surprising, therefore, that this highly nationalistic administration did not decisively support the promotional
activities of NAFIN. It was more concerned with restoring the
public trust and that of the private sector (domestic) in the
activities of the federal government. Still, as Calvin Blair
argues, by the end of this period NAFIN had become ". . . a
reasonably robust institution with 18 million pesos (nominal) in
total assets, 47 employees, and a sense of destiny. It had tried
everything and found its character: industrial promotion."[38]
Blair's comment is apt, for by the end of 1940 and through
1947, promotion of basic industry would occupy center stage
in NAFIN's overall operations.

THE INDUSTRIALIZATION DRIVE: 1941-47

This reorientation of the bank's basic goals, as embodied
in the organic law of 1940,* coincided with a change in administration that saw Avila Camacho assume the presidency of
Mexico. Like Cárdenas and Rodríguez before him, he saw the
role of the state as one of complementing the workings of the
market. Despite Camacho's pro-business feelings, as Cárdenas'
handpicked candidate he encountered stiff opposition from
"conservatives whose candidate had widespread backing of anti-
reform interests."[40] In fact, it is hard to say what the margin
of victory was, since the government counted the votes and
"Cárdenas had decided beforehand to rig the election, rather
than risk seeing his reforms swept away by a loss to the
right-wing candidate."[41] Once Camacho was in office, many of
the fears of the private sector proved to be unfounded, for
the newly elected president sought the cooperation and advice
of private entrepreneurs. Besides, the Camacho administration
was more interested in maintaining intact the reforms that

------

*The organic law of December 30, 1940, gave NAFIN
three fundamental functions:

1. To exercise supervision and regulation of the national
securities and long-term credit markets

2. To promote capital investment in the organization and
expansion of industrial enterprises

3. To act as trustee and agent of the federal government
in the issue, contracting, and supervision of government
securities.[39]

Cárdenas had instituted, rather than pursuing further reforms and risking what had already been gained. The private sector was further reassured by the fact that Cárdenas, although still a powerful public figure, in no way attempted to exercise political power over his successor in the manner that had been so prevalent under the rule of Calles. This gave the Camacho administration, if not political independence, a greater degree of flexibility in the implementation of an industrialization program that, among other things, ". . . stimulated private investment, encouraged foreign capital to come in, and tried to improve relations with the U.S."[42]

It should not be inferred from the above remarks, however, that there was a sharp break between the Camacho administration and that of his predecessor. This is shown by the fact that personnel in key financial positions served in both administrations. For instance, Cárdenas's secretary of treasury (*secretario de hacienda*), Eduardo Suárez, retained the same position in the subsequent administration of Avila Camacho, as did Antonio Espinoza de los Mateos, general director of NAFIN.[43] Camacho helped his cause a great deal by conveying the image of a man with bourgeois values and a modicum of religious faith. This enabled him to gain the trust and respect of the business community and perhaps, as a result, NAFIN could become a powerful instrument for extending the state's role in the economy. A similar move under an administration that was perceived as nationalistic and agrarian ". . . might have deterred private investment or provoked a reaction which could have hamstrung NAFIN's operations."[44]

Another important factor contributing to the emergence of NAFIN as a banker of industry and promoter of industrial activity was World War II. The administration of Avila Camacho was faced with severe shortages of consumer and capital goods as a result of the world conflict. This state of affairs called for the implementation of an import-substitution policy in which the major financial institutions of the country would play a key role. The development of industry to produce what was previously imported was financed in part by high levels of foreign exchange and heavy borrowing in foreign capital markets. Wartime demand for agricultural and mineral exports by the United States and Great Britain was responsible for the former, while an agreement between the United States and Mexico to service the Mexican external debt during 1942 contributed to the latter. Calvin Blair notes that from 1942 on, "NAFIN's intervention in foreign capital markets on behalf of credit-seeking private firms was perhaps as important as its own investments were in promoting industrial development."[45]

Thus, after beginning as an institution originally created
to restore liquidity to the banking system and to support government policy in a number of areas, NAFIN found its character
by embarking upon an ambitious program whose objective was
to channel domestic and foreign long-term capital to enterprises that would create new sources of wealth and new centers
of employment.[46] Its investments in stocks, bonds, and other
securities rose from 25 million real pesos in 1940 to over 207
million in 1945, while investment in discounted paper, loans,
and credits jumped from over 12 million pesos in 1940 to 76.4
million in 1945. More importantly, loans and investments to
basic industry increased from 641 million pesos in 1945 to 888
million pesos by 1947, a 38.3 percent increase. Table 3.1 dramatically illustrates this extraordinary increase in NAFIN's
operations.

Not only did Nacional Financiera promote industrial growth
via its credit and security investments but—a first for this
period and one that is of most interest to this study—it
directly participated in the creation of industrial projects and
firms. A case in point is NAFIN's involvement in the formation
of an integrated steel mill at Monclova in the state of Coahuila.
Altos Hornos de México, as the new plant came to be called,
was originally the idea of private bankers and investors, but

TABLE 3.1

Basic Statistics of Nacional Financiera, S.A., 1934–46
(balance in millions of real pesos on December 31
of each year; 1954 = 100)

	1934	1940	1946	Percent [*] Increase (1940–46)
Total financing	90.3	42.3	1,509.4	189.0
Net worth	118.8	40.2	68.9	71.4
Total assets	123.9	76.9	1,207.1	176.1
Credits granted	52.8	9.6	631.0	194.0
Investments and securities	36.9	32.6	1,066.0	322.6

*Computed using an average of 1940 and 1946 figures
as a base.

Sources: El mercado de valores 24, no. 27 (July 6,
1964): 388; La economía mexicana en cifras (México, D.F.:
NAFIN, 1978), pp. 229–31.

the financial and technical requirements of such an undertaking
were far beyond the resources of the original investors. NAFIN
negotiated a credit with the U.S. Export-Import Bank for $6
million to help finance the project.[47] The entrepreneurial functions, however, went beyond the purely financial aspects, for
NAFIN played a crucial role in acquiring the necessary machinery and equipment for the plant. The greater part of it was
secondhand and was obtained primarily in the United States.
For instance, an idle blast furnace was acquired in St. Louis,
a steel roller in Indiana Harbor, and an abandoned train
trestle from the state of Kentucky.[48] In addition, NAFIN se-
cured the technical services of Armco International Corporation*
for the training and advising of young Mexican engineers and
skilled personnel. The success of this venture is attested by
the fact that at the start of its operations in 1944, Altos Hornos
produced only 5,880 tons of steel ingots, which represented
3.4 percent of the national output. Four years later it produced 96,618 tons, one-third of the total in the country.[49]

Similar developments took place with the creation of a
paper and wood company at Atenquique in the state of Jalisco.
NAFIN became a founding stockholder of this company, which
obtains from wood the cellulose that is the main material for
the manufacture of paper. The economic payoff was immediate,
for in 1948, a year after the start of its operations, it was producing 25,773 metric tons of kraft paper (58.4 percent of total
production). Moreover, costly imports of kraft paper were drastically reduced from 10,539 tons in 1947 to 1,438 tons in 1948
even though national consumption remained at roughly its trend
value.[50] Many other examples of enterprises in whose formation
or expansion NAFIN has taken part could be cited; however,
such a discussion is best left for chapter 4, where a detailed
analysis of NAFIN's entrepreneurial activities is taken up. For
now it is sufficient to present Table 3.2, with a complete list
of the companies formed by NAFIN that started operations
between 1941 and 1947.

The full impact of NAFIN's promotional activities is more
precisely revealed by the fact that its real financing to industry increased from 85.4 million pesos in 1942 to 1,228.7 million
pesos by the end of 1947. Relative to the total financing provided to industry by the banking system, its share increased
from 4.8 to 26.7 percent of the total.[51] Also, NAFIN's security

---

*In exchange for $5,335,000 worth of stock in Altos Hornos.

TABLE 3.2

Companies Formed by Nacional Financiera that
Commenced Operations between 1941 and 1947

Year	Name of Company
1941	Chapas y Triplay, S.A.
1942	Nueva Cia. Eléctrica de Chapala y Anercos
1943	Carbonífera Unida de Palau, S.A.
1943	Cementos Guadalajara, S.A.
1943	Unión Forestal de Jalisco y Calimo, S.A.
1944	Altos Hornos de México, S.A.
1944	Guanos y Fertilizantes de México, S.A.
1945	Empacadoras Calidad, S.A.
1947	Cia. Industrial de Atenquique

Source: NAFIN, *NAFINSA and the Economic Development of Mexico* (Mexico City: NAFIN, 1964), p. 77.

investments as a proportion of its productive financing* averaged 79.2 percent for 1941-47. As a result of its promotional activities, by 1947 NAFIN had

> . . . increased to 89 the number of corporations
> in which it held stocks and bonds. One third of
> the 89 corporations were located in the Federal
> District and the neighboring state of Mexico, the
> rest were distributed over seventeen other states.
> NAFIN had invested in practically all of the
> larger enterprises of recent vintage in Mexico.[53]

At this juncture one may well ask why it was necessary for Nacional Financiera to undertake such promotion. In other words, why didn't the private sector go into these areas? One possible explanation is that private investment flowed to traditional sectors, such as commerce and real estate, where the expected return was not necessarily higher, but the degree of risk was considerably lower, than that

---

*Productive financing is the sum of credits and security investments in real terms (1954 = 100).[52]

prevailing in the emerging industrial sector. Another possible explanation is that even when private investors and bankers finished the initial phase of the operations, they could not bring the project to completion because of a lack of necessary capital, technical expertise, and official representation abroad. A good example of such a situation was provided by the establishment of Altos Hornos de México. Needless to say, it was by no means unique to the steel industry, for it occurred in many other industries, including the paper industry. Sugar magnate Aaron Saenz and a group of private entrepreneurs formed the Cia. Industrial de Atenquique in 1941, but before long the financial and technical requirements of the project strained the resources of the group. Government participation was therefore welcomed, and "NAFIN stepped in with financing, first in the form of bonds and preferred stock, but later involving a majority equity position."[54]

This brings us to the final explanation, a political one, for the administration of Avila Camacho, and that of Cárdenas before him, regarded the intervention by the state in the Mexican economy as justifiable when projects of critical importance to national industrialization were at stake. The leaders of Mexico understood that their country needed a variety of investments that exceeded "either the risk-taking proclivities of the private sector or its capacity to mobilize the capital for the venture."[55] To be sure, the state's intervention in a variety of industries initially produced cries of protest from conservative businessmen and political leaders, but they soon died out because it is hard to imagine a set of policies designed to benefit private industry more than those of the Mexican government and NAFIN in particular.

This list by no means exhausts the possible explanations for the unwillingness or inability of the private sector to become actively engaged in the promotion of industry, but it does suggest fruitful avenues for future research. We consider some of them in the remainder of this chapter as well as in subsequent chapters. This is especially true with regard to the last explanation, since the special relationship of NAFIN to the private sector has been influenced, to a greater or lesser extent, by changes in the administration of the federal government.

SUSTAINED INDUSTRIALIZATION AND THE BANK

The third period in NAFIN's evolution as a banker of industry and promoter of industrial activity had begun by 1947, when the bank shifted its emphasis ". . . from investments in

particular firms to greater interest in development of what is
now referred to as infrastructure and heavy industry."[56] Some
indication of the extent to which the bank altered its basic
policy can be obtained by comparing the period between 1940
and 1946 with that from 1946 to 1952. In the former interval—
the industrial promotion phase—investments in securities rose
from 32 million pesos to over 1 billion, while credits—a major
source of financing to infrastructure and heavy industry—rose
only from over 9 million to approximately 443 million real pesos.
The opposite was the case for the latter period, when investments in securities grew from roughly 1 billion to about
1,036.0 million pesos, while credits increased dramatically, to
2,133.6 million pesos, about five times as much.[57]

The reorientation of NAFIN's basic development strategy
can be traced to a combination of economic, social, and political factors. In what follows, we shall concentrate on those
elements that students of the bank's history consider to be the
most telling. To begin with, Blair observes, as Mosk had before him, that by the end of World War II "rapid industrial
expansion had 'caught up' to Mexico's overhead capital facilities. Transport and communication were becoming limiting
factors on the efficient use of industrial capacity and on the
creation of further investment opportunities."[58]

That bottlenecks and shortages of key raw materials were
becoming a major problem is revealed by the fact that the index of volume of manufacturing production dropped almost
3 percent between 1946 and 1947, after averaging an increase
of 7.3 percent per year in 1941-46.[59] Officials at the Bank of
Mexico and NAFIN were aware of this situation and cited the
following factors as responsible for a decrease in the rate
of manufacturing production:

(1) credit intended for productive endeavors
was directed to commercial operations;
(2) deficiencies in the distribution of fuel,
mainly petroleum;
(3) shortages in the supply of electric power;
(4) inadequate railroad service;
(5) labor-management conflicts in basic industries.[60]

To reverse this trend, the Mexican government, under
the leadership of President Miguel Alemán, began to actively
promote the expansion and strengthening of infrastructure
and basic industry. Domestic, and especially foreign, funds

were allocated to irrigation projects, the supply of electric power and fuel, and the creation of an efficient communications system. NAFIN, as the public sector's major investment bank, played a key role. Table 3.3 provides further evidence of the overall change in the bank's direction.

It is readily apparent from Table 3.3 that not only did NAFIN's investments flow to social infrastructure, but that an increasing share of those investments was devoted to the modernization of the nation's railways, highways, maritime traffic, and the construction of important bridges. NAFIN's financing of transportation and communication increased by over 500 percent between 1945 and 1952, at an average rate of 62.6 percent per year.

TABLE 3.3

Distribution of Industrial Financing of NAFIN:
Selected Years, 1945-52
(percent of total)

	1945	1947	1952
Infrastructure	7.6	28.5	54.5
Electricity	1.7	6.3	19.0
Transport and communication	5.9	22.2	35.5
Basic industries	60.4	27.4	17.7
Petroleum and coal	23.4	5.9	3.0
Iron and steel	24.4	15.9	9.3
Cement and construction materials	12.6	5.6	5.4
Other industries	32.0	44.1	27.8
Food and beverages	1.0	4.1	4.7
Textiles and clothing	5.5	6.4	2.7
Other	25.5	33.6	20.4
All industries, percent	100.0	100.0	100.0
All industries, millions of real pesos (1954 = 100)	572.8	888.8	1,659.9

Sources: Derived from Calvin P. Blair, "Entrepreneurship in a Mixed Economy," in Raymond Vernon, ed., *Public Policy and Private Enterprise in Mexico* (Cambridge, Mass.: Harvard University Press, 1964), p. 241; NAFIN, *La economía mexicana en cifras* (México, D.F.: NAFIN, 1978), p. 229.

Another factor explaining NAFIN's shift in policy is one
that, according to Robert T. Aubey, "can never be ignored
when discussing policy in Mexico."[61] He is referring to the
land reform program, the foundations of which were incorporated in article 27 of the 1917 constitution. Its economic and
social impact, however, was not felt until the Cárdenas administration, some 17 years later. During that administration
more land was redistributed to peasants than under all of the
previous revolutionary regimes. Statistically speaking, the
results were impressive: between 1930 and 1940 the *ejido* sector, consisting of communities receiving land, increased its
ownership of total irrigated land from 13.1 percent to 57.3 percent.[62] Some 9.1 percent of the total surface of Mexico was
redistributed, compared with a total of 3.9 percent by the
presidents from Carranza to Cárdenas.[63]

By the time Camacho assumed the presidency of Mexico,
and especially in the administration of Miguel Alemán, the
emphasis shifted away from land redistribution to a general
program that ". . . called for greater expenditures on irrigation and rural electrifiction and for other facilities necessary
to promote agricultural production."[64] An indication of this
commitment to improving productivity may be obtained by noting that between 1940 and 1952, the land benefiting from government irrigation programs jumped from 267,095 to 1,441,736
hectares, compared with a total of only 118,495 hectares during the Cárdenas administration (1934-40).[65] The financing of
these projects and the provision of technical assistance were
entrusted to the agricultural banks and NAFIN. The latter's
role became especially prominent in securing long-term loans
for irrigation projects from such well-known institutions as the
International Bank for Reconstruction and Development (World
Bank) and the Inter-American Development Bank.[66]

The final factor explaining NAFIN's overall change of
direction is directly related to the change in administration
during 1946 that brought Miguel Alemán—a conservative who
sought to allay the fears of certain segments of the business
community that believed that Nacional Financiera was becoming
too competitive—to the presidency. The businessmen we are
referring to are called the New Group by Mosk; they were
". . . composed chiefly of owners of small manufacturing
plants that came into being during the Second World War to
supply articles no longer available from foreign sources in sufficient quantity to satisfy the Mexican market."[67] Moreover,
they were distinctly hostile to joint ventures with foreign interests (especially U.S.), since this process usually involved

the Mexican government in the creation of large enterprises
that had little in common with the firms represented by them.
Thus, in the Reform Law that president Alemán submitted to
Congress, he emphasized the need for the bank to shift away
from active industrial promotion in all areas and to more pro-
tection of private industry and emphasis on the development
of infrastructure. To enable NAFIN to meet its new obligations,
article 5 of the Reform Law increased NAFIN's authorized capital to 100 million nominal pesos from an original 50 million
pesos.[68] The new law also

> . . . confirmed NAFIN as the only institution to
> handle issues of public securities, designated NAFIN
> as sole agent for medium and long-term foreign
> credits requiring government guarantee, and re-
> quired all public agencies and enterprises to obtain
> NAFIN's approval before borrowing abroad.[69]

The reorientation of the bank's goals, although sudden,
was persistent, if we confine ourselves to the method of inserting resources into the economy: more emphasis was placed
on credits than on risk capital as a means to foster industrial
growth. This is attested to by the fact that security investments as a proportion of productive financing declined from
64.2 percent in 1946 to 30 percent in 1955. However, this
evolution of NAFIN's nature and functions did not mean that
its real financing to industry declined; its real financing of
industry as a proportion of the real financing granted by the
banking system steadily increased during the administration of
Adolfo Ruíz Cortínez, from a level of 36.4 percent in 1952 to a
high of 50 percent in 1955. This financial, as opposed to
entrepreneurial, commitment to the promotion of heavy (basic)
industry and infrastructure was continued by the administrations of Adolfo López Mateos (1958-63), Gustavo Díaz Ordaz
1963-69), and Luis Echeverría Alvarez (1970-76). Table 3.4
reveals that in the 1950s, infrastructure began to absorb
about two-thirds of the total real financing by Nacional Financiera, with a sizable share going to electricity and transportation.
   The concentration placed on credits and underwriting to
finance industrial growth since 1948 did not mean the bank's
role in the field of enterprise creation via direct participation
was over. For example, Constructora Nacional de Carros de
Ferrocarril, S.A., was established in 1952 to meet "the growing
demand for railway equipment, the rental of which was costing
large quantities of foreign exchange."[70] Nacional Financiera

TABLE 3.4

Nacional Financiera, S.A.: Financing Granted
by Economic Sector, Selected Years, 1940-74
(percent)

Sector	1940	1953	1963	1974
Total	100.0	100.0	100.0	100.0
Infrastructure	14.5	58.6	60.3	61.5
Industry	11.4	32.6	35.6	30.6
Basic	8.2	18.8	18.4	10.3
Nonbasic	3.2	13.8	17.2	20.3
Other activities	74.1	8.8	4.1	7.9

Sources: NAFIN, Informe anual (México, D.F.: NAFIN,
1953, 1963, 1974); Raymond W. Goldsmith, The Financial Development of Mexico (Paris: OECD, 1961), p. 101.

aided in the promotion of this enterprise through its provision
of risk capital, loans, and underwriting. In 1956 Nacional
Financiera became the founding stockholder of Fertilizantes de
Monclova, S.A., which was to produce nitrogenous fertilizers;
until then, they had mostly been imported. Besides these companies, the bank has provided risk capital to numerous firms
whose activities range from the production of DDT to the
production of electrolytic copper.[71]
    Still, the promotional activities of the bank diminished
in importance relative to its financial and fiduciary functions
as the Mexican economy expanded and developed. Other institutions, such as the private financieras, began to provide
those services. Moreover, a deficiency in effective demand
was becoming less of a constraint on the rate of capital formation as a class of entrepreneurs, the New Group, began to
emerge. As these businesses began to expand, they needed
funds that were not forthcoming from the private banking system, since the latter provided credit to large and well-established industries. Thus, NAFIN, as fiduciary for the federal
government, was given the task of supervising several important funds designed to meet the financial and technical requirements of small and medium-size industry. Of particular
interest are the creation of the Guarantee and Development

Fund for the Promotion of Industry (FOMIN) and the Guarantee and Development Fund for Small and Medium Industry
(FOGAIN).

The latter was created in late 1953 to serve the financial
needs of, as well as provide technical assistance to, medium
and small industry. This development fund was one of the first
of its kind in Latin America to assist labor-intensive industry
through an assortment of financial instruments. The fund's
importance can be appreciated when one considers that in 1976
it authorized 20,617 loans for an amount of 1,879.9 million real
pesos, compared with 12,017 credits for a value of 1,584.8 million pesos in 1972. In 1976 these loans were distributed among
10,712 enterprises, with an average value of 177,000 real pesos
per enterprise, while in 1972 they were distributed among 6,163
firms with an average value of 257,000 real pesos per firm.[72]
The importance of these firms, as of 1976, for the economic
development of the country can be evaluated from the following
indicators:[73]

They represented 14 percent of the total number of
medium-to-small enterprises operating within the country.

They gave employment to about 368,000 workers, practically 39 percent of the labor force employed in small-to-
medium firms.

Their annual sales represented 27 percent of the total
value of annual production by small and medium industrial
concerns.

Their retained earnings represented about 20 percent of
the total assets that these enterprises possess.

Further evidence of the financial resources and employment provided by these firms, according to size, is provided
by Table 3.5.

More than 80 percent of the enterprises give employment
to, at most, 50 workers, and these firms have a capital value
that represents almost 50 percent of the total capital invested
by these 10,712 firms financed by FOGAIN. These industrial
concerns represent lines of activity ranging from textile production to the curing and processing of leather.

FOMIN was created during the Echeverría administration
to promote industry with minor equity investments. By the
late 1970s it was responsible for the evaluation and financing
of 291 projections, 105 of which were provided with risk
capital.[74] This manner of inserting resources into the economy

TABLE 3.5

FOGAIN: Financial Support of Enterprises
According to the Employment They Provide
(millions of real pesos)

	No. of Firms		Capital	
Level of Employment	Absolute	Percent	Absolute	Percent
Total	10,712	100.0	5,617.8	100.0
$\leq$ 50	8,707	81.2	2,726.4	48.5
> 50, $\leq$ 100	1,295	12.2	1,332.4	23.7
> 100	710	6.6	1,559.0	27.8

Sources: El mercado de valores 36, no. 39 (September 27, 1976); NAFIN, *La economía mexicana en cifras* (México, D.F.: NAFIN, 1978), pp. 229-31.

has continued, for, by 1983, "58% of funds channeled by FOMIN were risk capital and the remaining 42% were subordinated loans convertible into shares."[75] Table 3.6 shows that the resources channeled by FOMIN were directed primarily to cement and building materials, food products, machinery and equipment, and chemical products. For fiscal year 1983 actual disbursements and repayments were 293.6 million and 35.1 million, respectively, with a balance in December of 489.3 million pesos. This represents a growth of -.63 percent for the second half of the year and of just 4.6 percent for the full year. This poor growth performance is explained by the worst economic crisis to hit Mexico in five decades. (In chapter 4 we shall review some of the domestic and international factors leading to Mexico's balance-of-payment crisis in 1982.)

Before concluding this section, we shall consider the role that Nacional Financiera played in the all-important mexicanization process initiated during the administration of López Mateos. This strategy was implemented in order to regulate and control the activities of multinational corporations (especially U.S.), and to protect and promote the growth of Mexican industry. Among the industries that have been affected by the vigorous pursuit of this policy are electric power and mining, both of which were characterized by heavy foreign investment. Mexicanization calls for Mexican investors to

TABLE 3.6

FOMIN: Resources Channeled by Economic Activity, 1982-83
(millions of real pesos)

Activity	Balance as of 12-31-82	Movements January-June Disbursements	Movements January-June Recoveries	Balance as of 6-30-83	Movements July-December Disbursements	Movements July-December Recoveries	Balance as of 12-31-83
Industry	463.2	187.8	3.6	489.3	105.8	19.4	486.5
Basic industry	90.0	12.7	0.9	101.8	9.4	—	72.6
Iron and steel	13.0	—	—	13.0	5.0	—	12.7
Cement and building materials	77.0	12.7	0.9	88.8	4.4	—	59.9
Other manufactures	373.2	175.1	2.7	387.5	96.4	19.4	413.9
Food products	73.5	79.1	—	108.1	69.5	2.1	156.4
Textiles	44.8	28.4	1.1	51.1	2.3	1.2	46.5
Wood and cork	19.4	—	—	13.8	—	—	12.3
Cellulose and paper	47.2	1.4	1.4	33.5	—	0.1	29.7
Chemical products	56.4	1.1	0.2	40.6	—	3.0	33.4
Machinery and equipment	63.6	35.5	—	81.2	10.4	6.7	75.6
Others	68.3	29.7	—	59.4	14.2	—	59.9
Other activities	4.4	—	14.2	3.1	—	6.3	2.8
Total	467.6	187.8	17.8	492.4	105.8	17.3	489.3

Sources: NAFIN, Informe anual (México, D.F.: NAFIN, 1983), p. 72; and La economía mexicana en cifras (México, D.F.: NAFIN, 1984), p. 217.

supply at least 51 percent of the equity capital in any joint
venture with foreign concerns. For a number of reasons, it
has often proved difficult for Mexican investors to undertake
the initial expense; thus the Mexican government promoted
mexicanization via tax incentives and concessions, and, more
importantly, it acted as an investor of last resort by using
NAFIN to supply the portion of the risk capital that Mexican
private investors were unwilling and/or unable to provide. For
instance, during 1971, when Anaconda's giant Cananea mine
was mexicanized, NAFIN played a crucial role.

> [It] helped put together the consortium of Mexican
> investors who purchased the 51 percent. Ten per-
> cent of the stock went to Banco Nacional de Mexico
> (a major private banking group), a smaller holding
> was reserved for workers and employees of the
> mine, a number of other private investors took
> small holdings, and NAFIN put in the rest (some
> through Cobre de Mexico, a subsidiary of NAFIN).[76]

A similar course of events took place in the agricultural
machinery industry with the mexicanization of the John Deere
Company. NAFIN had to supply the risk capital because, even
after several years, no private Mexican investors showed any
interest in the equity issues of the company.[77] An incomplete
list of the companies mexicanized between 1967 and 1974 in
which NAFIN has acted as entrepreneur of last resort is provided below.[78]

Azufrera Panamericana, S.A.

Compañía Minera Cananea, S.A.

Compañía Minera Autlán, S.A.

Alimentos del Fuerte, S.A.

John Deere, S.A.

Motores Perkins, S.A.

La Tabacalera Mexicana, S.A.

Condumex, S.A.

Swecomex, S.A.

THE PORTILLO YEARS: 1976-82

The final phase in NAFIN's evolution took place in the administration of José López Portillo, with a renewed emphasis on the promotion of basic industry and especially undertakings requiring large commitments of capital and specialized manpower. Some indication of this development is provided by Table 3.7.

The share of financing channeled to infrastructure declined by about 67 percent between 1974 and 1982 (see Table 3.4), while industry's share increased by about 77 percent. In particular, the fraction going to basic industry increased significantly, especially if we compare 1979-82 with 1969-74. During the latter years (Echeverría presidency) basic industry's share averaged approximately 11.0 percent, while during the former period it averaged 28.0 percent. Most of this increase is explained by a greater financing of the petroleum, steel, chemical, and capital goods industries.[79]

The greater promotion of basic industry is also revealed by the increased willingness of the bank to assume an entrepreneurial role. For example, between 1977 and 1980 the number of enterprises in which NAFIN participated with its own risk capital grew from 74 to 87, an increase of approxi-

TABLE   3.7

Nacional Financiera, S.A.: Financing Granted
by Economic Sector, 1979-83
(percent)

Sector	1979	1980	1981	1982	1983
Infrastructure	55.7	55.0	45.6	20.0	20.5
Industry	28.4	29.0	32.4	54.1	54.0
1. Basic	16.7	17.0	23.1	41.8	41.4
2. Nonbasic	11.7	12.0	9.3	12.3	12.6
Other activities	15.9	16.0	22.0	25.9	25.5
Total	100.0	100.0	100.0	100.0	100.0

Sources: NAFIN, *Informe anual* (México, D.F.: NAFIN, 1980-83); and *La economía mexicana en cifras* (México, D.F.: NAFIN, 1984).

TABLE 3.8

Nacional Financiera, S.A.: Newly Created Enterprises, 1980–81
(millions of current pesos)

Enterprise and Partners	(1)	(2)	(3)	(4)	(5)
Turalmex, S.A.	540.0	1,058.0	348	7–80	1983
NAFIN	405.0				
Brown, Boveri & Co., Ltd.	135.0				
Industrial Group NKS, S.A.	5,895.0	16,074.0	2,062	9–80	1984
Kobe Steel (Japan)	1,945.4				
NAFIN	1,974.8				
SIDERMEX	1,974.8				
Nitro-cellulose Industries of Mexico, S.A.	260.0	667.0	117	10–80	1983
Defense Department	104.0				
NAFIN	78.0				
Union of Explosives/Río Tinto, S.A. (Spain)	39.0				
Hispanic–Mexican Coinversion Fund	39.0				
Productora Mexicana de Tubería, S.A.	1,300.0	3,700.0	1,110	11–80	1982
Sumitomo Metal Industries (Japan)	520.0				
NAFIN	442.0				
SIDERMEX	338.0				

80

	(1)	(2)	(3)	(4)	(5)
Tubinas y Equipos Industriales, S.A.	144.0	1,800.0	617	7-81	1983
NAFIN	100.8				
Suizer Brothers, Ltd. (Swiss)	43.2				
Tractor factory	1,100.0	4,050.0	760	9-81	1983
NAFIN	660.0				
Ford	440.0				

(1) = Capital subscribed.
(2) = Total investment.
(3) = Employment generated.
(4) = Date of initiation.
(5) = Date of actual operation.

Source: NAFIN, *Informe anual* (México, D.F.: NAFIN, 1981), pp. 132–33.

mately 18 percent. The majority of these firms were in the
steel, chemical, and capital goods industries, and generated
over 40,000 jobs, about a 36 percent increase.[80] Moreover,
during this period NAFIN entered into a number of joint ventures with foreign concerns: the creation of Turalmex, S.A.
(July 1980), with the Swiss firm Brown, Boveri and Co. Ltd.,
and the creation of a tractor factory with Ford Motor Company
(September 1981). An exhaustive list of the joint ventures
initiated during 1980-81 and the employment generated by
them, along with other relevant statistics, is provided by
Table 3.8.

These figures are of special interest because of the high
proportion of risk capital subscribed by NAFIN—for instance,
in the case of Turalmex, S.A., its share hovers around 75
percent. A more complete picture of NAFIN's entrepreneurial
activities is given by Table 3.9, which displays the sectoral
distribution of the bank's equity investments for 1980-82. By
and large, these investments are concentrated in iron and
steel, chemical products, and electrical products and machinery.

TABLE 3.9

Nacional Financiera, S.A.: Stock Movements and
Balances by Branch of Economic Activity, 1980-82
(percent)

Sector	1980	1981	1982
Infrastructure	3.8	1.4	1.4
Industry	93.2	95.2	95.6
Basic	53.7	50.1	46.8
Iron and steel	44.5	41.3	37.3
Mining	5.7	5.8	4.0
Other	3.5	3.0	5.8
Nonbasic	39.5	45.1	48.8
Chemical products	21.8	30.8	25.7
Machinery and electrical products	7.9	8.0	16.4
Textiles	1.6	1.3	3.2
Other	8.2	5.0	3.5
Other activities	3.0	3.4	3.0
Total	100.0	100.0	100.0

Source: NAFIN, Informe anual (México, D.F.: NAFIN,
1981-83).

On an aggregate level, NAFIN's share in the total equity
investments of the banking system in industry rose from
31.3 percent in 1973 to approximately 40 percent by 1977,
an increase of about 27.8 percent.[81] One final indication of
this trend is that the development bank's share in total real
financing to industry jumped from 34.9 percent in 1973 to
45.9 percent in 1979, the latest year for which we have reliable figures.[82]

In light of these and other indicators, it is evident that
NAFIN's role in enterprise creation and supervision is far from
over in the 1980s. Still, in comparison with the industrialization drive of the 1940s, NAFIN's promotional efforts have become more specialized; the bank is no longer delving into
every type of industrial activity, but concentrating its promotional activities on specific sectors, such as chemicals
and steel. It has delegated responsibility for many of the
activities in which it was once directly involved to trust funds
and specialized agencies that have, by and large, assumed a
life of their own. Moreover, private *financieras* and long-term
credit institutions have emerged to meet the ever-increasing
financial needs of certain industrial sectors once served by
NAFIN. Thus, as mentioned in chapter 2, NAFIN is in the
process of becoming one of a group of specialized institutions
providing entrepreneurial and financial services to leading
foreign and domestic economic interests.

One area in which the development bank has played, and
still plays, a prominent role is the acquisition of long-term
capital from international agencies and foreign banks. Between
1981 and 1983 Nacional Financiera's external debt increased by
49 percent, compared with a growth of 25 percent for 1979-81.
Its balance outstanding on foreign borrowings rose from
$9,451.9 million to $12,948.6 million, resulting in a net indebtedness of $3,496.7 million.* As can be seen from Table 3.10,
the greater part of this debt has been in the form of direct
loans, especially long-term.**

The relative importance of these figures is clearly indicated by Table 3.11, which shows that NAFIN's external debt
for 1979-83 averaged over 22 percent of the total public sector

---

*The difference of $123.2 million is explained by fluctu-
ations in the exchange rate during this period.

**An increasing proportion of these loans has been ob-
tained from foreign, especially U.S., banks.

TABLE 3.10

Nacional Financiera, S.A.: Total External Debt, 1979–83
(millions of dollars)

	1979	1980	1981	1982	1983
Direct loans	5,684.2	6,079.7	7,084.7	10,854.7	10,591.2
Long-term*	5,567.2	6,059.7	6,424.7	8,537.1	8,105.5
Short-term	117.0	20.0	660.0	2,317.6	2,485.7
Guarantees and endorsements	1,880.9	2,068.6	2,367.2	2,456.9	2,357.4
Total	7,565.1	8,148.3	9,451.9	13,311.6	12,948.6

*Contracted for one year or more.
Sources: NAFIN, Informe anual (México, D.F.: NAFIN, 1980–83); El mercado de valores 42,
no. 47 (November 22, 1982): 200.

TABLE 3.11

NAFIN's Share in the Total Public Sector Debt, 1979–83
(millions of dollars)

Year	Total Public Sector Debt	Annual Increase (percent)	NAFIN's Share (percent)	Total Public Sector Long-term Debt	NAFIN's Share (percent)
1979	29,757.2	13.3	25.4	28,315.0	20.1
1980	33,812.8	13.6	24.1	32,322.0	18.8
1981	52,960.6	56.6	17.8	42,206.7	15.2
1982	58,874.2	11.2	22.6	49,548.7	17.2
1983	63,874.2	8.5	20.3	63,874.2	12.7

Sources: Computed from NAFIN, *Informe anual* (México, D.F.: NAFIN, 1980–84), and *La economía mexicana en cifras* (México, D.F.: NAFIN, 1984), p. 241.

debt. NAFIN's role in securing long-term loans has diminished, as indicated by a fall in its share from 20.1 percent of the total in 1979 to 12.7 percent in 1983. The sharp fall between 1982 and 1983 was the direct result of the financial and economic crisis afflicting the country. NAFIN did not receive any new funds during 1982 from the international commercial banks. An indication of their importance to NAFIN's overall operations is revealed in Table 3.12, which shows the structure of NAFIN's total foreign debt by source for 1982-83. Along with multilateral agencies such as the World Bank and the Inter-American Development Bank, international commercial banks provided NAFIN with over 80 percent of its direct debt. Although private banks are important suppliers of both long-

TABLE 3.12

Nacional Financiera, S.A.: Structure of Foreign Debt (millions of dollars)

Item	Balance as of 12-31-82	Percent	Balance as of 12-31-83	Percent
Total	13,311.6	100.0	12,948.6	100.0
Direct debt	10,782.4	81.0	10,591.2	81.8
Private banks	6,509.4	48.9	6,262.3	48.4
Organizations and suppliers	4,273.0	32.1	4,328.9	33.4
EXIMBANK	186.4	1.4	218.3	1.7
World Bank	1,983.4	10.5	1,368.0	10.5
IDB	1,397.7	14.9	2,028.9	15.7
IDA	39.9	0.3	31.3	0.2
IFAD	1.1	0.0	7.8	0.1
Other creditors	665.6	5.0	674.6	5.2
Guarantees	2,529.2	19.0	2,357.4	18.2
EXIMBANK	252.9	1.9	227.2	1.7
World Bank	639.0	4.8	567.3	4.4
Other creditors	1,637.3	12.3	1,562.9	12.1

Source: NAFIN, Informe anual (México, D.F.: NAFIN, 1983), p. 52.

TABLE 3.13

NAFIN: Direct Loans Granted to NAFIN
by the World Bank, 1949-82
(thousands of dollars)

Use	Amount Approved	Structure (percent)
Total	4,976,700	100.0
Irrigation	1,165,500	22.4
Industrial	964,300	18.5
Agriculture and livestock	925,000	17.7
Electric power	704,800	13.5
Rural development	511,000	9.8
Highway	266,800	5.1
Tourism	114,000	2.7
Higher education	90,000	1.7
Other*	235,300	4.6

*Includes potable water, pollution control, mining, air-
ports, and ports.
Source: NAFIN, Informe anual (México, D.F.: NAFIN,
1982), p. 103.

and short-term loans, international institutions such as the
World Bank specialize in the provision of soft long-term loans
to projects deemed of critical importance to the country. Thus,
they play a far more important role in enabling the bank to
meet its development objective. From the World Bank, for instance, between January 1949 and December 1981, NAFIN
obtained 65 medium-to-long-term loans with a total value of
over $4.8 billion. In 45 of these NAFIN is sole debtor, in 17
a partner in debt, and in the remaining 3 endorser.[83] A high
proportion of these funds has been channeled to the rural
sector, which, as of December 1981, had received direct loans
having a cumulative value of $1,205 million. Other sectors that
have benefited substantially from the intervention of NAFIN
are energy (especially electricity and petroleum), transportation, and communications. Table 3.13 gives an indication of
the magnitude and structure of the credits granted by the
World Bank to NAFIN as of June 30, 1982.

The Inter-American Development Bank granted direct
loans to NAFIN with a total value of $2,194 million through

TABLE 3.14

NAFIN: Loans Granted by the IDB as of June 30, 1982
(thousands of dollars)

Use	Amount Approved	Structure (percent)
Total	2,326,419	100.0
Irrigation	829,987	35.7
Agriculture and livestock	409,482	17.6
Industrial	342,479	14.7
Rural development	175,275	7.6
Mining	145,416	6.3
Higher education	112,336	4.8
Small- and medium-scale industry	107,642	4.6
Tourism	72,748	3.1
Export financing	59,046	2.5
Other*	72,008	3.1

*Includes fishing, potable water, and housing.
Source: Computed from NAFIN, Informe anual (México,
D.F.: NAFIN, 1982), p. 102.

June 30, 1981. Table 3.14 reveals that the greater part of
these credits has been directed to irrigation projects and
infrastructure, although close to $107 million has been granted
to small and medium industry. NAFIN has also established
global lines of credit with 15 countries, among which the
United States, Japan, England, and France occupy prominent
positions.[84] During the 1979-80 fiscal year, new lines of
credit were opened with Norway, Poland, Canada, and Sweden
to finance the importation of machinery and equipment. The
terms under which the debt was contracted were preferential,
if we confine ourselves to length of amortization and interest
payments. For example, on March 11, 1980, Nacional Financiera and the Skandinaviska Enskilda Banken opened a line of
credit for $15 million. The interest was 7.5 percent annually
for loans with an amortization period of up to five years, and
7.75 percent[85] for those between five and ten years. Also
during this fiscal year the development bank issued bonds at
fluctuating rates in the United States, in addition to obtaining
loans from banks in that country.

Notwithstanding these accomplishments, the flow of international and domestic funds for development purposes slowed considerably during 1982-83, a direct result of the reduction in public expenditures caused by the severe economic recession of 1982. During 1983 NAFIN's international operations were, by and large, confined to restructuring foreign debt and negotiating credits for the importation of basic inputs.[86] For example, beginning in late August 1983,

> The total debt restructured by NAFIN was 3,207.5 million dollars, consisting of four currencies: U.S. dollars (98%); Japanese Yen (1.6%); Deutsche Marks (0.4%); and Canadian dollars (0.1%). In total, 357 loan agreements with 216 foreign banks were subject to renegotiation.[87]

In recognition of the improved maturity profile of NAFIN's foreign liabilities, the World Bank and the IDB granted NAFIN loans with a total value of $381 million during 1983. Foreign official institutions, encouraged by the improved performance, also extended lines of credit, primarily to finance the purchase of capital and food imports.[88]

SUMMARY AND CONCLUSIONS

The foregoing discussion has traced Nacional Financiera's financial and institutional development in light of the historical and economic realities of Mexico. It was observed that the role of the state in fostering economic growth and maintaining political stability has had a long and rich tradition that goes as far back as the Porfiriato. In fact, the excesses of the Díaz regime paved the way for a social and institutional revolution that would further extend the powers of the state in economic and financial matters. Thus, under the leadership of Cárdenas, and Calles before him, the state embarked upon a number of undertakings whose immediate objectives were to revive the moribund financial system and to lay the foundations for a legal-institutional environment conducive to business activity. These efforts culminated in the creation of a national party and a number of key financial institutions, including the Bank of Mexico, the Agrarian Credit Bank, and Nacional Financiera, S.A.

The discussion then proceeded to examine the financial and institutional evolution of NAFIN through key periods in

its history. Of particular interest to this study was the
emergence of the bank, during the Camacho administration,
as an entrepreneurial instrument for initiating many of the
industrial projects of the time. No less important was the
reorientation of its operations during the 1950s and 1960s so
as to better serve the changing economic and financial needs
of a growing economy along private lines. NAFIN's operations
became more specialized and its entrepreneurial functions
began to diminish vis-à-vis its purely financial operations.
Last, the bank's renewed promotion of industry during the
Portillo years was reviewed, as well as its critical role in
securing long-term funds from private banks and multilateral
agencies. It was shown that most of the projects undertaken
with the bank's funds were connected in some way with the
petroleum industry.

NOTES

1. Raymond W. Goldsmith, *The Financial Development
of Mexico* (Paris: OECD, 1961), p. 10.
2. Philip Russell, *Mexico in Transition* (Austin, Tex.:
Colorado River Press, 1977), p. 22.
3. James Cockcroft, *Intellectual Precursors of the Mexican Revolution, 1900-1913* (Austin: University of Texas
Press, 1968), pp. 47-70.
4. Russell, op. cit., p. 22.
5. Roger Hansen, *Mexican Economic Development: The
Roots of Rapid Growth* (Washington, D.C.: National Planning
Association, 1971), p. 15.
6. Ibid.
7. Alfredo Navarrete R., "The Financing of Economic
Development," in *Mexico's Recent Economic Growth* (Austin:
University of Texas Press, 1967), p. 109.
8. Daniel Cosio Villegas, *Historia moderna de México*,
VII, *El Porfiriato—vida económica* (México, D.F.: Editorial
Hermes, 1965), p. 1155.
9. Ibid.
10. Hansen, op. cit., p. 24.
11. Russell, op. cit., p. 23.
12. Hansen, op. cit., p. 25.
13. See Jesús Silva Herzog, *Breve historia de la Revolución mexicana*, I (México, D.F.: Fondo de Cultural Económica, 1972), p. 57.

14. Kenneth Paul Erickson and Kevin J. Middlebrook, "The State and Organized Labor in Brazil and Mexico," in Sylvia A. Hewlett and Richard S. Weinert, eds., *Brazil and Mexico: Patterns in Late Development* (Philadelphia: ISHI, 1982), pp. 213, 221.

15. Arnaldo Cordova, *La ideología de la revolución mexicana* (México, D.F.: E.R.A., 1974), p. 247.

16. Hansen, op. cit., p. 28.

17. Robert J. Shafer, *Mexico, Mutual Adjustment Planning* (New York: Syracuse University Press, 1966), p. 40.

18. Hansen, op. cit., p. 28.

19. Douglas Bennett and Kenneth Sharpe, "The State as Banker and Entrepreneur: The Last Resort Character of the Mexican State's Economic Intervention, 1917-1970," in Sylvia A. Hewlett and Richard S. Weinert, eds., *Brazil and Mexico: Patterns in Late Development* (Philadelphia: ISHI, 1982), p. 176.

20. Ibid.

21. Ibid., p. 177.

22. Leopoldo Solis M., *La realidad económica mexicana: Retrovisión y perspectivas*, 11th ed. (México, D.F.: Siglo xxi Editoriales, 1981), p. 85.

23. Russell, op. cit., p. 40.

24. Ibid., p. 42.

25. See Hansen, op. cit., p. 31.

26. Bennett and Sharpe, op. cit., p. 181.

27. Calvin P. Blair, "Entrepreneurship in a Mixed Economy," in Raymond Vernon, ed., *Public Policy and Private Enterprise in Mexico* (Cambridge, Mass.: Harvard University Press, 1964), p. 206.

28. *El mercado de valores* 42, no. 42 (1982): 1193.

29. Blair, op. cit., p. 206.

30. Ibid.

31. Rosa Olivia Villa M., *Nacional Financiera: Banco de fomento del desarrollo económico de México* (México, D.F.: NAFIN, 1976), p. 4.

32. Blair, op. cit., p. 208.

33. Villa, op. cit., p. 4.

34. Blair, op. cit., p. 209.

35. Ibid.

36. José Hernández Delgado, *The Contribution of Nacional Financiera to the Industrialization of Mexico* (Mexico City: NAFIN, 1961).

37. Gerrit Huizer, *La lucha campesina en México* (México, D.F.: Centro de Investigaciones Agrarias, 1970), p. 71.

38. Blair, op. cit., p. 210.

39. *NAFINSA and the Economic Development of Mexico* (Mexico City: NAFIN, 1964), p. 12.

40. Russell, op. cit., p. 45.

41. Ibid.

42. Ibid.

43. Nora Hamilton, "Mexico: The Limits of State Autonomy," *Latin American Perspectives* 2, no. 2 (Summer 1975): 96.

44. Blair, op. cit., p. 211.

45. Ibid.

46. *NAFINSA and the Economic Development of Mexico*, p. 15.

47. Villa, op. cit., p. 4.

48. William Patton Glade, Jr., "Las empresas gubernamentales descentralizadas," *Problemas agrícolas e industriales de México* 6 (January 1959): 162.

49. *NAFINSA and the Economic Development of Mexico*, p. 58.

50. Ibid., p. 77.

51. NAFIN, *La economía mexicana en cifras* (México, D.F.: NAFIN, 1978), pp. 229-31.

52. Ibid.

53. Blair, op. cit., p. 222.

54. Bennett and Sharpe, op. cit., p. 185.

55. Raymond Vernon, "Public Policy and Private Enterprise," in Raymond Vernon, ed., *Public Policy and Private Enterprise in Mexico* (Cambridge, Mass.: Harvard University Press, 1964), p. 6.

56. Robert T. Aubey, *Nacional Financiera and Mexican Industry* (Los Angeles: University of California Press, 1966), p. 44.

57. *El mercado de valores* 24, no. 27 (July 6, 1964): 388.

58. Blair, op. cit., p. 222.

59. Computed from NAFIN, *Statistics on the Mexican Economy* (Mexico City: NAFIN, 1966), p. 89.

60. Sanford A. Mosk, *Industrial Revolution in Mexico* (Los Angeles: University of California Press, 1950), p. 117.

61. Aubey, op. cit., p. 46.

62. Russell, op. cit., p. 75.

63. See Hansen, op. cit., Table II-10, p. 30.

64. Aubey, op. cit., p. 46.

65. *NAFINSA and the Economic Development of Mexico*, p. 20.

66. Ibid., pp. 22-23.

67. Mosk, op. cit., p. 21.
68. *El mercado de valores* 42, no. 47 (November 22, 1982): 1193.
69. Blair, op. cit., p. 221.
70. *NAFINSA and the Economic Development of Mexico*, pp. 22-23.
71. Ibid., pp. 56-97.
72. Villa, op. cit., p. 41.
73. *El mercado de valores* 36, no. 39 (September 27, 1976): 761-66.
74. *El mercado de valores* 42, no. 24 (June 14, 1982): 592.
75. NAFIN, *Informe anual* (México, D.F.: NAFIN, 1983), p. 30.
76. Bennett and Sharpe, op. cit., p. 189.
77. Ibid.
78. Villa, op. cit., p. 49.
79. NAFIN, *Informe anual* (México, D.F.: NAFIN, 1974-83).
80. Ibid. (1981), p. 141.
81. *El mercado de valores* 39, no. 28 (July 28, 1979): 569-78.
82. NAFIN, *La economía mexicana en cifras*, pp. 229-31.
83. *El mercado de valores* 42, no. 20 (May 17, 1982): 503.
84. NAFIN, *Informe anual* (México, D.F.: NAFIN, 1981), p. 101.
85. Ibid. (1980), p. 27.
86. Ibid. (1983), p. 19.
87. Ibid.
88. Ibid.

4

NAFIN's Financing And Promotion Of The Industrial Sector

INTRODUCTION

In this chapter, we shall examine in greater detail the promotional and financial activities of the development bank in the industrial sector. Particular attention will be given to the changing role of NAFIN within the limits set by the general strategy of financial development and industrialization pursued by the public sector. However, in contrast with the earlier chapters, the analysis will be conducted along empirical lines by developing a number of bank-performance indicators and testing a reduced-form statistical model for key periods in Mexico's history.

To begin with, we shall review Mexico's financial experience and rapid economic growth during 1940-75. It is hoped that such an investigation will bring into sharper focus the well-recognized, but elusive, relationship between the nation's financial development and economic expansion. More important, perhaps, for our purposes is that it will provide a general framework within which to evaluate the performance of Nacional Financiera, S.A. Next, we shall develop a classification system designed to determine whether the bank's provision of financial resources to industry can be considered satisfactory. This evaluation will be conducted from the bank's vantage point, as well as relative to the banking system in general and private *financieras* in particular.

Third, we shall estimate a dynamic production function that relates the change in real industrial output during the current period to, among other variables, lagged changes in real financing to industry by NAFIN. The flow of long-term funds and equity capital provided by private *financieras* is incorporated for purposes of comparison. Fourth, we shall give a more detailed account of NAFIN's participation in the renewed promotion of basic industry undertaken during the Portillo years. By and large, we shall focus our investigation on NAFIN's contribution to the establishment of a group of 20 enterprises, mainly in the capital goods and petrochemical industries. Finally, we shall draw appropriate conclusions regarding the past and future roles of NAFIN in the industrial sector.

FINANCIAL DEVELOPMENT AND ECONOMIC EXPANSION: AN OVERVIEW OF 1940-75

Throughout the entire period under consideration, and especially from the mid-1950s on, the Mexican economy experienced a remarkable diversification and growth of its financial and industrial sectors. In what follows, we shall examine some of the factors responsible for enabling the Mexican economy to capitalize most effectively on opportunities to increase the pace of industrialization. Not surprisingly, our analysis will emphasize the role played by monetary and nonmonetary institutions in channeling private and public funds to expand Mexico's infrastructure and basic industry.

The Economy's Performance

Few countries in the world, developed or underdeveloped, have been able to record the real rates of economic growth that Mexico experienced during 1940-75. Its gross domestic product grew at better than 8 percent per year from 1960 to 1970, and no less than 5 percent between 1970 and 1975. On a per capita basis, the rate exceeded 3 percent in the earlier period, and hovered around 2 percent in the later. In addition, for over 30 years industrial production rose at a rate of at least 8 percent per year. Agricultural output, on the other hand, after registering an impressive growth rate of over 8 percent in the 1940s, dropped to approximately 4 percent during the 1950s and 1960s. Throughout the first half of the 1970s, however, it registered a dismal increase of less than 1 percent per year, as can be seen from Table 4.1.

TABLE 4.1

Mexican Economic Indicators, 1940-75
(real average annual growth rates, 1960 = 100)

Item	1940-50	1950-60	1960-70	1970-75
Gross domestic product	7.1	7.3	8.8	5.3
Population	3.4	3.2	3.6	3.1
Per capita product	3.7	4.1	5.2	2.2
Industrial output	8.0	9.0	12.0	6.2
Agricultural output	8.2	4.3	3.9	0.6

Source: Computed from NAFIN, *La economía mexicana en cifras* (México, D.F.: NAFIN, 1978), pp. 19-45.

On a sectoral basis, there were substantial shifts in both output and employment during the period under review. For instance, the primary sector employed over 65 percent of the economically active population and accounted for approximately 20 percent of gross domestic product in 1940; in 1975 it employed no more than 35 percent of the labor force and its output share had fallen to less than 10 percent. In contrast, the industrial sector made substantial gains during this period, especially in manufacturing, construction, and energy. As of 1975, it employed 25 percent of the economically active population and accounted for close to 36 percent of gross domestic product. These figures represent increases of 61 and 44 percent, respectively, over those shares prevailing in 1940.[1] Further evidence of the industrial sector's dynamism is given by the fact that between 1957 and 1975, the average product per person rose by close to 82 percent, or 4.3 percent per year. By contrast, productivity in the agricultural and service sectors increased at 3.7 and 1.2 percent per year, respectively.[2] A more detailed account of the changing structure of the Mexican economy is provided by Tables 4.2 and 4.3.

The rapid growth rate and structural transformation of the Mexican economy was, in contrast with other Latin American countries, achieved with considerable price stability, especially between 1957 and 1970. During this interval, the general price index for Mexico City grew at an annual rate of only 2.9 percent, as compared with a rate of 15 percent per year during 1940-53. Goods produced, such as construction materials, energy, and vehicles and accessories, registered an

TABLE 4.2

Economically Active Population by Sector, 1940-75
(percent of total employment)

Year	Agriculture	Industry	Services
1940	65.5	15.5	19.0
1950	58.0	16.0	26.0
1960	54.0	19.0	27.0
1970	37.5	23.1	39.4
1975	34.3	25.0	40.7

Source: Computed from NAFIN, La economía mexicana en cifras (México, D.F.: NAFIN, 1978), pp. 44-45.

TABLE 4.3

Gross Domestic Product by Sector, 1940-75
(percent of GDP)

Category	1940	1950	1960	1970	1975
Agricultural output	19.4	19.2	15.9	11.6	9.6
Industrial output	25.0	27.0	29.2	34.4	35.9
Manufacturing	15.4	17.1	19.2	23.3	23.7
Mining	3.7	2.0	1.5	1.0	0.9
Electricity	2.5	0.7	1.0	1.8	2.0
Petroleum	0.7	3.0	3.4	3.8	4.0
Construction	2.7	4.2	4.1	4.5	5.3
Services	55.6	53.8	54.9	54.0	54.5
Total	100.0	100.0	100.0	100.0	100.0

Source: Computed from NAFIN, La economía mexicana en cifras (México, D.F.: NAFIN, 1978), pp. 25-34.

annual rate of price increase of only 2.2 percent in 1957-70, while during 1940-53 they rose at a rate approximately equal to that of the general price index.[3] In the next section, "The Financing of Development," we shall explore some of the reasons why the financing of development was inflationary during initial industrialization. For now, it is sufficient to note that the manner in which expenditures were financed changed decisively from 1956 on.

Turning to the country's external sector, it becomes evident that the developments taking place there are a reflection of the changing requirements of the economy, as well as of the industrialization policies pursued by the public sector. For instance, the country's balance on current account was in the black for seven of the eleven years between 1940 and 1950—especially during the war years. This is not surprising, considering that the demand for Mexican goods by the United States and Great Britain was high, and the Camacho administration implemented an import-substitution industrialization program in order to relieve the severe shortage of consumer and capital goods that the economy experienced during this period.

As can be seen in Table 4.4, exports grew at an average annual rate of 12.3 percent between 1940 and 1950, while imports lagged behind at 8.2 percent per year. During the 1950s the demand for Mexican exports declined substantially, and the "inward-looking" policies followed by the administrations of Miguel Alemán (1946-52) and Adolfo Ruíz Cortínez (1952-58) did not help matters. They were more concerned with implementing a variety of protective measures to ". . . entice domestic producers into import-substitution enterprises."[4] The figures do not belie this, for not only did the share of imports and exports in GDP decline between 1950 and 1960, but their growth rates fell to 6.0 and 4.5 percent per year, respectively.

By the late 1950s and early 1960s, the "easy" phase of import substitution was coming rapidly to a close as the high-yield, short-payout projects declined in number.[5] Mexican industrialists and policy makers were forced to turn their eyes to international markets in order to effectively use the installed capacity. Moreover, it soon became apparent that as a result of the higher capital-output ratios of the new projects, a limit to the compression of the import coefficient had been reached; the growing industrial sector necessitated imports of sophisticated machinery and equipment that could not be produced domestically. It has been estimated that by 1965, the pro-

TABLE 4.4

Major External Indicators, 1940-75
(millions of U.S. dollars)

	1940	1950	1960	1970	1975
Exports of goods	94.4	493.4	738.7	1,281.3	2,861.0
Imports of goods	132.4	596.7	1,186.4	2,326.8	6,580.2
Net capital inflow (long-term)	2.5	51.2	109.5	503.9	4,318.0
Net capital inflow (short-term)	-3.1	62.1	182.4	498.7	-460.0
Reserves of the Bank of Mexico	22.0	172.0	-8.6	102.1	165.1
Shares (percent)					
Exports/GDP	6.3	9.7	6.1	4.3	4.3
Imports/GDP	8.8	11.8	9.8	7.8	10.0

Growth Rates (average annual rates, percent)				
	1940-50	1950-60	1960-70	1970-75
Exports of goods	12.3	4.5	6.7	12.7
Imports of goods	8.2	6.0	8.7	15.9
Net capital inflow (long-term)	17.4	10.4	32.7	126.2

Sources: Computed from various issues of Banco de
México, *Informe anual* (México, D.F.: Banco de México, 1950-
76; NAFIN, *La economía mexicana en cifras* (México, D.F.:
NAFIN, 1978).

portion of imports rigidly determined by the requirements of
industry had reached 45.9 percent of total imports.[6]
    Faced with having to pay for this increasing and chang-
ing volume of imports, Mexican policy makers devised a
variety of fiscal and financial measures to improve the competitive position of export industries and attract large volumes
of foreign capital into the country. In the case of exports,
these policies consisted in part of subsidies in the form of
exemptions from the payment of taxes on imports of key raw

TABLE 4.5

Exports of Manufactured Goods, 1940-74

(1)	(2)	(3)	(4)
1940-44	57.0	14.7	-1.2
1945-49	5.8	22.1	11.6
1950-54	1.6	9.6	7.8
1955-59	13.8	12.6	2.0
1960-64	21.9	23.6	0.0
1965-69	10.5	27.4	0.0
1970-74	30.1	42.8	0.0

(1) = Period.
(2) = Average annual growth rate during period (percent).
(3) = Share of manufactured exports in total exports (percent).
(4) = Variations in the exchange rate. The exchange rate was fixed at 12.5 pesos per dollar between 1955 and 1975.
Sources: NAFIN, *La economía mexicana en cifras* (México, D.F.: NAFIN, 1978), pp. 227-28; and various issues of *Anuario estadístico de los Estados Unidos Mexicanos* (México, D.F.: 1940-75).

materials used by export industries. Also, the Law of Federal Receipts stipulated that predetermined fractions of the revenues generated from the General Tariff on Imports would be destined for a trust fund to aid Mexican exporters.[7] Under the Mateos administration (1958-64), the National Bank of Foreign Commerce authorized deposit banks and private *financieras* to provide a part of their legal reserves in the form of low-cost loans to firms exporting a high proportion of manufactured goods.[8] From Table 4.4 it can be ascertained that these various measures had an overall beneficial impact, for the rate of growth of Mexican exports jumped from 4.5 percent during the 1950s to 6.7 percent during the 1960s, an increase of about 49 percent. Their share in gross domestic product declined because the latter grew at an even faster rate.

A more significant indicator of the success of these policies is given by Table 4.5, where the evolution of Mexico's
exports of manufactured goods is revealed.

Beginning in the early 1960s, Mexico experienced an
impressive growth rate in its export of manufactured goods,
and their share in total exports increased continuously. The
latter development occurred in spite of the fact that the exchange rate remained fixed at 12.5 pesos per dollar between
1960 and the mid-1970s.

Insofar as net foreign capital inflow is concerned, it is
evident from Table 4.4 that its rate of growth accelerated considerably during the 1960s, and especially between 1970 and
1975. By far the greater part of the debt contracted during
these years was public—contracted directly by public agencies
or by private institutions with the guarantee of the government or of public institutions such as NAFIN. For example,
between 1960 and 1975 Mexico's external public debt as a percentage of gross domestic product rose from 9.7 to 24.4 percent. By comparison, the public debt-product ratio of Latin
America as a whole increased from 11 percent in 1960 to about
21 percent in 1975.[9] More importantly, Mexico's external financial solvency—as measured by the public debt-service ratio*—
deteriorated considerably during this period. From an average
of 21.5 percent between 1960 and 1970, it increased to 26 percent by the end of 1975. The latter was well above the figure
for Latin America as a whole, which stood at 14.8 percent.[10]

In many respects, this increasing external dependence
was the direct outcome of the stabilization policies followed by
the Mexican government throughout the late 1950s and the
1960s. Foreign sources of funds became the most important
adjustment mechanism for financing the growing public-sector
deficits and current-account imbalances. In the opinion of the
noted economist Rosario Green,

. . . the external public debt came to be viewed
as a readily accessible expedient, and certainly
less dangerous than a devaluation, an excessive
emission of money, a rationalization of public
expenditures, fiscal restructurization or, for that
matter, any other political adjustment that would

---

*Defined as the relationship between the debt-service pay-
ments and the current value of exports of goods and services.

disturb the equilibrium of the social forces in the country.[11]

It became quite apparent that in order for the Mexican state to maintain its growing rate of public investments without inflation, it had no choice but to turn to external official and private sources of funds. Since 1966 the latter have become especially prevalent: of the total authorized public debt of $4,524.0 million between 1965 and 1970, 67 percent originated from private sources. And of the total private debt contracted during this period, 50 percent came from banks (a great number of them in the United States.)[12]

At this point, it is worth mentioning that practically all of the external credits received by public enterprises were obtained with the intervention of Nacional Financiera. Some indication of where these funds have been channeled is given by Table 4.6, which shows the sectoral distribution of funds contracted from official sources of financing between 1958 and 1964.

The greater part of these funds were concentrated in infrastructure and basic industry, followed closely by agriculture.

TABLE 4.6

Sectoral Distribution of Funds Obtained
from Official Sources of Financing, 1958–64
(millions of dollars)

Sector	Amount	Percent
Transport	190.5	27.0
Electrification	153.8	22.0
Industry	82.8	12.0
Agriculture	75.5	11.0
Housing	50.0	7.2
Other*	145.7	20.8
Total	698.3	100.0

*Includes irrigation projects, secondary education, and public health.

Source: Derived from Rosario Green, El endeudamiento público externo de México: 1940-73 (México, D.F.: Colegio de México, 1976), p. 141.

The Financing of Development

We have so far examined the performance of the Mexican economy without any detailed reference to the flow of national and foreign resources in support of investments. In this section, therefore, we shall review the record of savings, investment, and resource allocation in accordance with national development programs. These figures reflect, perhaps more clearly than any others, the institutionalization of the growth process.

The ratio of gross national savings to gross domestic product is a rough indicator of internal resource mobilization. As can be seen from Table 4.7, the savings coefficient increased continuously throughout 1940-75. From a low of 12.7 percent during the 1940s, it reached a high of 18 percent between 1971 and 1975. This overall improvement in internal resource mobilization, however, was accompanied by a declining ratio of gross national savings to gross domestic investment. The latter development indicates the growing importance of net external resources in investment financing. In Table 4.7 it can be seen that during the periods 1940-50, 1951-60, 1961-70, and 1971-75 the proportions of investment financed with foreign resources were, respectively, 1.3, 7.5, 16.3, and 17.4 percent.

An analysis of the investment coefficients reveals an increase of 9.1 percentage points between 1940 and 1975, with almost half of it coming during the first two decades of the period. Of particular interest to this study, the investment coefficient rose to a high of 18.2 percent by the end of 1941-47. This figure would not be surpassed until 1965, when the ratio stood at 18.4 percent.[13] In addition, the share of the state in total investment was quite significant during these initial years. For example, the ratio of public-sector investments to total investment averaged 52.5 percent—attaining an all-time high of 70.7 percent in 1943.[14] Further evidence of the commitment of the Mexican government to industrialization—particularly during the administrations of Avila Camacho (1940-46), Miguel Alemán (1946-52), and Adolfo Ruíz Cortínez (1952-58)—is given by Table 4.8.

Between the beginning of the period and the late 1960s, public investments to industry increased by 27 percentage points, or approximately 219.5 percent. In fact, throughout the three and a half decades, public investments in industry and infrastructure did not fall below 56 percent of the total. Most of the increase in industrial investments between 1961 and 1975 is explained by the growing importance of the petroleum

TABLE 4.7

Aggregate Financial Indicators, 1940-75
(percent)

Item	1940-50	1951-60	1961-70	1971-75
Gross domestic investment / GDP	12.8	17.0	20.3	21.9
Gross national savings / GDP	12.7	15.7	17.0	18.0
Gross national savings / Gross domestic investment	98.7	92.5	83.7	82.6

Sources: Various issues of Banco de México, *Informe anual*; "Economic and Social Progress in Latin America," in *IDB, 1980-81 Report* (Washington, D.C.: Inter-American Development Bank, 1981).

TABLE 4.8

Distribution of Gross Public Investment, 1940-75
(percent)

Period	Total	Agriculture	Industry	Transport and Communication	Other*
1940-46	100.0	17.3	12.3	57.7	12.7
1947-53	100.0	21.1	25.6	45.3	8.0
1954-60	100.0	10.7	30.0	26.5	34.6
1961-70	100.0	10.9	39.3	22.2	27.6
1971-75	100.0	16.4	37.6	22.7	23.3

*Includes social welfare, administration, and defense expenditures.

Source: Computed from NAFIN, *La economía mexicana en cifras* (México, D.F.: NAFIN, 1978), pp. 369-73.

industry. Public investments in the latter grew at an average
annual rate of 11.6 percent between 1961 and 1970, while
during 1971-75 the rate rose to 35.5 percent per year.[15] As
we observed in chapter 3, Nacional Financiera played a key
role in channeling funds to industry and infrastructure, especially during the 1940s and 1950s, when most of its long-term
financing was directed ". . . to basic import-substitution
industries, including iron, steel, and oil."[16] More recently,
and in accordance with national industrialization programs, it
has promoted and financially assisted the petroleum and capital goods industries.

Along with the government's ever-increasing public investment projects came the need to finance its growing deficits.
During 1940-54 the Bank of Mexico ". . . underwrote government sector deficits almost singlehandedly, the responsibility
for financing deficits elsewhere in the economy was largely
assumed by private financial institutions and the various
specialized national credit institutions."[17] For instance, between 1940 and 1950 the Bank of Mexico accounted for 80 percent of the total claims of the banking system on the government sector.[18] Much of the same pattern is found for 1951-54.
Thus, the Mexican state financed its growing public-sector
deficits via the creation of money—which, undoubtedly, contributed to the inflation experienced by the country throughout
these years. According to Roger D. Hansen, the reason the
government chose the straightforward monetization of deficits
rather than financing them via direct taxation, is that

> Those responsible for government policy . . .
> apparently felt that growth with price stability
> was impossible at that time, they feared that in-
> creases in taxation would simply undermine all
> other investment incentives. So taxes were not
> raised and prices continued to average 10 percent
> a year through 1955.[19]

Beginning in 1955, the government had to reassess its
development policy, for the devaluation of the previous year
(see Table 4.5) had brought about sharp increases in prices
(see Table 4.9) and, more important, harsh and outspoken
criticism by the private sector. The administration of Adolfo
Ruíz Cortínez decided to grant a higher priority to price stability while maintaining its commitment to increased capital
formation. These seemingly incompatible goals were achieved
by compelling private deposit banks and private *financieras*

TABLE 4.9

Selected Nominal and Real Interest Rates, 1947-77

(1)	(2)	(3)	(4)	(5)	(6)	(7)
1947	10.6	4.9	—	—	—	5.7
1948	10.7	3.4	9.7	2.4	—	7.3
1949	10.9	1.4	10.6	1.1	—	9.5
1950	10.3	1.0	10.7	1.4	-1.3	9.3
1951	10.6	-2.1	11.4	-1.3	-4.7	12.7
1952	10.4	6.7	11.3	7.6	4.3	3.7
1953	10.3	12.2	10.6	12.5	9.9	-1.9
1954	10.5	1.2	11.5	2.2	-1.2	9.3
1955	10.2	-3.4	11.4	-2.2	-5.6	13.6
1956	9.5	4.8	12.0	7.3	3.3	4.7
1957	9.6	5.3	12.6	8.3	3.9	4.3
1958	9.6	5.2	13.0	8.6	3.8	4.4
1959	10.9	9.7	13.4	12.2	7.0	1.2
1960	12.0	7.1	14.0	9.1	3.3	4.9
1961	—	—	14.5	13.6	7.5	0.9
1962	—	—	14.4	12.5	6.7	1.9
1963	—	—	13.7	13.2	8.5	0.5
1964	—	—	12.4	8.2	4.8	4.2
1965	—	—	—	—	7.1	1.9
1966	—	—	—	—	7.7	1.3
1967	—	—	—	—	6.1	2.9
1968	—	—	—	—	7.1	1.9
1969	—	—	—	—	6.7	2.6

(continued)

TABLE 4.9 (continued)

(1)	(2)	(3)	(4)	(5)	(6)	(7)
1970	—	—	—	—	3.3	5.9
1971	—	—	—	—	5.3	3.7
1972	—	—	—	—	7.3	2.9
1973	—	—	—	—	-5.5	15.7
1974	—	—	—	—	-10.0	22.5
1975	—	—	—	—	1.9	10.6
1976	—	—	—	—	-7.0	22.2
1977	—	—	—	—	—	—

(1) = Year.
(2) = Nominal mortgage rate (percent).
(3) = Real mortgage rate (percent).
(4) = Nominal average yield on the assets of private banking institutions (percent).
(5) = Real average yield on the assets of private banking institutions (percent).
(6) = Real yields on long-term financial bonds (percent).
(7) = Rate of inflation for Mexico City.

Sources: Mortgage rates, whose yearly publication was discontinued after 1960: Sidney Homer, *A History of Interest Rates*, 2nd. ed. (New Brunswick, N.J.: Rutgers University Press, 1977), p. 590; average yields on assets of private banks: Dwight S. Brothers and Leopoldo Solis M., *Mexican Financial Development* (Austin: University of Texas Press, 1966), pp. 74, 192-93; real yields on long-term financial bonds: G. Ortiz and L . Solis, "Mexican Financial Data and Exchange Rate Experience," *Journal of Developmental Studies*, 1977, pp. 518-19; price data: NAFIN, *La economía mexicana en cifras* (México, D.F.: NAFIN, 1978).

to supply the new deficit financing required by the government, and increasing the public sector's reliance on external financing.[20] The former objective was achieved via the Bank of Mexico's extensive control over the legal reserve requirements of the private banking system.[21] Basically, it induced privately owned deposit banks (and subsequently private *financieras*) to meet their reserve requirement ratio by acquiring government bonds or issues of public enterprises. The yields on these securities were not competitive with those realized by the banks on other investments. However, they ". . . did provide an interest return, and in this respect were preferable from the banks' viewpoint to an equal amount of non-earning cash reserves."[22] Some indication of the success of this policy is provided by the following figures:

> Between 1950 and 1955, over 33 percent of the increase in total banking system claims on the government was acquired by the central bank. Between 1956 and 1961, the holdings of the central bank fell—not only relatively, but absolutely—from 2.1 billion pesos to 1.3 billion. Over the latter period private financial institutions increased their share of the banking system's claims on the government from 23 percent to 63 percent of the total.[23]

Thus, not only did the central bank (Bank of Mexico) shift the burden of financing public-sector investments to the private sector, but it was also able to neutralize the creation of excess reserves that, presumably, would have been made available to other borrowers. In particular, loanable funds to the private sector became steadily more scarce and costly, as indicated by the real rates presented in Table 4.9.

The average yield on assets of private banks fell continuously until the mid-1950s, after which it stabilized and then experienced a sharp rise. This tendency was short-lived, however, for by the mid-1960s and through the remainder of the decade interest rates at first declined and then stabilized. These developments indicate that during initial industrialization (1940-55), the Mexican economy adjusted primarily via price increases, while during stabilizing development (1956-72), increases in the real rate of interest became the mechanism of adjustment. The latter attracted massive inflows of financial capital to the domestic economy, and thus helped offset any "crowding out" of private investment that might have taken place. This new financial capital was instrumental in financing the ever-growing deficits the country began to experience after 1962.

The successful transition of the Mexican economy into growth without inflation or sustained industrialization was a direct outcome of the stabilization process. Even if in the beginning it sacrificed economic growth to price stability, it eventually increased the resources available for financing economic development by ". . . enabling savers and investors, as well as financial intermediaries providing the linkage between them . . . to respond to the real factors governing domestic market conditions,"[24] and increasing the inflow of foreign savings via an assortment of measures ranging from placing bond issues in the U.S. and European capital markets to encouraging foreign direct investment to enter the country on terms established by the Mexican government.[25] (As we observed in chapter 3, the policy of mexicanization called upon foreign investors to offer opportunities for equity participation by Mexican investors. NAFIN played, and still plays, a key role in its implementation.)

The response of the private financial sector to these efforts by the Mexican government to achieve domestic stability without a slowdown in infrastructure expenditure is clearly revealed in Table 4.10 by the changing structure of the banking system's claims on public and private enterprises.

During the 1940s and early 1950s, a significant proportion of the credits extended to enterprises and individuals originated from deposit banks and national development banks such as NAFIN. Throughout this period, the Banco de México almost singlehandedly financed federal, state, and local expenditures while contributing marginally to the deficit spending of enterprises and individuals. The figures above do not belie this pattern, especially between 1945 and 1955, when the Banco de México's financing to both public and private enterprises declined both relatively and absolutely. However, after 1955 the burden of financing both government and public enterprise expenditures shifted to other credit institutions, such as deposit banks, national development banks, and private *financieras*. This enabled the Banco de México to make available an increasing volume of financial resources to enterprises and individuals during 1955-64. Between 1955 and 1962 the supply of funds to both private and public enterprises increased from a low of 511.7 million real pesos to an all-time

TABLE 4.10

Banking System Financing of Enterprises
and Individuals, 1940–75
(millions of real pesos; 1960 = 100)

| | Monetary System | | Other Credit Institutions | | |
| | Banco de | Deposit | National | Private | |
Year	México	Banks	Banks	Financieras	Other*
1940	477.6	1,837.4	1,564.4	27.0	698.9
1945	1,395.6	2,772.7	1,996.7	1,160.5	1,565.9
1950	803.9	3,756.5	5,593.7	1,548.6	1,799.4
1955	511.7	4,900.2	8,607.0	2,117.3	2,646.8
1960	3,221.0	5,584.9	15,937.8	7,135.4	3,467.9
1965	955.3	13,140.8	27,788.9	15,018.9	2,948.5
1970	1,738.5	22,372.8	43,516.0	39,109.4	9,673.4
1975	2,388.9	24,763.7	56,306.7	38,949.8	12,913.8

*Includes claims on both private and public enterprises.
Source: Various issues of Banco de México, Informe
anual; NAFIN, La economía mexicana en cifras (México, D.F.:
NAFIN, 1978), pp. 231–33.

high of 6,817.8 million real pesos in 1962.[26] After 1964 the
bank once again began to acquire an ever-increasing quantity
of government securities while leaving it to deposit banks and
other credit institutions to meet the financial needs of public
and private enterprises.

In this respect, the provision of financing by private
financieras to deficit spending units in the private and public
sectors was particularly impressive. For example, as shown
in Table 4.10, between 1955 and 1970 not only did the credits
provided by these intermediaries increase absolutely, but
their share in the total real financing granted by credit
institutions rose from 15.8 to 42.4 percent. Moreover, under
the impetus of the Mexican government, a high proportion of
this financing was channeled to industry, as can be attested
by the fact that in 1965, over 50 percent of their credits
were directed to industry.[27] Also revealed in Table 4.10 is
the rapid growth of credits extended by national development
banks to selected enterprises in the public and private sectors. As we have seen in this and previous chapters, a sig-

nificant proportion of the funds of these intermediaries has been obtained from foreign sources, both official and private.

Thus, the stabilization policies pursued by the Mexican government not only increased the participation of credit institutions other than the Bank of Mexico in financing public-sector deficit spending but also, and more importantly, stimulated the growth and development of private credit institutions by creating an economic environment free from the misallocations induced by rapid inflation.* It is here that the essential difference between the Díaz regime's approach to finance and that of the revolutionary governments is found. As pointed out by the Mexican minister of finance in 1924:

> . . . under the previous law [of 1897] the guarantee of [bank] liabilities was the essential thing and, once accomplished . . . the banks could use their funds in the manner in which they wished. On the other hand, the new law indicates a new orientation in that its article five states that the credit institutions have in common the function of facilitating the use of credit and are distinguished one from the other by the nature of the liabilities which they issue or by the services they render the public. This last concept marks a completely new tendency, since it follows the intent of the State to channel the capital invested in the credit industry toward accomplishing specific objectives. Under the new system it is not enough that the liabilities issued by credit institutions are well secured; it is necessary that the capital obtained through issues of such liabilities goes to enrich sources of public wealth and this capital may not be used as an instrument in creating monopolies for certain industries or individuals.[28]

AN EVALUATION OF THE BANK'S OPERATIONS

The foregoing discussion of the policies pursued by the Mexican government to finance the growth and development of

---

*See Appendix C for more detail.

the economy should better prepare us to assess the impact of
NAFIN during initial (1940-55) and later industrializations
(1956-71). In the present section, we attempt to test empirically whether the bank's provision of financial resources to
industry has been satisfactory. This evaluation, it will be
recalled, is conducted from the bank's vantage point, as well
as relative to that of the banking system as a whole. In view
of the historical and institutional evolution of both NAFIN and
the Mexican financial system, we would expect the bank's
performance to be significantly better during initial industrialization.

Following the lead of Joseph A. Kane, we consider two
factors that would appear to be significant in determining
whether the provision of real financing can be considered
satisfactory: the rate of growth (positive or negative) of
financing and the real value or level of financing relative to
levels attained in the previous periods. Thus, we will say
that the provision of financing is satisfactory the greater the
rate of growth, and the higher the current provision relative
to past levels of financing. The following ranking system
incorporates both of these conditions:

A = Provision of financing attains a new peak that is at
least x percent greater than that of any period in the past.

A- = Provision of financing attains a new peak that is
less than x percent greater than that of any period in the past.

Both of these rankings imply that the rate of growth
from one year to the next is > 0 and that the level of financing
provided in the last period is greater than that of any previous period.

B = Provision of financing increases by at least x percent over the previous period, but is at a nonpeak level.

B- = Provision of financing increases by less than x percent over the previous period, and is at a nonpeak level.

Both of these rankings imply that the rate of growth
from one year to the next is > 0 and that the level of financing
provided in the current period is locally, but not globally,
at a maximum relative to other periods.

C = Provision of financing declines by less than x percent from one year to the next, and the previous period was
ranked in either the A or the B category.

C- = Provision of finance declines by at least x percent, and the previous period was classified as either A or B.

Both of these rankings imply that the rate of growth is < 0, and that provision of financing vis-à-vis the previous peak or nonpeak level was lower.

D = Provision of finance declines by less than x percent, and the previous period was classified as C or C-.

D- = Provision of finance declines by at least x percent, and the previous period was in either the C or the C- category.

E = Provision of finance decreases by less than x percent, and the previous period was D, D-, E, or E-.

E- = Provision of finance declines by at least x percent, and the previous period was in the D, D-, E, or E- category.

We can also assign a numerical scale to our categories by giving the better-ranking a higher numerical value, as shown below.

Category	Numerical Scale
A	100
A-	90
B	80
B-	70
C	60
C-	50
D	40
D-	30
E	20
E-	10

70-100 = Satisfactory (S).
50-60 = Inconclusive (I).
10-40 = Unsatisfactory (U).

To begin our investigation, let us examine NAFIN's provision of productive financing for the period between 1940 and 1976. To avoid any misunderstanding, "productive financing means the total real value of medium-to-long-term loans plus equity investments. This is a stock concept, and a dynamic notion can be obtained by observing changes in the variable over time. Table 4.11, in addition to providing the various

TABLE 4.11

Nacional Financiera: Productive Financing, 1939-76
(millions of real pesos)

(1)	(2)	(3)	(4)	(5)	(6)
1939	46.8	—	—	—	91.8
1940	50.2	A–	90	S	59.7
1941	166.5	A	100	S	88.8
1942	814.4	A	100	S	94.3
1943	1,307.7	A	100	S	93.8
1944	1,178.9	C	60	I	90.9
1945	1,567.3	A	100	S	90.4
1946	1,541.1	C	60	I	87.7
1947	1,568.0	A–	90	S	77.9
1948	1,999.4	A	100	S	82.8
1949	2,242.2	A	100	S	83.1
1950	2,553.1	A–	90	S	82.8
1951	2,735.7	A–	90	S	82.0
1952	3,169.3	A–	90	S	79.1
1953	4,102.5	A	100	S	79.0
1954	4,326.0	A–	90	S	71.4
1955	3,664.4	C	60	I	65.9
1956	3,575.9	D	40	U	60.0
1957	3,655.5	B–	70	S	57.8
1958	4,169.1	B–	70	S	60.3
1959	4,361.5	A–	90	S	59.6

(continued)

ratings, displays data on absolute levels of real productive
financing and the proportion of the bank's total financing in
productive form.

From the general rating it is evident that the level of
productive financing has been satisfactory throughout the
period, especially between 1940 and 1955, when no single
year was evaluated as unsatisfactory. The specific categories
also reveal the intense promotional phase in the bank's history,
for during six of the nine years between 1940 and 1948, the

TABLE 4.11 (continued)

(1)	(2)	(3)	(4)	(5)	(6)
1960	6,767.0	A	100	S	68.6
1961	8,679.2	A	100	S	66.7
1962	9,939.6	A-	90	S	63.5
1963	10,390.0	A-	90	S	71.3
1964	11,045.5	A-	90	S	65.0
1965	11,185.8	A-	90	S	66.1
1966	12,370.3	A-	90	S	68.0
1967	14,467.9	A-	90	S	71.0
1968	16,697.0	A-	90	S	74.0
1969	18,562.9	A-	90	S	76.1
1970	19,950.2	A-	90	S	77.4
1971	20,545.8	A-	90	S	77.5
1972	22,757.5	A-	90	S	79.5
1973	21,303.2	C	60	I	79.1
1974	20,904.6	D	40	U	73.2
1975	25,740.6	A-	90	S	78.2
1976	34,611.5	A-	90	S	75.3

(1) = Year.
(2) = Real productive financing.
(3) = Rating scale with 25 percent threshold.
(4) = Numerical scale with 25 percent threshold.
(5) = General scale with 25 percent threshold.
(6) = Share of productive financing in total financing.
Source: Computed from NAFIN, La economía mexicana en
cifras (México, D.F.: NAFIN, 1978), p. 299.

level of productive financing attained new peaks that were at
least 25 percent greater than those of any previous period.
The share of financing in productive form for this nine-year
period averaged over 85 percent, reaching an all-time high of
94.3 percent in 1942. In recent years this proportion has
dropped somewhat, but it is still quite high, averaging 77 percent for 1969-75.

Our second test pertains to NAFIN's provision of security
investments (equity and bonds) to private and public enter-

prises. This variable is in many respects a better indicator of
the entrepreneurial role of the development bank, since it
involves the latter in a long-term commitment to the firm. We
proceed as before, first evaluating the rate of growth in real
equity investments, and second looking at the share of productive financing in equity form.

The results in this case are not as unambiguous as
before, but they do indicate that during the administration
of Avila Camacho, the bank assumed an entrepreneurial role.
As can be observed from Table 4.11, between 1940 and 1943
the level of equity capital provided by NAFIN attained a new
peak at least 25 percent greater than any previous period. In
addition, throughout the first half of the 1940s the proportion
of productive financing in equity form averaged over 85 percent. However, once Miguel Alemán took office, the latter proportion dropped sharply and the absolute levels of equity
investment decreased, as attested by the unsatisfactory rating
given to three consecutive years. The reorientation in the
bank's operations, it will be recalled, was a direct outcome of
a policy that emphasized the use of credits to promote infrastructure and basic industry. This shift is clearly discernible
from Table 4.11, where it is shown that for 1947-52 the bank's
provision of productive financing attained new peaks each
year.

Still, it was not until sustained industrialization that the
promotional activities of NAFIN took a back seat to the financial operations of the development bank. This is revealed in
Table 4.12 by the fact that after 1962 the proportion of financing in equity form consistently registered figures below 20
percent. (As mentioned in chapter 3, this trend was reversed
somewhat during the administration of José López Portillo.)

So far we have only considered the performance of
Nacional Financiera from its own vantage point. Let us now
evaluate NAFIN's performance relative to that of other financing of the industrial sector.

To begin with, let us look at NAFIN's financing of
industry as a proportion of the total financing of industry by
the banking system. If the data indicate that during initial
industrialization the bank is financing an increasing proportion of the total credit of the banking system, the hypothesis
of limited impact outlined in chapters 1 and 2 is not supported,
ceteris paribus. We may formalize this test by introducing the
following notation:

TABLE 4.12

Nacional Financiera, S.A.: Security Investments, 1939-76*

(1)	(2)	(3)	(4)	(5)	(6)
1939	36.5	—	—	—	78.0
1940	39.7	A	100	S	79.0
1941	131.4	A	100	S	78.9
1942	745.0	A	100	S	91.5
1943	1,249.3	A	100	S	95.5
1944	1,064.9	C	60	I	90.3
1945	1,173.6	B-	70	S	75.0
1946	989.7	C	60	I	64.2
1947	920.3	D	40	U	58.7
1948	883.0	E	20	U	44.2
1949	839.2	E	20	U	37.4
1950	1,026.6	B-	70	S	40.2
1951	740.0	C-	50	I	27.0
1952	1,035.7	B	80	S	32.7
1953	1,261.4	A-	90	S	30.7
1954	1,256.5	C	70	I	29.0
1955	1,087.1	D	40	U	29.7
1956	1,080.6	E	20	U	30.2
1957	1,119.0	B-	70	S	30.6
1958	1,088.6	C	60	I	26.1
1959	885.5	D	40	U	20.3
1960	1,304.0	A	100	S	19.3

(continued)

TABLE 4.12 (continued)

(1)	(2)	(3)	(4)	(5)	(6)
1961	2,060.9	A	100	S	23.8
1962	1,500.4	C-	60	I	15.1
1963	1,358.8	D	40	U	13.0
1964	1,744.4	B	80	S	15.8
1965	2,112.5	A-	90	S	18.9
1966	2,275.7	A-	90	S	18.4
1967	3,300.3	A	100	S	22.8
1968	3,244.9	C	60	I	19.4
1969	2,238.2	D-	30	U	12.0
1970	3,127.6	B	80	S	15.7
1971	2,984.6	C	60	I	14.5
1972	3,145.8	B-	70	S	13.8
1973	2,869.7	C	60	I	13.6
1974	3,030.7	B-	70	S	14.5
1975	3,779.0	A	100	S	14.7
1976	4,964.2	A	100	S	14.3

*Equity investments consistently represent practically 90 percent of all security investments. Hence, this variable is a good indicator of the bank's entrepreneurial commitment.

(1) = Year.

(2) = Security investments.

(3) = Rating scale with 25 percent threshold.

(4) = Numerical scale with 25 percent threshold.

(5) = General scale with 25 percent threshold.

(6) = Security investments as percent of productive financing.

Source: NAFIN, *La economía mexicana en cifras* (México, D.F.: NAFIN, 1978), p. 299.

B_t = total stock of financing to domestic industry provided by the banking system at time t.

N_t = total stock of financing to domestic industry provided by NAFIN at time t.

b,n = Average annual rates of growth in B and N, respectively.

If $b > n$, then $N_0/B_0 > N_1/B_1$ and the hypothesis of limited impact is supported, ceteris paribus. If $b < n$, then $N_0/B_0 < N_1/B_1$ and the hypothesis is not supported. In other words, if $b < n$, NAFIN's provision of financing to industry has grown more rapidly than the financing to industry provided by the the banking system, and consequently its share has risen. Table 4.13 provides us with the information needed to make such an evaluation.

Between 1942 and 1954 the average annual rate of growth of real financing to industry was 420 percent for NAFIN and 159 percent for the banking system. This can be more readily ascertained from NAFIN's increasing share in total financing to industry. This proportion reached a peak of 50 percent of the total in 1955, despite a drop in the real level of financing between 1954 and 1955 due to the economic crisis faced by the country.

A similar pattern can be discerned in Table 4.14, where the banking system's investments in bonds and equity issues of private and public enterprises are compared with those of NAFIN.

In particular, the right-hand column indicates that between 1941 and 1947, NAFIN's share in the total security investments of the banking system to enterprises averaged 49.1 percent, reaching an all-time high of close to 68 percent in 1942. Thus, the hypothesis of limited impact is rejected for the period in question—a period of intense industrialization in which, as we have argued elsewhere, national development banks such as NAFIN played a crucial role.

However, after the stabilization policies of the late 1950s were implemented, the relative importance of NAFIN and other national development banks began to diminish. This trend is clearly revealed by Tables 4.13 and 4.14. Despite an increase of almost 232 points in NAFIN's real financing to industry between 1955 and 1970, its share in the total financing to industry by the banking system fell from a high of 50 percent in 1955 to a low of 29.7 percent in 1970. Similarly, NAFIN's share in the total security investments provided by

TABLE 4.13

Nacional Financiera, S.A.: Share in
Total Real Financing to Industry, 1942-77
(millions of real pesos; 1954 = 100)

(1)	(2)	(3)	(4)	(5)	(6)
1942	1,775.8	17.3	85.4	1.8	4.8
1943	2,209.4	21.5	271.4	5.9	12.3
1944	2,625.0	25.5	394.2	8.5	15.0
1945	3,116.6	30.3	749.5	16.2	24.0
1946	3,596.6	35.0	859.3	18.5	23.9
1947	4,604.6	44.8	1,228.7	26.5	26.7
1948	5,401.7	52.5	1,528.9	33.0	28.3
1949	5,665.2	55.0	1,877.8	40.5	33.1
1950	6,063.4	59.0	2,013.8	43.5	33.2
1951	6,597.3	64.2	2,040.0	44.0	30.9
1952	7,098.7	69.0	2,584.8	55.8	36.4
1953	8,355.6	81.3	3,419.0	73.8	40.9
1954	10,282.0	100.0	4,635.0	100.0	45.1
1955	9,165.5	89.1	4,584.5	98.9	50.0
1956	10,074.9	98.0	4,925.2	106.3	48.9
1957	11,119.4	108.1	5,180.6	111.8	46.6
1958	12,478.8	121.8	5,891.9	127.1	47.2
1959	14,460.0	140.6	6,284.0	135.6	43.5
1960	17,499.6	170.2	8,037.8	173.4	45.9
1961	21,908.5	213.0	9,803.3	211.5	44.8
1962	27,331.2	265.8	11,254.8	242.8	41.2

(continued)

TABLE 4.13 (continued)

(1)	(2)	(3)	(4)	(5)	(6)
1963	27,284.3	265.4	11,100.7	239.5	40.7
1964	31,459.2	306.0	12,692.8	273.8	40.4
1965	32,923.1	320.2	12,501.7	269.7	38.0
1966	35,940.5	349.6	13,805.6	297.9	38.4
1967	40,505.0	393.9	14,460.6	312.0	35.7
1968	44,288.4	430.7	15,784.0	340.5	35.6
1969	51,103.5	497.0	16,388.3	353.6	32.1
1970	56,893.7	553.4	15,321.2	330.6	29.7
1971	61,986.2	602.9	19,664.9	424.3	31.7
1972	67,554.7	657.0	21,149.7	456.3	31.3
1973	63,524.4	617.8	19,779.4	426.7	31.1
1974	59,020.5	574.0	21,477.6	463.4	36.4
1975	73,186.3	711.8	25,548.8	551.2	34.9
1976	78,023.0	758.8	30,833.5	672.6	39.5
1977	71,487.4	695.3	32,508.1	701.4	45.5

(1) = Year.
(2) = Total real financing by the banking system to industry.
(3) = Index of real financing by the banking system, 1954 = 100.
(4) = Real financing by Nacional Financiera to industry.
(5) = Index of real financing by Nacional Financiera, 1954 = 100.
(6) = Share of Nacional Financiera in total real financing.
Sources: NAFIN, *La economía mexicana en cifras* (México, D.F.: NAFIN, 1978), pp. 229-31; *Informe Anual* of the Central Bank of Mexico for 1975-77.

TABLE 4.14

Investment in Securities of Enterprises, 1940–66
(millions of real pesos)

Year	(1) Banking System	(2) NAFIN	(2)/(1) × 100
1940	253.1	39.7	15.7
1941	488.2	131.4	26.9
1942	1,098.2	745.0	67.8
1943	1,883.0	1,249.3	66.4
1944	1,732.0	1,064.9	61.5
1945	1,980.3	1,173.6	59.3
1946	1,913.7	989.7	51.7
1947	2,103.9	920.3	43.7
1948	2,124.6	883.0	41.6
1949	2,432.4	839.2	34.5
1950	2,327.3	1,026.6	44.1
1951	1,962.5	740.0	37.7
1952	2,473.5	1,035.7	41.9
1953	2,476.9	1,261.4	50.9
1954	2,797.5	1,256.5	44.9
1955	2,160.0	1,087.1	50.4
1956	2,323.7	1,080.6	46.5
1957	2,721.2	1,119.0	41.1
1958	3,279.2	1,088.6	33.2
1959	3,194.7	885.5	27.7
1960	3,839.3	1,304.0	33.9
1961	5,068.5	2,060.9	40.6
1962	4,917.0	1,500.4	30.5
1963	5,107.0	1,358.8	26.6
1964	5,722.6	1,744.4	30.5
1965	6,455.9	2,112.5	32.7
1966	7,189.2	2,275.7	31.7

Source: Banco de México, S.A., Informe anual, various issues.

the banking system to enterprises experienced a precipitous
drop of over 45 percent between 1955 and 1959. These figures
indicate that alternative sources of long-term funds and equity
financing became available to prospective entrepreneurs; from
private *financieras* and other private credit institutions. A
clear indication of this trend is given by Table 4.15, which
displays the real financing to industry provided by private
financieras between 1955 and 1968—the latest date for which
we have disaggregated data.

TABLE 4.15

Private *Financieras*: Real Financing to Industry, 1955-68
(millions of real pesos)

(1)	(2)	(3)	(4)	(5)	(6)
1955	937.5	—	—	—	14.9
1956	1,081.0	A-	90	S	16.0
1957	1,614.5	A	100	S	22.7
1958	1,688.4	A-	90	S	20.8
1959	2,394.9	A	100	S	27.7
1960	3,137.2	A	100	S	28.4
1961	3,832.8	A-	90	S	28.5
1962	4,746.9	A-	90	S	30.7
1963	5,660.9	A-	90	S	37.0
1964	5,788.2	A-	90	S	38.9
1965	7,647.6	A-	90	S	44.6
1966	8,740.6	A-	90	S	46.0
1967	9,833.6	A-	90	S	49.4
1968	10,926.6	A-	90	S	50.3

(1) = Year.
(2) = Real financing to industry by private *financieras*.
(3) = Rating scale with 25 percent threshold.
(4) = Numerical scale with 25 percent threshold.
(5) = General rating with 25 percent threshold.
(6) = Share in total financing granted by Nacional
Financiera.
Source: Computed from various issues of *Informe anual*
of the Banco de México, 1955-68.

It is readily apparent from the figures presented in this table that throughout this period, private *financieras* exhibited a high growth rate in their level of real financing to industry. Of particular interest is the fact that their share in the total financing granted by NAFIN to industry rose to over 50 percent by the end of 1968. In recent years, though, particularly since 1974, this fraction has declined as NAFIN's share in total financing to industry increased to 45.5 percent in 1977 (see Table 4.13). This development is in large measure explained by the intensive promotion of the petrochemical and capital goods industries under the presidency of José López Portillo.

The foregoing investigation of NAFIN's performance during initial and sustained industrialization does not lend support to the hypothesis of limited impact. On the contrary, it suggests that during 1940-54 NAFIN was among a handful of intermediaries to which public and private enterprises could turn for promotional and financial support.

EMPIRICAL ANALYSIS OF NAFIN'S IMPACT ON THE INDUSTRIAL SECTOR

As a measure of the economic impact of Nacional Financiera, we estimated a dynamic production function of the following general form:

$$Q(t) = \phi(\overset{+}{L(t)}, \overset{+}{K^M(t)}, \overset{+}{N(t)}, \overset{+}{t})$$

where

Q   = industrial output (millions of real pesos)[29]

L   = labor force actively employed in the industrial sector (thousands)

K^M = capital imports (machinery and equipment) for industry (millions of real pesos)

N   = real financing provided by NAFIN to industry (millions of real pesos)

t   = time (years).

The +'s indicate the expected direction of the relationship.

The change in output over time is given as

$$\frac{dQ}{dt} = \frac{\partial\phi}{\partial L}\frac{dL}{dt} + \frac{\partial\phi}{\partial K^M}\frac{dK^M}{dt} + \frac{\partial\phi}{\partial N}\frac{dN}{dt} + \frac{\partial\phi}{\partial t}$$

and

$$\frac{dL}{dt}, \frac{dK^M}{dt}, \frac{dN}{dt} > 0$$

The first three terms on the right side of the equation indicate the change in output due to increased inputs of labor, capital imports, and real financing, respectively. The last term on the right indicates the change in output due to disembodied technical change.[30] Put differently, it captures those shifts in the production function resulting from a reorganization of inputs over time.

The actual model estimated by ordinary least squares (OLS) is given below:

$$\Delta Q_t = \alpha_0 + \beta_1\Delta L_t + \beta_2\Delta K_t^M + \beta_3 \sum_{i=1}^{n} \Delta N_{t-i} + \varepsilon_t$$

where

$$\Delta Q_t = Q_t - Q_{t-1}$$
$$\Delta L_t = L_t - L_{t-1}$$
$$\Delta K_t^M = K_t^M - K_{t-1}^M$$
$$\Delta N_t = N_t - N_{t-1}$$

and

$$\alpha_0, \beta_1, \beta_2, \beta_3 > 0$$

Before presenting the results, however, a note on methodology is in order.

First, the reasons for incorporating changes rather than levels are that the underlying process being described is above all a dynamic one, since it involves the conversion of financial resources into real resources, and the introduction of change injects more variability into the sample data, thus

helping to avoid the problem of serial correlation and multi-
collinearity that is often encountered in time-series studies.
Second, the financial variable has been lagged into the past
because it takes time for financial resources to become transformed into new plant, machinery, and equipment. Third,
three regressions were estimated: for 1940-76, 1940-56, and
1957-76. The reason for partitioning the data in this manner
is that it may allow us to determine whether the bank's impact
during initial industrialization was significant, and to what
extent it has ceased to be significant in recent years. Finally,
a multiple regression with disaggregated lagged changes in the
financial variable was run in order to determine at which
point in the past this variable became significant.

The estimated models are presented in Table 4.16, beginning with the disaggregated version, which suggests that the
change in the financial variable does not become significant
until two periods, or two years, into the past; viz., the
financing provided by NAFIN in 1968 does not become transformed in plant, machinery, and equipment until 1970. This is
not entirely surprising, given that most projects financed by
NAFIN take two to three years to commence operations in ear-
nest. The ensuing fit aggregates over the lagged changes in
the financial variable, and for all variables in this equation we
reject the hypothesis of no relationship at $\alpha = .005$. All coefficients have the expected signs; and the interpretation, say,
of the estimate of the financial variable in the first equation
goes as follows:

If the sum of the lagged changes in real financing to
industry two and three periods ago is equal to 1 million real
pesos, then the change in real industrial output is equal to
1,130 thousand pesos, ceteris paribus. The β elasticity for
this estimate is .44, which means that an increase in the sum
of the lagged changes of 10 percent gives rise to a change in
real industrial output of 4.4 percent during the current period.

The remaining regressions fit the data reasonably well,
as indicated by their adjusted R^2 ($\bar{R}^2$). Also, they do not
exhibit serial correlation at both the 5 and 1 percent significance levels. More importantly, they suggest that NAFIN contributed significantly to the industrial growth of the country
during 1940-56. A glance at the coefficients and t ratios of the
financial variable confirms this. Last, the capital import coefficient and the constant term increase in magnitude and significance during 1957-76. The former development may suggest
that imported capital inputs have become more important in
Mexico's industrial growth, while the latter may indicate the

TABLE 4.16

Estimates of Dynamic Production Function*

Period		R^2	$\bar{R}^2$	D.W.
1940–76**	$\Delta Q_t = -1,122.6 + 30.9 \Delta L_t + 1.1 \Delta K_t - .1 \Delta N_t$ (−1.6) (3.5) (3.3) (−.44) $+ .1 \Delta N_{t-1} + 1.0 \Delta N_{t-2} + .83 \Delta N_{t-3}$ (.40) (3.87) (2.7)	.74	.71	1.57
1940–76	$\Delta Q_t = -971.1 + 29.7 \Delta L_t + 1.1 \Delta K_t + .96 \sum_{i=2}^{3} \Delta N_{t-i}$ (−1.45) (4.78) (3.17) (4.93)	.73	.70	1.6
1940–56	$\Delta Q_t = -47.3 + 12.5 \Delta L_t + .2 \Delta K_t^M + 1.05 \sum_{i=2}^{3} \Delta N_{t-i}$ (−.17) (13.5) (.65) (2.8)	.95	.94	1.93
1957–76	$\Delta Q_t = 2,927.6 + 13.3 \Delta L_t + 1.14 \Delta K_t^M + .24 \sum_{i=2}^{3} \Delta N_{t-i}$ (3.1) (5.5) (2.23) (1.0)	.91	.89	1.25

*Numbers in parentheses are t ratios.

**See appendix at the end of chapter.

Source: Compiled by author (see note 29 for data source).

increasing importance of disembodied technical change and/or
the omission of other significant variables. One possible candidate, in light of the rapid growth of private *financieras* since
the mid-1950s, is the flow of long-term funds provided by the
latter to industry.[31]

To test this hypothesis, we estimated a model with the
change in real financing to industry by private *financieras*.
The period under consideration, however, had to be short-
ened, since specific data for the private financial variable was
unavailable after 1968. Still, the results are suggestive and
are given below.

Period		R^2	$\bar{R}^2$	D.W.

$$1957\text{-}68 \quad \Delta Q_t = 715.5 + 10.72\Delta L_t + 2.06\Delta K_t^M \qquad .99 \quad .98 \quad 2.09$$
$$\phantom{1957\text{-}68 \quad \Delta Q_t = } (1.08) \quad (6.4) \qquad (5.25)$$

$$-.19\,\Delta N_{t-2} + 3.37\,\Delta P_{t-2}^F$$
$$(-.92) \qquad (3.75)$$

where

$$P_t^F \; = \; \text{real financing to industry by private } \textit{financieras}$$
$$\text{(millions of real pesos)}$$

and

$$\Delta P_t^F \; = \; P_t^F - P_{t-1}^F$$

The addition of this variable has improved the fit to the
data, as indicated by both an increase in the adjusted R^2 and
a decrease in the magnitude and significance of the constant
term. Also, the sample data do not exhibit serial correlation,
and we reject the hypothesis of no relationship for the private
financial variable at $\alpha = .005$. Last, the coefficients for labor
and capital remain positive and significant, while that for
NAFIN reverses sign and continues to be insignificant.

NAFIN'S PROMOTION OF BASIC INDUSTRY
DURING THE PORTILLO ADMINISTRATION

Before concluding this chapter, it will be expedient to
consider in greater depth NAFIN's promotion of basic industry
during the Portillo years. The present discussion relates the
bank's renewed promotional activities to the economic policies
pursued by the public sector.

Historical Background

Between 1957 and the early 1970s Mexico experienced economic growth and financial diversification without inflation. This was largely the result of a general policy that shifted the burden of financing public-sector deficits from the Bank of Mexico to the private financial sector and foreign savers. The stability that the country enjoyed throughout this period made it attractive not only to the latter but also to domestic savers, especially in view of the fact that real yields on deposits were generally high (see Table 4.9). A clear indication of this development is given by Figure 4.1, which shows that voluntary savings—as measured by the ratio of banking liabilities to gross domestic product—rose from 28 to 50 percent between 1960 and 1970.

However, the "Mexican economic miracle" wrought by the stabilization process aggravated the distribution of income, as attested by the rise in the Gini coefficient from .54 in 1963 to .57 in 1975.[32] Moreover, the persistent annual growth rates in population, on the order of 3.6 percent (see Table 4.1), accentuated the already serious problem of unemployment and

FIGURE 4.1

Coefficient of Voluntary Savings, 1940-70

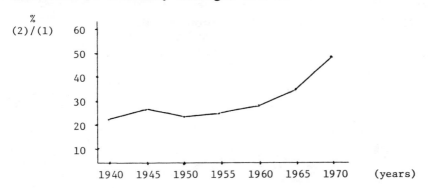

(1) = Real gross domestic product (millions of 1960 pesos).
(2) = Real obligations of the banking system (millions of 1960 pesos).

Source: Various issues of *Informe anual* of the Banco de México, 1940-72.

underemployment. The economically active population as a proportion of the total population declined from 32.4 percent in
1960 to 26.9 percent in 1970.[33]

Faced with this unfavorable economic evolution and mount-
ing social criticism, the Echeverría administration (1970-76)
decided to abandon the stabilization process of the 1960s. Beginning in 1972, it embarked upon an ambitious economic program designed to "prop up" effective aggregate demand via a
higher rate of public spending and to accelerate the process
of import substitution in the capital goods sector.[34] The former action was obviously designed to alleviate the employment
problem (and therefore the distribution of income), and the
latter was counted upon to reduce the ever-growing current-
account deficits the country had been experiencing since 1967.
Given the inadequacy of the private financial sector to finance
the higher rate of government expenditure, the Bank of Mexico
began, once again, the direct monetization of the public-sector
deficits. As can be seen in Figure 4.2, the public sector deficit grew continuously throughout the Echeverría administration, attaining a high of practically 10 percent of gross
domestic product by the end of 1975.

The increase in the annual rate of growth of the money
supply from 7.5 percent in 1971 to almost 25 percent by the

FIGURE 4.2

Public Sector Deficit as a Proportion of GDP, 1970-77*

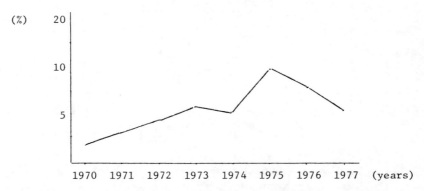

*Real gross domestic product (millions of 1960 pesos).

Sources: Secretaría de Hacienda y Crédito Público,
Cuenta de la hacienda pública federal (México, D.F.: 1978);
NAFIN, La economía mexicana en cifras (México, D.F.: NAFIN,
1978).

end of 1974 had a telltale impact on inflation.[35] This is readily apparent from Table 4.9, which shows that during 1971 the rate of inflation for Mexico City was only 3.7 percent, while during 1974 it had accelerated to almost 23 percent. Not surprisingly, real yields on financial bonds and deposits became negative (see Table 4.9), which discouraged domestic savings, as can be seen from Figure 4.1.

Still, the Echeverría administration was not willing to reduce the rate of public expenditures, which meant that it had no recourse but to increase the public sector's external indebtedness. That indebtedness rose on a net basis from $1,679.9 million in 1974 to an unprecedented $3,053.8 million in 1975, an increase of practically 83 percent.[36] By 1976 the economic situation worsened considerably, as a result of the growing debt-service ratio, which had reached an all-time high of 31.6 percent, and the failure of export revenues to increase as anticipated during the first half of the year.[37] This caused a deterioration in the Bank of Mexico's reserves that was well beyond the capacity of the nation to acquire short-term debt. This led to a growing uncertainty among private investors as to whether the exchange rate—which had been fixed since 1954 at 12.5 pesos per dollar—could be maintained. There was a flight of capital from the country that, according to Leopoldo Solis, reached a level of approximately $4 billion.[38]

Faced with these unfortunate economic events, Mexico devalued the peso from 12.5 to 19.7 per dollar by the end of 1976. In addition, talks with the International Monetary Fund were initiated that culminated in an economic package calling for the economic contraction of the state and the liberalization of commerce. The following guidelines were adopted:[39]

1. The increase in nominal salaries should not exceed that of the principal countries with which Mexico trades.

2. The prices and tariffs of the goods and services produced by the public enterprises should reflect the real costs of production.

3. External commerce should be liberated completely.

4. Inflation should be controlled by repressing the rate of expansion of the economy.

5. The public-sector deficit should be reduced by 6 to 7 percent.

6. Employment in the public sector should not increase by more than 2 percent during 1977.

7. The net external debt should not exceed $3 billion for 1977.

8. The rate of exchange should vary so as to maintain equilibrium in the foreign exchange market.

9. The rate of growth of the money supply should be restricted so as to increase the cost of credit.

To a greater or lesser extent, these measures were implemented during 1977, with the expected results: a reduction in the rate of growth of gross domestic product to 3.4 percent; a deceleration of the rate of price increases; an increase in the reserves of the Bank of Mexico to $504.2 million from -$320.9 the previous year; and an increase of 28 percent in the voluntary savings of the public.[40] Fortunately, the employment situation did not deteriorate, as evidenced by the slight drop in the proportion of the population economically active from 27.9 percent in 1976 to 27.8 percent in 1977.[41]

TABLE 4.17

Proven Reserves and Annual Production
of Oil and Natural Gas, 1970–81
(millions of barrels)

Year	Total Reserves	Annual Production	Years of Reserves
1970	5,567.5	310.6	18
1971	5,428.4	306.0	18
1972	5,387.8	326.9	16
1973	5,431.7	335.6	16
1974	5,773.4	402.0	14
1975	6,338.4	464.8	14
1976	11,160.9	500.0	22
1977	16,001.7	545.6	29
1978	40,194.0	672.2	60
1979	45,803.4	803.6	57
1980	60,126.4	1,039.1	58
1981	72,008.4	1,228.8	57

Source: PEMEX, Memoria de labores 1970–1981 (México, D.F.: Subdirección de Planeación, 1984).

TABLE 4.18

Mexican Economic Indicators, 1976-82
(real annual growth rates)

Item	1976	1977	1978	1979	1980	1981	1982
Gross domestic product	4.2	3.4	8.2	9.2	8.3	7.9	-0.5
Population	3.2	3.2	3.1	3.0	3.0	2.9	2.8
Per capita product	1.0	0.2	5.1	6.2	5.3	5.0	-3.3
Industrial output	5.0	3.5	9.8	10.8	7.2	7.0	-2.9
Agricultural output	-1.0	10.3	8.1	-5.9	10.0	8.0	-2.9
Employment	2.0	3.9	3.7	5.4	6.2	6.4	-1.0
Rate of inflation*	19.6	30.4	16.7	20.3	28.7	26.7	61.9

*GDP deflator with 1970 = 100.
    Source: Computed from NAFIN, La economía mexicana en
cifras (México, D.F.: NAFIN, 1984).

The three-year austerity program recommended by the IMF
was short-lived, if not de jure, then certainly de facto, for by
1978 it was discovered that Mexico had 40,194 million barrels
of proven oil and gas reserves, compared with 6,338 million
barrels in 1976. Table 4.17 shows that, as of 1981, its proven
reserves stood at an impressive 72 billion barrels, and that at
existing annual production levels they would last well into the
twenty-first century. Thus, the country was transformed over-
night into an energy colossus capable not only of meeting its
internal needs but also of developing its export capacity, especially at a time when the world supply of oil was by no means
guaranteed. From 1978 through 1981, Mexico embarked once
again upon a path of increased government expenditures—particularly from 1979 on—that was designed to alleviate unemployment
while renewing the development of the petrochemical and capital
goods industries. The results were impressive, if one chooses
to consider certain macroeconomic variables. Table 4.18 reveals
that real gross domestic product grew at an annual rate of better than 8 percent between 1978 and 1981, and manufacturing
output rose at a rate of practically 11 percent during 1979. Employment growth rates averaged close to 6 percent per year
in 1979-81 and, more significantly, the government's efforts to
reduce the country's stubbornly high population growth rates
seemed to be taking effect. However, other variables pointed
in another direction that was plain to see but, in the optimism

TABLE 4.19

External Public-Sector Debt Indicators, 1977–82
(millions of 1970 pesos)

Year	GDP (1)	External Public Debt (2)	(2)/(1) (percent)	Exports of Goods and Services (3)	Public Debt Service (4)	(4)/(3) (percent)
1977	657,632.5	185,254.8	28.2	73,687.4	28,593.9	38.8
1978	712,187.0	181,851.9	25.5	80,836.7	43,613.9	54.0
1979	776,982.4	171,868.9	22.1	93,182.7	58,771.3	63.1
1980	841,828.8	154,794.1	18.4	113,044.1	34,702.2	30.7
1981	912,738.7	215,832.6	23.6	116,384.7	39,430.8	33.9
1982	888,182.8	545,748.7	61.4	n.a.	n.a.	—

Source: Computed from NAFIN, La economía mexicana en cifras (México, D.F.: NAFIN, 1984), pp. 242, 271.

134

of the moment, they were overlooked or given lip service by policy makers in the government. One of these variables was the increasing dependence of the country on revenues derived from oil exports, particularly from 1979 on. For example, between 1979 and 1981 the value of oil exports rose from $3.9 billion to $14.5 billion and their share in total exports increased from 45.0 percent to slightly over 75 percent.[42] Another discouraging trend, which had been rectified somewhat during 1977, was the country's growing public-sector debt. From a reduction of $343.1 million between 1976 and 1977, it rose by $813 million during 1978 and more than doubled between 1979 and 1981.[43]

Moreover, as shown in Table 4.19, the share of external public debt service in the value of exports of goods and services registered an alarming figure of 63.1 percent by the end of 1979. At about the same time, the rate of inflation began to accelerate (see Table 4.18) along with a deterioration in domestic savings. The events of 1976 were repeated with a vengeance in 1982, when, as a result of the recession in the developed nations and a decrease in world oil exports, the country failed to generate an anticipated flow of $7 billion.[44]

NAFIN's Promotion of Basic Industry

As the country's major development bank, it is not surprising that NAFIN played a key role in the overall development of the petrochemical and capital goods industries during the Echeverría and López Portillo administrations—particularly the latter. In this respect, it was observed earlier that beginning in 1974, NAFIN's share in the total financing to industry by the banking system was on the rise. This trend is reflected in its promotional operations, as can be observed in Table 4.20.

In particular, of the 20 enterprises created by the bank between 1977 and 1982, all but one were in the industrial sector. Moreover, 11 of these industrial plants came into existence in 1980 or later.

Also revealed in Table 4.20 is NAFIN's greater participation in the paid-in capital stock of the industrial group of enterprises. The majority of these enterprises were created in the steel, chemical, and capital goods industries.

NAFIN's 14 capital goods projects between 1977 and 1982 represented one-third of the total of such projects promoted by the various public and private enterprises of the country.[45]

TABLE 4.20

Salient Features of the NAFIN Group of Enterprises, 1977–82
(millions of real pesos)

Item	1977	1978	1979	1980	1981	1982
Number of companies	74	76	79	87	94	94
Industrial	69	71	73	81	88	88
Services	5	5	6	6	6	6
Joint paid-in capital stock	—	—	—	38,133.3	46,217.8	45,480.9
Industrial	—	—	—	35,930.7	44,177.9	42,325.4
Services	—	—	—	2,202.6	2,039.9	3,155.5
Direct participation by NAFIN	—	—	—	13,198.0	17,811.5	17,641.0
Industrial	—	—	—	12,837.3	17,534.7	17,179.3
Services	—	—	—	360.7	276.8	461.7
Percentage of participation by NAFIN	—	—	—	35	38	39
Industrial	—	—	—	36	40	41
Services	—	—	—	16	16	15

Sources: NAFIN, *Informe anual*, 1977–82; Banco Nacional de México, *Mexico Statistical Data, 1970–79* (México, D.F.: BANAMEX, 1980).

136

These industrial plants produce goods that had not previously been manufactured in Mexico.[46] In compliance with the guidelines of the policy for industrial development designed by the federal government, the majority of these firms have been located outside the Federal District and the other traditional industrial areas, such as Monterrey and Guadalajara.[47] These 14 companies, along with information on location, number of employees, and product manufactured, are presented in Table 4.21.

Among the companies formed by NAFIN, those that stand out are the Groupo Industrial NKS, S.A. de C.V., and Productora Mexicana de Tubería, S.A. de C.V. The former, constituted in September 1980 as a joint promotion of SIDER-MEX, NAFIN, and the partner supplying the technology, has completed its basic engineering and almost all of its detailed engineering. Its industrial premises are being constructed at Lázaro Cárdenas in the state of Michoacán, and it is scheduled to start operations in the third quarter of 1984. Once in operation, it will provide employment for more than 2,000 persons. The latter company was formed in November 1980 and is in the process of beginning operations in the industrial port of Lázaro Cárdenas, Michoacán. The project was promoted jointly, with SIDERMEX and the Japanese partner supplying the technology. Its purpose is to manufacture welded seamed pipes in the dimensions required by Petróleos Mexicanos (PEMEX) for the transportation and distribution of hydrocarbons, up to a maximum of 48 inches in diameter. At the present time, it provides work for more than 1,000 persons.[48]

In Morelia, also in the state of Michoacán, three companies have just begun producing turbomachinery components: Turalmex, Turbinas y Equipos Industriales, and Sistemas de Energía Autónoma. In Guadalupe, Zacatecas, a factory for agricultural tractors with a productive capacity of 13,600 tractors of medium size (70, 86, and 135 HP) per year is ready to commence operations. It will provide almost 800 jobs. Of particular interest to this study is that it was constituted with NAFIN as majority stockholder and Ford Motor Company as minority stockholder and supplier of technology.[49] Manufacturera de Cigueñales de México, S.A. de C.V., has two manufacturing installations, one in Tenango del Valle, state of México, which started operations at the beginning of 1981, and one in Ramos Arizpa, Coahuila, which initiated production on March 13, 1982. The former installation produces VAM six-cylinder and Chrysler six- and eight-cylinder crankshafts; total output capacity is 120,000 units per year. The latter

TABLE 4.21

Capital Goods Industries Constituted by NAFIN, 1977-82

Company	Partners	Total Investment (millions of pesos)[a]	Subscribed Capital Stock (millions of pesos)[b]	Date Set Up	Year Operations Began	Location	Number of Employees	Product Manufactured
Grupo Industrial NKS, S.A. de C.V.	NAFINSA (33.5%) SIDERMEX (33.5%) Kobe Steel (Japan) (33.0%)	18,923.0	5,895.0	9/1980	1984	Lázaro Cárdenas, Mich.	2,062	cast and forged products and machining service
Productora Mexicana de Tubería, S.A. de C.V.	NAFINSA (34.0%) SIDERMEX (26.0%) Sumitomo Metal Industries (Japan) (40.0%)	6,075.0	1,300.0	11/1980	1983	Lázaro Cárdenas, Mich.	1,100	seamed pipe in diameters between 16" and 48"
Tuborreactores, S.A.	NAFINSA (14.0%) Aeroméxico (35.5%) Cía. Mexicana de Aviación (35.5%) International Support Systems (USA) (15.0%)	5,700.0	1,400.0	5/1980	1982	Querétaro, Qro.	298	maintenance and repair service for jet engines
Productora de Engranes y Reductores, S.A. de C.V.	NAFINSA (32.5%) SIDERMEX (32.5%) Technocommerz (GDR) (35.0%)	4,500.0	1,100.0	9/1981	1984	Cd. Xicotencatl, Tlax.	654	gears and speed reducers up to 18,000 HP
Fábrica de Tractores Agrícolas, S.A.	NAFINSA (60.0%) Ford Motor Co. (USA) (40.0%)	5,973.8	1,100.0	9/1981	1983	Guadalupe, Zac.	760	agricultural tractors of 70, 86, and 135 HP
Turalmex, S.A.	NAFINSA (75%) BBC Brown, Boveri & Co., Ltd. (Switzerland) (25%)	2,553.2	1,020.0	7/1980	1983	Morelia, Mich.	412	steam turbines and electric generators for alternating current from 1 to 110 MW
Turbinas y Equipos Industriales, S.A.	NAFINSA (70.0%) Sulzer Brothers, Ltd. (Switzerland) (30.0%)	1,474.0	720.0	7/1981	1982	Morelia, Mich.	617	hydraulic turbines of 10 to 350 MW
Compañía de Manufacturas Metálicas Pesadas, S.A. de C.V.	NAFINSA (60.0%) Fondo Franco-Mexicano de Coinversiones (31.1%) Construction Métallique de Provence (France) (8.9%)	890.0	225.0	5/1979	1982	Tampico, Tamps.	300	pressure vessels, tower or column reactors, and spherical tanks
Interruptores de México, S.A.	NAFINSA (67.0%) Siemens (FRG) (33.0%)	674.0	200.0	7/1977	1980	Villa Corregidora, Qro.	130	SF_6 circuit breakers for up to 400 kV

Company	Ownership				Year	Location		Products
Sistemas de Energía Autónoma, S.A. de C.V.	NAFINSA (11.0%) FOMIN (25.0%) Fondo Israelí-Mexicano de Coinversiones (24.0%) Ormat Turbines Ltd. (Israel) (40.0%)	933.0	50.0	9/1981	1983	Morelia, Mich.	400	closed-cycle turbo-generators based on nonconventional sources of energy
Telettra Industrial, S.A.	NAFINSA (14.0%) Fondo Italo-Mexicano de Coinversiones (33.0%) Private investors (4.0%) Telettra Internazionale (Italy) (49.0%)	363.0	100.0	8/1978	1978	Federal District	160	transmitters and receivers for telephone systems and for long-distance communication; telecontrol equipment
KSB Mexicana, S.A.	NAFINSA (26.0%) BANAMEX (25.0%) KSB (FRG) (49.0%)	131.0	40.0	3/1980	1983	León, Gto., and Lagos de Moreno, Jal.	199	high-volume pumps with electric motor, and special pumps
Tecno Industrial Mexicana, S.A.	Fondo Germano-Mexicano de Co-inversiones (33.0%) Private investors (18.0%) Mannesmann Anlagenbau (FRG) (49.0%)	100.0	20.0	10/1978	1981	San Martín Texmelucan, Pue.	140	prefabricated tubing, supports, and supporting structures
Manufacturea de Cigüenales de México, S.A. de C.V.	NAFINSA (50.0%) SOMEX (50.0%)	1,650.0	800.0	11/1978	1981	Tenango, Mex., and Ramos Arizpe, Coah.	604	automotive crankshafts
TOTAL		49,940.0	13,970.0				7,836	

[a] At June 1982 prices and exchange rate of 50 pesos per dollar.

[b] At June 1982.

Source: Various issues of NAFIN, *Informe anual*, 1977-82.

TABLE 4.22

Nacional Financiera, S.A.: Financial Performance
of the Industrial Group, 1977-81
(millions of real pesos)

Year	(1)	(2)	(3)	(4)	(5)	(6)	(7)	(8)
1977	69	37,588.2	198.2	.39	.10	.04	.12	113,861
1978	71	40,369.8	229.3	.44	.03	.01	.04	125,355
1979	73	42,531.7	281.7	.53	.02	.01	.03	137,559
1980	81	48,918.0	299.3	.51	.04	.02	.04	154,376
1981	88	53,161.1	305.0	.44	.03	.01	.03	175,072

(1) = Number of companies.
(2) = Paid-in capital stock.
(3) = New sales per day.*
(4) = Total asset turnover.
(5) = Profit margin on net sales.
(6) = Return on total investment (ROI).
(7) = Return on net worth.
(8) = Employees.
*For convenience, the financial community generally uses
360 rather than 365 as the number of days in the year.
Sources: Computed from various issues of NAFIN, *Informe
anual*, 1977-82, Banco Nacional de México; *Mexico Statistical
Data, 1970-79* (México, D.F.: BANAMEX, 1980), p. 32.

manufactures Chrysler four-cylinder crankshafts and can produce 270,000 units annually. The two industrial plans presently
employ 604 persons.[50] NAFIN and Fomento Industrial SOMEX
provided equal parts of the risk capital of this company.

So far we have examined in some detail the promotional
activities of NAFIN in the industrial sector. Let us now assess
the performance of the companies promoted by the development
bank in the industrial sector, using the limited information at
our disposal. The evaluation is undertaken via a ratio analysis
of the financial data taken from the industrial group's balance
sheets and income statements for 1977-81.[51] A summary of the
various financial ratios used, along with other relevant information, is presented in Table 4.22.

As of December 31, 1981, the NAFIN industrial group
was made up of 88 companies; on the same date two years
earlier it had consisted of 73 companies. This reveals the

intense promotion of basic industry undertaken by the public
sector beginning in 1978. Column (2) reveals that the paid-in
capital stock of the companies increased in real terms at a
rate of 8.2 percent per year between 1977 and 1981. By the
end of 1981, the total subscribed capital stock of the 88 industrial enterprises amounted to 117 billion real pesos, of which
53.2 billion was paid—an increase of 35 percent over the previous year. As was indicated in Table 4.20, the direct participation of NAFIN in the paid-in capital stock was 21.7 billion
real pesos, 41 percent of the total. At the end of 1981, the
stock holdings of Nacional Financiera were mainly in the sub-
groups of iron and steel (Altos Hornos) (47.5 percent); chemicals (27.8 percent); mining (10 percent); automotive industry
(3.6 percent); cellulose, pulp, and paper (Atenquique), and
mechanical machinery and parts (2.7 percent).[52]

Next, we consider the financial ratios displayed in columns 3-7. The first two of these are activity ratios, and
measure how effectively the firms are using their resources;
the remaining columns are profitability ratios, and measure
management's overall effectiveness as shown by the returns
generated on sales and investment.

The first activity ratio, given by column 3, is defined
as the ratio of net real sales to the number of days in the
years. Throughout the period this variable exhibited a positive rate of growth, especially between 1978 and 1979, when it
registered an increase of almost 23 percent. A more precise
measure is given by the turnover of all the firms' assets,
reported in column 4. Calculated by dividing net real sales by
total real assets, it provides information to determine whether
the companies are generating a sufficient volume of business
for the size of their total investment. This ratio attained a
high of .53 in 1979 before declining for two years in a row,
particularly between 1980 and 1981. The latter development
reflects the fact that even though net sales increased at a
satisfactory rate during this period, they were not sufficient
to offset the intense pace of investment of 1979-81.

We now turn to a consideration of the profitability
ratios, beginning with the profit margin on sales reported in
column 5. The latter, computed by dividing net income after
taxes by net sales, gives the profit per real peso of net
sales. It is evident that the profit margin of these companies
experienced a precipitous drop of 70 percent between 1977
and 1978. In fact, since 1978 their average profit margin has
been only 3 percent, perhaps indicating that the companies'
sales prices are relatively too low or that their costs are

relatively high, or both. Not surprisingly, the ratio of net
profit to total assets, the ROI as it is frequently called, is
also quite low, since it is computed as follows:

net profits/net sales × net sales/total assets = ROI

In other words, the low ratios displayed in column 6
result from the low profit margin on sales and/or from the low
turnover of total assets—the product of columns 4 and 5.
Next, we consider the rate of return on net worth, the stockholders' investment. It is computed by dividing the net worth
of these companies into the net profit after taxes. Since the
latter declined for two consecutive years while the former
steadily increased throughout the period, it is no wonder that
the ratios in column 7 were so low for 1978-81. Column 8 reveals the employment record of the NAFIN industrial group.
The rate of employment creation of almost 11 percent per year
for these companies was superior to the national annual rate
of 4.9 percent.[53]
Thus, on the basis of the financial ratios and other
information presented in Table 4.22, it can be said that the
overall performance of these companies was, by and large,
satisfactory until 1980. However, from the stockholders' point
of view, the years after 1977 left much to be desired. This
trend is not likely to be reversed in the near future, since
many of these firms have experienced, and are experiencing,
severe liquidity problems as a result of the financial and economic crisis of 1982. For example, during the first half of
1983 the board of directors of NAFIN agreed to transfer to
the state and workers those companies whose activities were
no longer deemed of "high" enough priority to justify the participation of the institution. In reality, this amounted to an
admission of the bank's inability to cover the substantial
losses incurred by these firms. A case in point was the sale
to the federal government of the bank's equity holdings in
FERDIMEX and SIDERMEX. The transfer of shares in Inter-
ruptores de México, S.A., has been completed, and the sale
of the institution's holdings in Productos Cowen is under
way.[54] The resources generated by these sales have been
applied to the support of the remaining companies in the
industrial group.

SUMMARY AND CONCLUSIONS

It should be apparent from the evidence presented in this chapter that during initial industrialization, Nacional Financiera, S.A., played a significant role in mobilizing the productive use of idle savings already in existence in Mexico. However, with the development and growth of the economy along private lines, and a result of the policies pursued by the public sector, the bank's role began to diminish vis-à-vis the banking system in general, and private *financieras* in particular. The stabilization policies pursued by the Mexican government stimulated the development of the private sector by creating an economic environment free from the misallocations induced by rapid inflation. By the same token, these policies exacerbated existing structural weaknesses endemic to the Mexican economy, and thus planted the seeds for their abandonment in the early 1970s. This turn of events paved the way for a renewed participation by the public sector in the promotion of industry and employment, particularly in the petrochemical and capital goods industries. NAFIN, in its capacity as a national industrial bank, once again assumed a leading role in the support and development of the companies that form a part of the productive infrastructure of the country.

APPENDIX: ALMON DISTRIBUTED
LAG MODEL RESULTS

An Almon lag model was fitted to the reduced form model of the section "Empirical Analysis . . ." because the results suggest that NAFIN's financing does not become important until two periods into the past. A Koyck lag model was not used because it assumes geometrically declining weights, and it violates the OLS assumptions by replacing the lagged independent variables with the lagged dependent variable.

The following results were obtained when running this lag structure:

Period
1940-76 $\Delta Q_t = -1,002.66 + 31.17 \Delta L_t + .91 \Delta K_t^M - .25 \Delta N_t$

   (-1.39)*   (3.32)***   (2.64)***   (-1.12)

$+ .48 \Delta N_{t-1} + .9 \Delta N_{t-2} + .87 \Delta N_{t-3}$

   (1.54)*   (2.25)**   (1.74)**

R^2	$Ad_j R^2$	D.W.	F	n
.71	.66	1.8	12.93***	37

   * = Significant at the 10 percent level.
  ** = Significant at the 5 percent level.
 *** = Significant at the 1 percent level.

Each period is a year. There is a lagged effect in the provision of financing by NAFIN to industry. Thus, NAFIN's financing to industry today does not have a full impact on industrial output until two to three years in the future. Also, notice the considerable improvement in the value for the Durbin-Watson statistic.

NOTES

1. NAFIN, *La economía mexicana en cifras* (México, D.F.: NAFIN, 1978), pp. 19-45.

2. Ibid., pp. 44-45.

3. Various issues of Banco de México, *Informe anual* (México, D.F.: Banco de México, 1950-76).

4. Roger Hansen, *The Politics of Mexican Development*, 2nd ed. (Baltimore: Johns Hopkins University Press, 1973), p. 48.

5. Dwight S. Brothers and Leopoldo Solis M., *Mexican Financial Development* (Austin: University of Texas Press, 1966), p. 164.

6. Jorge Eduardo Navarrete, "Las dos caras de la moneda," in Navarrete, ed., *Questiones económicas nacionales* (México, D.F.: Banco Nacional de Comercio Exterior, 1971), p. 365.

7. Ricardo Torres Gaitan, "La política de commercio exterior," in Jorge Eduardo Navarrete, ed., *Questiones económicas nacionales* (México, D.F.: Banco Nacional de Comercio Exterior, 1971), p. 299.

8. Ibid., p. 300.

9. "Economic and Social Progress in Latin America," in *IDB, 1980-81 Report* (Washington, D.C.: Inter-American Development Bank, 1982), p. 98.

10. Ibid., p. 102.

11. Rosario Green, "La deuda externa del gobierno mexicano," in Nora Lustig, ed., *Panorama y perspectivas de la economía mexicana* (México, D.F.: Colegio de México, 1980), p. 487.

12. Rosario Green, *El endeudamiento público externo de México: 1940-73* (México, D.F.: Colegio de México, 1976), pp. 130-31, 154.

13. Banco de México, *Información económica: Producto interno bruto y gasto, cuadernos 1960-77* (México, D.F.: Banco de México, 1971): IPI/B6-001-00-08-78.

14. Ibid.

15. NAFIN, op. cit., pp. 370-72.

16. Hansen, op. cit., p. 45.

17. Brothers and Solis M., op. cit., p. 95.

18. Banco de México, *Informe anual* (México, D.F.: the Bank, 1940-50).

19. Hansen, op. cit., p. 50.

20. For further details see Dwight S. Brothers, "El financiamiento de la formación de capital en México, 1950-61," in Jorge Eduardo Navarrete, ed., *Questiones económicas nacionales* (México, D.F.: Banco Nacional de Comercio Exterior, 1971), pp. 79-103.

21. Brothers and Solis M., op. cit., pp. 59-61.

22. Ibid., p. 61.

23. Hansen, op. cit., p. 5.

24. Brothers and Solis M., op. cit., p. 203.

25. Hansen, op. cit., p. 54.

26. See NAFIN, op. cit., p. 256.

27. Banco de México, *Informe anual* (México, D.F.: the Bank, 1964-66).

28. "Secretaría de Hacienda y Crédito Público, Dirección General de Crédito," *Legislacion bancaria* (México, D.F.: the Secretariat, S.H.C.P., 1957), I, pp. 27-28.

29. Data have been transformed into real terms (1960 = 100). They were obtained from NAFIN, op. cit., as well as from various issues of the *Anuario estadístico de los Estados Unidos Mexicanos* (México, D.F.: Secretaría de Programación y Presupuesto (S.S.P), 1940-53).

30. Robert M. Solow, "Technical Change and the Aggregate Production Function," *Review of Economics and Statistics* 39 (1957): 312-20.

31. Raymond W. Goldsmith, *The Financial Development of Mexico* (Paris: OECD, 1961).

32. Manuel Gollas, "Orígenes de la desigualdad en la distribución del ingreso familiar en Mexico," in Nora Lustig, ed., *Panorama y perspectivas de la economía mexicana* (México, D.F.: Colegio de México, 1980), p. 141.

33. For further information see NAFIN, op. cit., pp. 3-13.

34. Leopoldo Solis M., "Reflexiones sobre el panorama general de la economía mexicana," in Hector E. Gonzales, ed., *El sistema económico mexicano* (México, D.F.: La Red de Jonas Premia Editora, 1982), p. 340.

35. NAFIN, op. cit., p. 226.

36. Ibid., p. 384.

37. "Economic and Social Progress in Latin America," *IDB, 1980-81 Report* (Washington, D.C.: Inter-American Development Bank, 1982), p. 102.

38. Solis M., "Reflexiones," p. 344.

39. Rene Villarreal, "De la industrialización sustitutiva a la petrodependencia externa y desustitición de importaciones," in Hector E. Gonzales, ed., *El sistema económico mexicano* (México, D.F.: La Red de Jonas Premia Editora, 1982), p. 31.

40. See NAFIN, op. cit., pp. 380-87.

41. Ibid., pp. 3-15.

42. Solis, "Reflexiones," p. 351.

43. Banco Nacional de México, *Mexico Statistical Data, 1970-79* (México, D.F.: BANAMEX, 1980), p. 55.

44. Solis, "Reflexiones," p. 352.

45. NAFIN, *Informe anual* (México, D.F.: NAFIN, 1982), p. 53.

46. Ibid.

47. Ibid., p. 52.

48. Various issues of NAFIN, *Informe anual* (México, D.F.: NAFIN, 1980-82).

49. NAFIN, *Informe anual* (México, D.F.: NAFIN, 1982), p. 57.

50. Ibid.

51. Various issues of NAFIN, *Informe anual* (México, D.F.: NAFIN, 1979-82).

52. NAFIN, *Informe anual* (México, D.F.: NAFIN, 1982).

53. "Statistical Report," *Financial Monthly Report* no. 5 (September 1983) (México, D.F.: S.H.C.P.), p. 89.

54. NAFIN, *Informe anual* (México, D.F.: NAFIN, 1984), p. 34.

5

NAFIN's Participation In
The Development Of
The Financial Sector

INTRODUCTION

The purpose of this chapter is to assess empirically the
contribution of NAFIN and private *financieras* to the growth
and development of the financial sector. The analysis is undertaken by relating the operations of these intermediaries to the
structure, organization, and institutional development of the
financial superstructure.

The chapter is organized as follows: First, it gives a
descriptive account of the principal characteristics of the
financial sector as it has evolved during initial and sustained
industrialization. Second, we employ the classification system
developed in chapter 4 to evaluate the performance of NAFIN
both from its own vantage point and relative to that of the
banking system. Third, various investment functions are estimated that incorporate both the long-term credits provided
by NAFIN and those of private *financieras*. In addition, a
supply-demand model similar to that presented in chapter 2
is estimated to determine the significance of the contribution
of NAFIN and private *financieras*. The chapter is brought to
a close by summarizing the major results and discussing their
implications for Mexico's future financial development.

PRINCIPAL CHARACTERISTICS OF THE FINANCIAL SECTOR
Basic Trends in Financial Development

The growth and development of Mexico's financial sector
since 1945 have paralleled those of its real sector, both in

TABLE 5.1

Real Assets and Obligations of the Financial Sector
in Relation to GDP,* 1945-75
(millions of real pesos)

Year	GDP (1)	Assets (2)	Liabilities (3)	2/1	3/1
1945	57,513.4	18,255.8	15,005.9	31.7	26.1
1950	75,400.4	22,860.7	18,222.6	30.3	24.2
1955	102,748.2	30,311.4	26,122.8	29.5	25.4
1960	150,511.0	48,676.7	42,787.8	32.3	28.4
1965	229,742.9	95,862.0	87,079.5	41.7	37.9
1970	330,726.7	174,826.3	164,640.0	52.9	49.8
1975	473,015.1	250,840.0	239,981.9	53.0	50.7

*The reserves of the system are obtained by subtracting
(3) from (2).
   Source: NAFIN, La economía mexicana en cifras (México,
D.F.: NAFIN, 1978), pp. 247-53, 18-19.

size and in the diversity of its private and public institutions.
Some indication of its growth is given by the fact that the
resources of all financial intermediaries rose from 18.3 billion
real pesos in 1945 to 250.9 billion real pesos in 1975—in percentage terms, an increase in excess of 173 percent.[1] A better
measure of the rapid expansion of the financial superstructure
is given by the ratio of either financial resources or liabilities
to gross domestic product, displayed in Table 5.1.

   The financial sector's ability to attract funds from surplus spending units—as measured by the ratio of total liabilities to GDP—increased rapidly after the implementation of the
stabilization policies discussed in the previous chapters. By
the end of 1972—the last year before these policies were
abandoned—the total liabilities:GDP ratio attained an all-time
high of 54 percent.[2]

   Besides the overall growth in the assets and obligations
of the financial sector, substantial changes occurred in the
relative position and number of the various financial entities
comprising the banking system. For instance, although private
credit institutions far outnumbered their counterparts in the
public sector in 1940, the total assets of the public institutions

represented over 64 percent of the total resources of the banking system.[3] Three decades later, private financial entities held both a numerical advantage as a percent of the total assets (resources) of the banking system and, as indicated in Table 5.2, a relative one.

Particularly noteworthy is the rapid growth of public *financieras* such as NAFIN during initial industrialization, and that of private *financieras* (development banks) after 1955. In fact, most of the growth of the private sector can be attributed to that of *financieras* and mortgage banks. The waning importance of the public sector between 1950 and 1970 can be attributed, by and large, to a reduction in the rate of growth of the Bank of Mexico's assets. This promotion of the private sector in general, and that of private *financieras* in particular, was consistent with the industrialization program pursued by the government, for the majority of the credits granted by the latter were, and are, long term.[4] By contrast, the credits granted by commercial banks (deposit and savings institutions), which experienced a relative decline between 1955 and 1972, are primarily for less than one year. In this respect, it can be argued that there is a sharp division of labor in Mexico's financial sector that is different from that found in the United States, for although private development banks

> . . . in the United States do make industrial loans, they are generally thought of as important consumer credit organizations. The commercial bank is about the only credit institution in Mexico that makes consumer loans, and these are usually on a thirty, sixty, or ninety-day note.[5]

One final trend brought to light by Table 5.2 is the re-emergence of public institutions as a result of the abandonment of the stabilization program. In particular, the Bank of Mexico began to acquire increasing amounts of bonds issued by government agencies and public enterprises. Also, the role of national banks in providing productive financing to government-approved projects has expanded. Although not shown in the table, NAFIN's assets as a share of the total resources of the banking system jumped from 7.9 percent in 1975 to 10.2 percent by the end of 1976.[6]

At this point it will be expedient to turn our attention to certain developments in Mexico's capital market or stock exchange. There are three organized stock exchanges in the country: the Bolsa de Valores de México, S.A., the Bolsa de

TABLE 5.2

Share of Resources of Credit Institutions in Resources of the Banking System, 1940–75
(percent)

Year	Private Institutions					Public Institutions			
	Total	Deposit and Savings	Financieras	Mortgage Banks	Other	Total	Bank of Mexico	NAFIN	Other
1940	34.9	31.8	—	1.3	1.7	65.1	48.5	0.8	15.8
1945	45.4	35.0	5.7	2.2	2.5	54.6	41.2	6.0	7.4
1950	42.8	32.5	5.9	1.2	3.2	57.2	36.2	7.8	13.2
1955	42.9	33.2	6.6	0.8	2.3	57.1	29.9	8.3	18.9
1960	45.8	27.9	15.5	0.8	1.6	54.2	22.7	13.3	18.2
1965	51.6	25.5	20.0	4.9	1.2	48.4	17.4	13.6	17.4
1970	57.7	21.5	29.2	6.2	0.8	42.3	14.5	13.5	14.3
1971	57.1	20.3	29.5	6.6	0.7	42.9	14.2	12.5	16.2
1972	54.2	19.0	28.0	6.6	0.6	45.8	18.9	11.9	15.0
1973	51.4	19.8	24.8	6.2	0.6	48.6	21.0	11.0	16.6
1974	47.7	18.6	22.7	5.9	0.5	52.3	23.7	10.2	18.4
1975	43.2	16.3	20.9	5.5	0.5	56.8	21.5	7.9	27.4

Source: Computed from NAFIN, *La economía mexicana en cifras* (México, D.F.: NAFIN, 1978), pp. 282–83.

150

TABLE 5.3

Registered Transactions on All Exchanges, 1940-75
(millions of real pesos)

	1940	1950	1955	1960	1965	1970	1975
Mexico City	29.1	103.0	275.4	5,103.7	19,521.4	26,660.7	64,602.7
Monterrey	—	2.5	21.3	175.1	725.7	2,917.1	18,567.3
Guadalajara	—	—	—	0.2	59.1	1,546.4	7,171.5

Sources: Banco de México, S.A., various issues of *Informe anual* (México, D.F.: the Bank, 1955-75); NAFIN, *La economía mexicana en cifras* (México, D.F.: NAFIN, 1978).

Valores de Monterrey, S.A., and the Bolsa de Valores de Guadalajara, S.A. The stock exchange in Mexico City, the Bolsa de Valores de México, is by far the largest and oldest of the exchanges. It was created in 1933, and the value of its registered transactions represented over 67 percent of that on all three exchanges in 1975.[7] The Bolsa de Valores de Monterrey came into existence in 1950, and that of Guadalajara was established a decade later. In Table 5.3 the real value of registered transactions on the three exchanges is given for 1940-75.

Not surprisingly, the real value of securities traded in the exchanges experienced a significant rise as a result of the monetary and financial stability that prevailed during the 1960s. This was the case not only with bonds and other fixed-yield securities, but also with equity or variable-income securities. As indicated in Table 5.4, the share of equity sales in the total transactions effected in the Bolsa de Valores de México rose from just over 3 percent in 1960 to almost 7 percent in 1965.

Still, the small importance of equity financing since 1956 among investors and savers has been the consequence of the refusal of Mexican entrepreneurs to "issue shares and thereby suffer loss of control over policies and profits as well as loss of secrecy as a result of being required to disclose their financial position,"[8] and the greater diversity and liquidity of financial instruments at the disposal of savers. Beginning in 1960, the Bank of Mexico induced private *financieras* to shift from short-term to long-term borrowing by imposing a ceiling of 12 percent per year on the rate of increase of the former. This policy became quite effective in stimulating the growth of the capital market, since the bonds issued by the *financieras*

TABLE 5.4

Transactions in the Bolsa de Valores de México, 1960-75
(percent)

Year	Total	Equity Issues	Fixed-Income Securities		
			Total	Public Sector	Private Sector
1960	100.0	3.1	96.9	44.1	52.8
1965	100.0	6.8	93.2	22.3	70.9
1970	100.0	2.1	97.9	23.7	74.2
1971	100.0	2.1	97.9	24.4	73.5
1972	100.0	3.0	97.0	10.8	86.2
1973	100.0	3.3	96.7	12.2	84.5
1974	100.0	2.6	97.4	11.6	95.8
1975	100.0	3.2	96.8	14.5	82.3

Source: Computed from various issues of the Boletín
mensual of the Comisión Nacional de Valores, 1960-75.

paid a relatively higher rate of interest, and the financieras
stood ready to repurchase their outstanding securities at any
time at par.[9] The popularity of these issues among individuals
and enterprises was so great that their share in the total
fixed-income securities in circulation in Mexico increased from
6.4 percent in 1960 to 23.4 percent in 1965.[10] In fact, ever
since 1965 the value of these securities in circulation has surpassed those of Nacional Financiera.[11]

At this point, it should be mentioned that private financieras, Nacional Financiera, and the Bank of Mexico generally
deal directly with purchasers and sellers of securities. Thus,
despite the rapid growth of the organized exchanges in
recent years, their share in the total volume of securities
traded in the country is still quite small. For instance, in
1972—the latest year for which we have reliable data—the total
transactions effected through these exchanges comprised only
9 percent of all securities traded in Mexico; the balance was
on the over-the-counter market.[12] Leopoldo Solis and Dwight
Brothers attribute this to the practice of public and private
credit institutions of maintaining the market price of their
obligations ". . . at the nominal or par value (face value) of
these instruments regardless of changes in basic supply and
demand conditions."[13] In turn, this general policy of sup-

porting bond prices was, and is, designed to insure lenders against the risk of capital losses, and thereby ". . . bolster public confidence in the financial sector."[14] The success of this measure in attracting surplus funds is attested by the rapid growth of fixed-income securities between 1960 and 1972. In 1960, the real value of these securities stood at 11,150.2 million pesos; by 1972 it had risen to 68,555.9 million pesos. Relative to the resources of the banking system, their share rose from 41.7 percent in 1960 to 48 percent in 1972.[15]

Still, the greater liquidity and high yield of these obligations not only implies distortions in the market rates of interest but also (and more importantly), during times of uncertainty and/or intense inflation, it may lead to a substantial flight of capital from the country. As observed in chapter 4, this is exactly what happened during 1976. To remedy this situation, the Ministry of Finance and Public Credit established by decree a central exchange in 1976, the Bolsa de Valores de México. The latter is the result of a merger of the existing exchanges, and it is hoped ". . . that a central exchange will help diversify the sources of financing, and widen the range of savings and investment instruments, improve the capitalization of companies, and stimulate increased stockholder interest in Mexico."[16]

Structure and Organization of the Financial Sector

At the center of Mexico's financial sector is the Bank of Mexico, which with the Ministry of Finance and Public Credit sets policies and regulations. The latter are implemented by the National Bank and Insurance Commission and the National Securities Commission.[17] As we have seen in this chapter and chapter 4, the Bank of Mexico exerts monetary control in accordance with the economic growth priorities established by the Mexican state. Thus, during the "stabilizing development" of the 1960s, the Bank of Mexico established obligatory reserves on additional or marginal deposits of commercial banks of up to 100 percent. (The practice of altering incremental deposits or marginal deposits taken in after a specified date is preferred, since it tends to be less disruptive to the normal operations of banks than if the requirements are imposed on total bank deposits.[18]) These could be dispensed with only if the banks were willing to make their new deposits available to deficit spending units in accordance with a scheme determined

TABLE 5.5

Legal Reserves Demanded of Commercial Banks
(percent)

	Sight Deposits[a]		
	Mexico City	Outside Mexico City	Time Deposits
Deposits in the Bank of Mexico	15	15	15
In security investments and loans	60	55	85
Industrial securities	5	5	5
Medium-term loans	15	15	15
Credit for productive activities	5	25[b]	25
Credit for consumer goods	—	—	25[c]
Securities of the federal government (5%)	25	10	15
Securities of the federal government (8%)	10	—	—
Freely disposable funds	25	30	—

[a]Includes time deposits with maturities of less than
30 days.

[b]Only for agriculture, livestock, and forestry.

[c]Can be invested in industrial securities with the ap-
proval of the monetary authorities.

Source: Obtained from Antonin Basch, *El mercado de capitales en México* (México, D.F.: Centro de Estudios Monetarios
Latinoamericanos, 1968), p. 53.

by the Bank of Mexico and the National Bank and Insurance
Commission. Table 5.5 shows the various proportions in which
commercial banks were obligated to invest their incremental
deposits if they wished to avoid the 100 percent legal reserve
requirement.

By far the greater part of these newly acquired funds
had to be made available to government-approved investment
projects or invested in government securities. Similar but less
restrictive measures were imposed on private *financieras* beginning in 1958.[19] Marginal deposits denominated in foreign

currency (mostly dollars) were subject to even stricter requirements. For example, 65 percent of incremental deposits in foreign currency had to be invested in government securities paying
an annual rate of interest of 3 percent.[20] The practice of regulating the composition of bank assets in order to influence
the allocation of resources among competing projects has continued into recent times. For instance, the legal reserve
requirement of private financial institutions as of January 31,
1977,

> . . . stipulated that 30% of each peso deposit was
> to be held as cash in the Banco de Mexico, 10%
> was to be invested in government securities, 40%
> was to be allocated to government-endorsed growth
> industries, and 20% could be invested freely.[21]

Besides these selective controls, the Banco de México
regulates the interest rates that private financial institutions
can pay on time deposits and their term obligations, as well as
those they can charge on loans. In fact, it will be argued subsequently that its policy with respect to interest rates was
instrumental in the impressive growth of private *financieras*.

Public Financial Institutions

By the end of 1976 there existed in Mexico 21 national or
public credit institutions besides the Banco de México. The
importance of these financial intermediaries to the overall development strategy cannot be emphasized enough, for through
them the Mexican government controlled over 35 percent of the
resources of the banking system (see Table 5.2). By far the
most important of these was, and is, Nacional Financiera (a detailed account of its institutional development was provided in
chapter 3). Still, the emphasis in chapters 3 and 4 was on its
promotion of industry, not its role in fostering the development
of a market for fixed-income securities. We will rectify this in
the next section when the bank's operations are evaluated, but
for now a brief examination of some of the other major public
credit institutions will be undertaken.

Banco Nacional de Obras y Servicios Públicos (BANOBRAS).
The country's major mortgage bank, this was established in
1933 to promote investments in public works at the federal and
state levels. It is also a primary source of funds for the construction of low-cost housing.[22] Some indication of its importance
is revealed by the fact that its resources as a share of those of

the banking system (excluding Banco de México) rose from
12.5 percent in 1960 to 17.5 percent in 1968.[23]

The bank's funds are obtained primarily from loans contracted domestically and abroad, the sale of its bonds (*bonos
hipotecarios*), and, to a lesser extent, its capital and reserves.
The credits granted to the bank from domestic and foreign
sources increased in real terms from 858.3 million pesos
(31.2 percent of its resources) to 4,486.0 million pesos (52.6
percent) between 1960 and 1968, an increase of approximately
423 percent.[24] A similar expansion in the outstanding bonds
of the bank occurred during this period, but in relative terms
their share in the total sources of funds declined from 45.5
percent to 30.4 percent.[25]

Banco Nacional de Comercio Exterior, S.A. This bank is primarily concerned with promoting the growth and diversity of
Mexican exports. Since 1966 it has intensified its financing
and promotion of manufactured exports. Most of its funds are
derived from the bank's own capital and reserves, and are
used in granting short-term loans and discounting paper for
public enterprises in the external sector.[26]

Banco Nacional de Crédito Rural (BANRURAL). Although established in 1975, the roots of this financial intermediary reach
far into the past. It is the result of a merger of three agricultural development banks: the Banco Nacional de Crédito
Agrícola, founded in 1926; the Banco Nacional de Crédito
Ejidal, established in 1936; and the Banco Nacional Agro-
pecuario, created in 1965. The first two were instrumental in
implementing the objectives of the agrarian reform program via
their working-capital and fixed-asset loans to small farmers and
peasants. The Banco Nacional de Crédito Agrícola specialized
in granting long-term loans at subsidized rates to small farmers, while the Banco Nacional de Crédito Ejidal channeled its
financial resources primarily to peasants working communal
lands (*ejidos*) that had been recently expropriated.[27] Both
banks experienced severe pecuniary difficulties, for "many
farmers and peasants considered the credits obtained through
them as subsidies or outright gifts, and consequently, did not
bother to meet their payments."[28]

To rectify this situation, the Banco Nacional Agro-
pecuario was established in March 1965 with an authorized capital of 1,500 million pesos (nominal), most of which was subscribed by the federal government, the Banco de México, and
Nacional Financiera.[29] The implicit, if not explicit, objective

of the bank was to gradually decentralize the system by indirectly supporting farmers and peasants through affiliated, but independent, local agricultural development banks. In this manner, direct and personalized transactions—the source of considerable inefficiency and preferential treatment—would be minimized.[30] Eventually, all three agricultural development banks fused to form the Banco Nacional de Crédito Rural, which, as of 1975, implemented its policies via nine affiliated agricultural banks at the regional level.

Private Financial Institutions

At the end of 1976 there were 628 private and private-leaning credit institutions in Mexico, with total assets worth 146,741.5 million real pesos.[31] As shown in Table 5.2, deposit and savings banks, along with private development banks, accounted for the lion's share of these resources. Mortgage banks and other credit institutions, such as capitalization banks and trust companies, comprised the remainder. Tables 5.6 and 5.7 contain data showing the impressive increase that occurred between 1940 and 1972 in the various types of private credit institutions as well as the growth in their assets.

TABLE 5.6

Number of Private Credit Institutions, 1940-72

	1940	1950	1955	1960	1965	1972
Banking system	140	517	572	580	590	621
Deposit banks	61	106	106	102	105	106
Savings banks	6	80	100	111	120	122
Private *financieras*	—	96	92	98	97	92
Mortgage banks	2	20	24	26	25	25
Trust companies	—	95	98	114	124	140
Savings and loan associations	—	5	4	3	3	3
Capitalization banks	8	16	16	12	13	12
Other*	63	99	132	114	103	121
Branches and agencies	99	559	836	2,378	3,379	5,518

*Includes the stock exchanges, general deposit warehouses, general house associations, and credit unions.

Source: Compiled from NAFIN, *La economía mexicana en cifras* (México, D.F.: NAFIN, 1978), pp. 237-44.

TABLE 5.7

Assets of Private Credit Institutions, 1940-72
(millions of real pesos)

	1940	1950	1955	1960	1965	1972
Deposit and savings banks	4,058.1	9,577.0	12,131.0	16,253.7	27,765.2	50,087.2
Private *financieras*	—	1,739.0	2,414.9	9,057.8	21,706.1	73,593.4
Mortgage loan banks	174.7	360.7	283.9	471.3	5,463.2	17,315.3
Other	340.8	925.2	845.4	933.8	1,217.7	1,602.0
Total	4,573.6	12,601.9	15,675.2	26,716.6	56,152.2	142,597.9

Source: Computed from NAFIN, *La economía mexicana en cifras* (México, D.F.: NAFIN, 1978), pp. 281-83.

During the 1940s and early 1950s, deposit and savings banks exhibited the highest rates of growth, both in numbers and in resources. This is not surprising, since they were simply ". . . reflecting the need of the economy for the relatively simple instruments which these institutions were capable of providing."[32] Of far more interest to this study is the rapid growth of private *financieras*, particularly of their resources, after 1955.

The relative advantage of private *financieras* vis-à-vis commercial banks was the direct outcome of less restrictive legal reserve requirements on added deposits and an absence of such requirements on funds obtained through the issue of fixed-income securities (*bonos financieros*). Furthermore, in light of the important role these intermediaries play in financing private investment, they were allowed by the monetary authorities to pay higher rates of interest on their nonmonetary obligations (4-6 percent in real terms) throughout the 1960s.[33] No such advantage was attached to their sight and time deposits, for they were subject to the same marginal reserve requirements as deposit and savings banks. A summary of the various changes in the legal reserve requirements of private *financieras* during the 1960s is presented in Table 5.8.

Beginning in January 1958, 20 percent of each additional peso had to be held either in government securities or in cash with the Banco de México. Otherwise, it became subject to a 100 percent legal reserve requirement—identical to that in existence for savings and deposit banks since 1955. These requirements were stricter for deposits denominated in foreign currency, especially after March 1959. Also shown in Table 5.8 are the higher reserve requirements imposed on *financieras* during 1960 for additional funds acquired via short-term instruments. If the latter exceeded 1 percent per month, they had to be held entirely as nonearning cash in the vaults of the Banco de México. This measure was adopted by the monetary authorities in accordance with a general policy designed to foster the development of a market for long-term funds.[34] In 1966 the Bank of Mexico induced private *financieras* to issue securities with maturities ranging between two and five years—the *certificados financieros*. As can be seen in Table 5.8, the funds acquired via their issue had to be invested primarily in government securities and/or other approved investments. As before, failure to do so meant that they had to be held as noninterest-bearing cash in the Banco de México.

Turning to Tables 5.6 and 5.7 once again, we can discern another significant development in the evolution of the

TABLE 5.8

Changes in the Legal Reserve Requirements of Private *Financieras*, 1958–66 (percent)

	January 1958 Domestic Monies	January 1958 Foreign Monies	March 1959 Foreign Monies	May 1960 Domestic Monies (a)	May 1960 Domestic Monies (b)	November 1966 Domestic Monies (c)	November 1966 Domestic Monies (d)
Deposits in the Banco de México	1	1	25	1	100	10	10
In obligatory investments and loans	19	24	75	99	0	90	90
Government securities	19	24	75	19	0	50	90
Other investments	0	0	0	80	0	40	0
Freely disposable	20	75	0	0	0	0	0

(a) = Applies to additional funds acquired after May 4, 1960.
(b) = Applies to increments in short-term obligations exceeding 1 percent per month.
(c) = Relevant to funds obtained via the issue of financial certificates before October 31, 1966.
(d) = Applicable to funds obtained via the issue of financial certificates after October 31, 1966.
Source: Derived from Antonio Gómez Oliver, *Política monetaria y fiscal de México, 1946–1976* (México, D.F.: Fondo de Cultura Económica, 1981), Table 19.

financial sector: the increasing concentration of resources among commercial banks and *financieras* after 1955. This is also revealed by the fact that even though the number of these institutions rose only slightly, their affiliated branches and agencies throughout the country grew by leaps and bounds. Moreover, within each group only a few institutions controlled the majority of assets and affiliated agencies. A case in point is that of the system of the Banco de Comercio, the largest in existence among deposit banks. It is composed of the Banco de Comercio, S.A., and 32 affiliated banks throughout the country. In 1964 the bank and its affiliates

TABLE 5.9

The Most Important Deposit Banks in Mexico, 1974
(millions of real pesos)

Institution	Resources	Resources as Percent of Total Assets of Commercial Banks[a]	Resources as Percent of Total Private Banking Assets
Sistema Bancos de Comercio	14,986.3	29.0	11.2
Banco Nacional de México, S.A.	14,016.1	26.9	10.5
Banco de Londres y México, S.A.	4,208.6	8.1	3.2
Banco Comercial Mexicano, S.A.	2,955.3	5.7	2.2
Banco Internacional, S.A.	1,267.5	2.4	1.0
Other[b]	3,942.0	7.6	3.0

[a]Savings banks are excluded.

[b]Includes Banco Mexicano, S.A.; Banco del Atlántico, S.A.; Banco Industrial de Jalisco, S.A.; First National City Bank; Banco Longoria, S.A.

Sources: Computed from *Anuario financiero de México,* XXXV (México, D.F.: Asociación be Banqueros de México, 1975); NAFIN, *La economía mexicana en cifras* (México, D.F.: NAFIN, 1978).

TABLE 5.10

The Most Important Private *Financieras*, 1974
(millions of real pesos)

Institution	Assets	As Percent of Total Assets of Private *Financieras*	As Percent of Total Private Banking Assets
Financiera Bancomer, S.A.	12,534.2	19.8	9.4
Financiera Banamex, S.A.	10,358.0	16.4	7.8
Financiera Acepta- ciones, S.A.	6,635.6	10.1	5.0
Sociedad Mexicana de Crédito Industrial, S.A.	4,416.1	7.0	3.3
Financiero Comermex, S.A.	4,398.0	6.9	3.3
Other*	9,027.7	14.2	6.8

*Includes Financiera del Norte, S.A.; Financiera del Atlántico, S.A.; Financiera Internacional, S.A.; Financiera Industrial, S.A.; Crédito Minero y Mercantil, S.A.; Financiera de Ventas Banamex, S.A.

Sources: Computed from *Anuario financiero de México*, XXXV (México, D.F.: Asociación de Banqueros de México, 1975); NAFIN, *La economía mexicana en cifras* (México, D.F.: NAFIN, 1978).

controlled 26 percent of the total assets of commercial banks, and ten years later their share had risen to 29 percent; the bank itself saw its share increase from 9.7 to 11.2 percent between 1964 and 1974.[35] A list of the most important deposit banks, arranged according to the size of their assets, is provided in Table 5.9.

The top three deposit banks, with their affiliated agencies and branches, controlled 64 and 24.9 percent of the assets of commercial banks and the private banking system, respectively. These figures underestimate the degree of concentration, for ". . . the large commercial banks control most of the large private development banks. . . ."[36] A glance at Table 5.7 reveals that the assets of the latter surpassed those of commercial banks in 1972. A list of the most important private *financieras* is presented in Table 5.10.

Although the degree of concentration is not as great as that of deposit banks, it is still quite high, especially since the resources of the top two *financieras* were greater than the combined assets of the next eight largest.

AN EVALUATION OF THE BANK'S OPERATIONS

In the previous section, we examined a number of significant developments in the evolution of the financial sector, as well as certain policies pursued by the monetary authorities to foster the development of a viable banking system. The present section attempts to evaluate NAFIN's contribution, if any, to the development of the financial sector—particularly that of the capital market. Again, a variety of tests similar to those employed in the previous chapter are used to assess the performance of the development bank during initial and sustained industrialization.

However, before proceeding to examination of the data, let us briefly consider the history and nature of the financial instruments issued by the bank.

It will be recalled from chapter 1 that one of the ways in which the bank can promote the emergence of a market for securities is by issuing its own bonds and/or debentures. In doing so, the development bank not only creates a market for its own financial instruments but also, and more importantly, it encourages savings on the part of surplus spending units by offering them the opportunity to hold a less risky and more diverse portfolio of assets. A case in point was NAFIN's issuance in 1941 of *certificados de participación* (certificates of participation). The latter became one of Mexico's most popular fixed-income securities and, until 1954, NAFIN's most reliable source of funds.[37] Their success among Mexican investors can be attributed to two major reasons: the bank stood ready to repurchase its outstanding securities at any time, at face value; and, as their name implies, they entitled holders to co-ownership of each and every one of the carefully selected securities that guaranteed their sale.[38] In the beginning, they were supported by government bonds; later, they were guaranteed by securities and bonds of NAFIN-supported enterprises.[39] These characteristics were especially attractive to Mexican investors, who have a strong preference for liquid financial assets. Besides, they offered relatively competitive

TABLE 5.11

Securities Circulated by NAFIN, 1937-75
(percent)

| | | In Domestic Currency | | | | In |
Year	Total	Certificates of Participation	Financial Bonds	Financial Titles	Other	Dollars Total
1937	100.0	—	—	100.0	—	—
1940	100.0	—	—	100.0	—	—
1945	97.4	93.0	—	4.4	—	2.6
1950	97.0	90.8	—	6.2	—	3.0
1955	82.3	80.7	—	1.6	—	17.7
1960	54.2	41.5	—	12.1	0.6	45.8
1965	82.5	26.4	—	56.1	—	17.5
1970	94.4	16.9	31.0	46.5	—	5.6
1975	96.3	15.0	9.6	30.8	49.0	3.7

Source: Nacional Financiera, S.A., Informe anual, various years.

interest rates that fluctuated between 6 and 7 percent during 1941-50, and have stayed at 5 percent since 1951. An indication of their importance to the bank's operations is shown in Table 5.11, which reveals that, as late as 1955, they represented at least four-fifths of NAFIN's total circulation of securities.

Besides the *certificados de participación*, two other highly successful securities have been circulated by the development bank: the *títulos financieros* (financial titles) and the *bonos financieros* (financial bonds). The former, as we mentioned in chapter 2, were issued as early as 1937, with a total nominal value of 500,000 pesos, while the latter began circulating in 1967, with a total nominal value of 64.1 million pesos.[40] The *títulos financieros* were not very successful until after 1960, when the annual rate guaranteed the Mexican investor was raised from 5 to 8 percent. Between that year and 1971, the real value of these outstanding bonds increased from 323.9 million pesos to 4,814.3 million pesos, more than 14 times. An even more impressive growth took place in the circulation of *bonos financieros*. Although it is not shown in

Table 5.11, between 1967 and 1972 the total real value of these
securities rose from 56.1 million to 4,522.4 million pesos. Their
rapid acceptance among Mexican investors was due to their
highly liquid nature and their attractive interest rates, which
ranged between 9.6 and 10.5 percent, for maturities of two
to nine years.[41]

Another development disclosed by Table 5.11 is the
rapid growth experienced by securities denominated in dollars
between 1955 and 1965. By far the most important of these
were the various series of *títulos financieros*. They became
attractive not only to domestic investors during "stabilizing
development" but also to foreign investors. Their attractiveness
lay in their liquidity and their relatively high average annual
real rates of interest (real yields between 5 and 7 percent)—
certainly higher than those prevailing in the United States at
the time.[42] However, toward the end of the 1960s, especially
after the stabilization program was abandoned, their popularity
waned.

Let us now proceed to evaluate NAFIN's performance in
the capital market. Following the lead of Hugh Patrick, we
shall consider the bank's performance satisfactory if its rate
of growth in issuing bonds and/or debentures is positive and
its current level is higher than peak levels attained in the
past. Table 5.12, in addition to providing the various ratings,
displays data on the real value of the bonds circulated by the
bank and their share in the total of such instruments in
circulation.

The first thing to notice is that between 1940 and 1951
the bank's performance was satisfactory except for two years.
Throughout this period NAFIN's issuance of bonds attained
peak levels five times, and its share in the total circulation of
fixed-income securities reached an all-time high of 32 percent
in 1951. After the stabilization program was put into effect,
the bank's securities began to lose ground as the monetary
authorities promoted the circulation of the *bonos financieros*
issued by private credit institutions. This may not appear to
be the case from Table 5.12—especially between 1960 and
1962—where it is shown that NAFIN's securities increased their
share in the total. However, those securities were used to support the issue of private bonds—particularly those of private
financieras—up to 25 percent of their value.[43] In fact, despite
the satisfactory performance of NAFIN's securities throughout
the 1960s, their relative importance diminished considerably
vis-à-vis that of private development banks, especially after

TABLE 5.12

Fixed-Income Securities Circulated by NAFIN, 1940-75
(millions of real pesos; 1960 = 100)

(1)	(2)	(3)	(4)	(5)	(6)
1940	1.7	A	100	S	0.4
1941	48.1	A	100	S	5.6
1942	217.6	A	100	S	17.3
1943	596.0	A	100	S	30.4
1944	652.8	A-	90	S	27.5
1945	709.5	A-	90	S	23.2
1946	694.3	C	60	I	19.9
1947	715.1	A-	90	S	18.3
1948	691.8	C	60	I	17.8
1949	826.1	A-	90	S	19.8
1950	1,449.5	A	100	S	29.8
1951	1,672.5	A-	90	S	31.6
1952	1,644.7	C	60	I	27.3
1953	2,105.4	A-	90	S	30.0
1954	1,797.7	C	60	I	27.0
1955	1,922.2	B	80	S	27.7
1956	1,788.3	C	60	I	25.1
1957	2,078.1	B	80	S	24.7
1958	1,946.1	C	60	I	19.5
1959	1,902.8	D	40	U	18.1
1960	2,673.5	A	100	S	24.0
1961	3,278.0	A-	90	S	25.7
1962	4,091.4	A	100	S	28.0
1963	5,027.2	A-	90	S	27.1

(continued)

TABLE 5.12 (continued)

(1)	(2)	(3)	(4)	(5)	(6)
1964	5,199.4	A-	90	S	23.6
1965	5,416.7	A-	90	S	20.6
1966	5,513.1	A-	90	S	17.1
1967	6,288.7	A-	90	S	15.0
1968	6,726.6	A-	90	S	14.0
1969	7,869.6	A-	90	S	14.9
1970	8,679.0	A-	90	S	15.4
1971	10,416.7	A-	90	S	16.4
1972	10,595.7	A-	90	S	15.5
1973	8,778.3	C	60	I	14.1
1974	7,529.3	D	40	U	12.7
1975	9,503.3	B	80	S	15.0

(1) = Year.
(2) = Real value of bonds circulated.
(3) = Rating scale with 25 percent threshold.
(4) = Numerical scale with 25 percent threshold.
(5) = General scale with 25 percent threshold.
(6) = Share in total circulation of bonds (percent).
Source: Computed from NAFIN, *La economía mexicana en cifras* (México, D.F.: NAFIN, 1978).

1965. This is clearly shown in Table 5.13, where the bonds
circulated by NAFIN are compared with those of private
financieras.

The securities circulated by NAFIN had a value practically twice as large as the securities of private *financieras*
in 1960. Eight years later, however, their value amounted to
only a little over one-fifth of the value of bonds circulated by
private development banks. Thus, it can be said that NAFIN
played a pioneer role during initial industrialization, when the
bank's securities were among a handful of financial instruments available to potential lenders, while during later indus-

TABLE 5.13

Bonds Circulated by Private *Financieras*, 1960-72
(millions of real pesos; 1960 = 100)

(1)	(2)	(3)	(4)	(5)	(6)
1960	1,351.3	A	100	S	197.8
1961	2,200.5	A	100	S	194.0
1962	2,590.8	A-	90	S	157.9
1963	3,972.5	A	100	S	126.6
1964	6,255.5	A	100	S	83.1
1965	10,050.9	A	100	S	53.9
1966	17,455.8	A	100	S	31.6
1967	24,848.1	A	100	S	25.3
1968	31,199.0	A	100	S	21.6
1969	35,095.2	A-	90	S	22.4
1970	38,069.5	A-	90	S	22.8
1971	43,124.2	A-	90	S	24.2
1972	46,195.7	A-	90	S	22.6

(1) = Year.
(2) = Real value of bonds circulated.
(3) = Rating scale with 25 percent threshold.
(4) = Numerical scale with 25 percent threshold.
(5) = General scale with 25 percent threshold.
(6) = NAFIN's share in the bonds circulated by private
financieras.

Source: Computed from NAFIN, *La economía mexicana en
cifras* (México, D.F.: NAFIN, 1978), pp. 276-80.

TABLE 5.14

Underwriting as a Share of NAFIN's Total Financing, 1941-70
(percent)

Year		Year		Year	
1941	13.4	1951	18.1	1961	33.3
1942	5.6	1952	20.9	1962	36.6
1943	6.2	1953	20.9	1963	38.8
1944	9.1	1954	28.7	1964	35.0
1945	9.6	1955	34.2	1965	34.0
1946	12.3	1956	40.0	1966	32.0
1947	22.1	1957	42.2	1967	28.9
1948	17.2	1958	39.7	1968	26.0
1949	16.9	1959	40.4	1969	24.0
1950	17.2	1960	31.4	1970	22.6

Source: Computed from NAFIN, *La economía mexicana en cifras* (México, D.F.: NAFIN, 1978), p. 299.

trialization, its role became supporting, as more diverse and attractive securities became available to surplus spending units at home and abroad.

The supporting character of Nacional Financiera is best exemplified by its underwriting, the insurance function of bearing the risks of adverse price fluctuations between the time the development banker pays the firm for its securities and the time it sells those bonds. As mentioned in chapter 1, this is a relatively new activity in underdeveloped capital markets, and to the extent that the development bank diverts an increasing share of its resources to this function, the greater is its promotion of the capital market. The value of NAFIN's underwriting services as a proportion of its total financing to individuals and enterprises is displayed in Table 5.14 for 1941-70.

Despite a gradual increase in the relative importance of NAFIN's underwriting services during initial industrialization, it was not until after 1953 that they displaced the bank's investments in securities as the second most important form of

financing.* In fact, between 1955 and 1966—except for
1963—they comprised at least 30 percent of the bank's total
financing. As mentioned earlier, some of the securities under-
written by the bank during this period were *bonos financieros*
of private development banks. NAFIN's underwriting services
go as far back as 1936. This is remarkable in and of itself,
because of the 189 development banks analyzed by Lucas
Salgado, during 1967, ". . . only 31 percent offered underwriting services. Most private development banks (65 percent)
provided underwriting services . . . and only 13 percent of
the public development banks . . . ."[44]

EMPIRICAL ANALYSIS OF NAFIN'S IMPACT ON THE INVESTMENT PROCESS AND LOANABLE FUNDS MARKET

NAFIN and the Investment Process

The objective of this section is to assess whether the
long-term funds provided by NAFIN and private *financieras*
have played a significant role in financing the capital expenditures of the country, thereby contributing to its economic
growth. The underlying assumption is that we are in a simple
Harrod-Domar world in which the change in capacity output is
some fixed proportion of the change in capital stock.[45] More
precisely, it is assumed that capital and labor are employed in
fixed proportions according to the following production function:

$$Q_t = \min(K_t/\nu, \; L_t/\eta) \tag{5.1}$$

and

$$1 = f(K, L + \delta) = f(K + \delta, L) \quad \nu > 0, \quad \eta > 0$$

where Q_t is capacity output in period t, K_t is the capital stock
in period t, and ν and η are the fixed capital-output and
labor-output ratios, respectively. Hence, if there is always a
sufficient amount of labor to ensure that it is not a significant
constraint on output, it follows from (5.1) that changes in
output and investment are related as follows:

———————————

*The bank's provision of long-term credits is the primary
form of financing.

$$dQ/dt = (1/\nu)I_t \qquad\qquad (5.2)$$

where $I_t = dK/dt$ is real gross domestic investment.

To determine whether this relationship holds in the case of Mexico, the following model was estimated by OLS:

$$\Delta GDP_t = \beta_1 I_t + \varepsilon_t$$

where

> GDP = real gross domestic product (millions of 1960 pesos)[46]
>
> I = real gross domestic investment (millions of 1960 pesos)
>
> ΔGDP_t = GDP(t) - GDP(t - 1)

and $\beta_1 > 0$

The regression results are as follows:

Period		R^2	S.E.	D.W.
1942–72	$\Delta GDP_t = .89\, I_t$ (14.07)	.87	9,793.0	1.67

and $\nu = 1.12$.

The linear equation through the origin fits the data reasonably well, as indicated by its coefficient of determination—especially in view of its simple nature. More importantly, the coefficient for real gross domestic investment has the expected sign and is highly significant, as revealed by its t-value in parentheses. In addition, the Durbin-Watson test failed to detect positive serial correlation at both the 5 and 1 percent levels of significance. Lastly, for purposes of comparison, the relationship was estimated with a constant term as well as in proportionate form. These results are given below.

Period		R^2	S.E.	D.W.
1947–72	$\Delta GDP_t = 7,199.52 + .72 I_t$ (2.78) (9.41)	.72	8,777.0	1.51
	$\Delta GDP_t/GDP = 1.1 I/GDP$ (4.86)	.44	.17	1.41

Thus, the evidence seems to suggest that, in Mexico, the change in gross domestic product is significantly related to real gross investment. Provided that this is the case, it will be argued below that whatever contributes to the formation of real gross investment indirectly promotes the growth of gross domestic product.

Economic theory suggests that real gross capital formation is negatively related to the real long-term rate of interest and the capital stock,* and positively related to levels or changes in real income. Besides these explanatory variables, Raymond W. Goldsmith argues that in Mexico ". . . the existence of a set of government financial institutions and the additional expenditures which they have provided, have played an important and essential role."[47] To test this hypothesis, we estimated an investment function that, among other variables, includes the flow of long-term funds provided by NAFIN to industry.

Before presenting the results, it should be mentioned that the capital stock is not included as an explanatory variable. The reason for this is simple, and unfortunate: there are no official published capital stock data for Mexico. Still, it could be argued that one way of remedying this would be to estimate the investment function in differenced form. Such a procedure would allow one to include the sum of lagged levels of investment as a proxy.[48] However, this method assumes that the investigator has sufficient information on the rate of depreciation for the economy at large to specify the appropriate length for the sum of lagged investment levels. Lacking such information, no attempt was made to estimate the investment function in differenced form.

The actual model estimated by OLS is given below:

$$I_t = \alpha_o + \beta_1(r - \dot{\pi})_t + \beta_2 \Delta GDP_t + \beta_3 \Delta N_t + \beta_4 D_t \qquad (5.3)$$

where

---

*If the capital stock is large relative to the desired capital stock, then the level of investment will be lower. Thus investment should be inversely related to the capital stock.

I_t = real gross domestic investment (millions of 1960 pesos)

$r - \overset{\bullet}{\pi}$ = real rate on long-term financial bonds (percent)

$\overset{\bullet}{\pi}$ = rate of inflation for Mexico City (percent)

ΔGDP_t = change in real domestic product (millions of 1960 pesos)

ΔN_t = real flow of long-term credits provided by NAFIN to industry (millions of 1960 pesos)

D_t = dummy variable designed to capture the impact of the rapid rate of investment expenditures during the Echeverría administration (1970-76)

and $\beta_2, \beta_3, \beta_4 > 0$, while $\beta_1 < 0$

The results obtained when running this model are summarized in Table 5.15. All coefficients have the expected sign and are significant at least at the 10 percent level. In particular, they suggest that NAFIN's long-term credits to industry contributed significantly to the financing of capital expenditures. Also, the overall fit of the multiple regressions is quite good and significant, as indicated by the R^2 and F values. The D.W. statistics suggest that the regressions do not exhibit serial correlation at the 5 and the 1 percent significance levels.

So far, the estimates discussed are for a period of time that comprises both initial industrialization and stabilizing development. It has been shown that private *financieras* assumed a leading role in providing long-term credits to industry during the later period. To test this proposition, a similar regression was estimated with the long-term credits to industry by private *financieras* included as an additional explanatory variable. Lacking any specific data for the funds provided by these institutions after 1972, the regression was run for 1955-72. The results are given below.

$$I_t = 9,407.7 - 785.0 \ (r - \overset{\bullet}{\pi})_t + 1.1 \ \Delta GDP_t + 3.3 \ \Delta N_t + 14.3 \ \Delta P_t$$

          (1.5)*   (-.9)   (3.27)***   (2.88)**   (5.43)***

R^2	F	D.W.	n	$r_{N \cdot P}$
.89	24.5***	1.7	18	.12

$$I_t = 5,932.3 - 550.1 \ (r - \overset{\bullet}{\pi})_{t-1} + 1.3 \ \Delta GDP_t + 3.5 \ \Delta N_t + 13.8P_t$$

          (1.47)*   (-1.0)   (3.5)***   (2.5)**   (5.6)***

R^2	F	D.W.	n	$r_{N \cdot P}$
.89	25.3***	1.68	18	.13

TABLE 5.15

Estimates of Investment Function, 1947–76

Gross Domestic Investment	Intercept	Independent Variables					R^2	F	D.W.
		$(r - \dot{\pi})_t$	$(r - \dot{\pi})_{t-1}$	ΔGDP_t	ΔN_t	D_t			
$I_t =$	4,243.5 (.81)	-905.71 (-1.97)**		2.64 (7.23)***	5.2 (5.08)**		.77	28.12	1.73
$I_t =$	3,308.47 (.72)		-1,406.9 (-3.05)***	2.92 (8.6)***	5.1 (5.4)***		.81	35.0	1.8
$I_t =$	8,588.9 (2.35)**	-475.44 (1.5)*		1.64 (5.32)***	5.2 (7.57)***	27,695.92 (5.53)***	.90	53.68	2.02
$I_t =$	7,399.18 (2.12)**		-604.04 (-1.6)*	1.84 (5.45)***	5.2 (7.5)***	25,626.8 (4.75)***	.90	54.5	2.1

Note: Numbers in parentheses are t-ratios.

   * = Significant at 10 percent level.

   ** = Significant at 5 percent level.

   *** = Significant at 1 percent level.

Source: NAFIN, *La economía mexicana en cifras* (México, D.F.: NAFIN, 1978). Interest rate data were obtained from Table 4.9.

where numbers in parentheses are t-ratios, levels of significance are as in Table 5.15, and

ΔP = real flow of long-term credits provided by private *financieras* to industry (millions of 1960 pesos)

It can be seen that the funds provided by private *financieras* were highly significant during this period, while those of NAFIN diminished in relative importance, as indicated by a fall in the absolute magnitude of the coefficient and t-ratio. These results may be misleading if the variables in question are highly collinear.[49] However, as can be seen by the low correlation coefficients, there is no evidence to suggest that this is the case for the sample in question. Finally, the models do not exhibit positive autocorrelation at the 1 percent level of significance.

One final testable hypothesis that naturally emerges from our discussion, given the nature and destination of the credits provided by NAFIN and private *financieras*, is whether they have contributed to a higher overall capital-output ratio. In some respects, this is similar to the proposition put forward by Griffin and Enos, to the effect that foreign capital inflow is associated with a higher incremental capital-output ratio.[50] For, as we have seen, these financial institutions have channeled substantial amounts of foreign capital into the country, particularly during later industrialization. To test this hypothesis, we estimated a number of simple regressions of the following general form:

$$I/\Delta GDP = \overset{+}{\phi}(F/GDP) \qquad\qquad (5.4)$$

where

$I/\Delta GDP$ = incremental capital-output ratio

F/GDP = long-term credits of NAFIN and/or private *financieras* as a share of gross domestic product

and the + indicates the expected direction of the relationship.

The regression results are displayed in Table 5.16. Despite the relatively low R^2s, all coefficients have the expected sign and are significant at least at the 5 percent level. Positive autocorrelation is not detected at the 1 and 5 percent levels of significance, with the possible exception of the first regression, whose D.W. statistic falls in the indeterminate region at the 5 percent level. When the funds provided by NAFIN are included as an explanatory variable, the magnitude

TABLE 5.16

Linear Estimates of Equation (5.4)

Period		R^2	S.E.	F	D.W.
1956–72	I/ΔGDP = .63 + 3.18 PF/GDP (4.2) (2.93)**	.36	.21	8.56	1.30
1956–72	I/ΔGDP = .50 + 9.69 NF/GDP (2.42) (2.68)**	.32	.22	7.19	1.39
1956–72	I/ΔGDP = .56 + 2.62(NF + PF)/GDP (3.39) (3.07)**	.39	.21	9.45	1.38
1942–55	I/ΔGDP = .52 + 19.7 NF/GDP (2.53) (2.55)**	.35	.42	6.49	2.0

**Significant at 5 percent level.

Sources: Data obtained from NAFIN, *La economía mexicana en cifras* (México, D.F.: NAFIN, 1978); various *Informes anuales* of the Banco de México, 1956–72.

of the coefficient rises considerably. This is possibly a reflection of the fact that a high proportion of NAFIN's funds goes to finance social infrastructure and basic industry, both of which exhibit relatively higher capital-output ratios. A glance at the last equation would suggest that this was even more the case during initial industrialization.

NAFIN and the Loanable Funds Market

To determine the impact of NAFIN and private *financieras* on the loanable funds market, the following supply-demand model was estimated via 2SLS (two-stage least squares):

Demand: $Q^D_{Lt} = \alpha_o + \beta_1(r - \dot{\pi}) + \beta_2 D^P_t + \beta_3 \Delta GDP_t + \epsilon^D_t$

Supply: $Q^S_{Lt} = \gamma_o + \phi_1(r - \dot{\pi}) + \phi_2 N^F_t + \phi_3 P^F_t + \epsilon^S_t$ (5.5)

and $\beta_2, \beta_3, \phi_1, \phi_2, \phi_3 > 0; \beta_1 < 0$

It is assumed that the market is cleared in every year, so that

$$Q_{Lt}^{D} = Q_{Lt}^{S} = Q_{Lt} \tag{5.6}$$

where

Q_{Lt} = quantity of long-term credits transacted in the market (millions of real pesos)

$(r - \dot{\pi})$ = real rate of interest on long-term financial bonds (percent)

ΔGDP_t = change in real domestic product (millions of 1960 pesos)

N_t^{F} = real resources of NAFIN (millions of 1960 pesos)

P_t^{F} = real resources of private *financieras* (millions of 1960 pesos)

D_t^{P} = real equity financing provided by NAFIN (millions of 1960 pesos)

Endogenous variables: QL_t, $(r - \dot{\pi})$

Exogenous variables: D_t^{P}, ΔGDP_t, N_t^{F}, P_t^{F}

Although the given model is similar to the one outlined in chapter 2, it is in certain respects less complete, and in others more refined. For instance, in addition to including equity investments on the demand side as a proxy for the entrepreneurial activities of the bank, it includes the change in real gross domestic output. The underlying rationale is that a faster rate of economic growth will induce entrepreneurs to invest in plant, machinery, and equipment, and thereby apply for long-term funds, ceteris paribus. The model also includes the financial resources of NAFIN and private *financieras* on the supply side—the greater these are, in real terms, the better suited these institutions are to meet the financial needs of the business community, ceteris paribus. However, the model is less complete in that it does not include the structural breaks that, in all likelihood, characterize the loanable funds market during initial industrialization.

With this in mind, it will be expedient to outline some of the assumptions and conditions underlying the model's estimation.

TABLE 5.17

Estimates for Supply-Demand Model

Period 1942-72 Coeff.	Demand Values OLS	Demand Values 2SLS	Demand t-statistic OLS	Demand t-statistic 2SLS	Coeff.	Supply Values OLS	Supply Values 2SLS	Supply t-statistic OLS	Supply t-statistic 2SLS
α_0	-21,400.32	-23,653.90	-5.3**	-3.52**	γ_0	2,526.59	2,413.73	7.54**	3.01**
β_1	-191.80	-3,354.47	-.40	-1.34*	ϕ_1	65.40	586.23	1.38*	1.00
β_2	14.12	12.60	4.20**	2.26**	ϕ_2	1.24	1.02	6.55**	2.02**
β_3	.80	1.18	5.13**	3.08**	ϕ_3	1.16	1.20	14.3**	6.18**

Demand (OLS)

R^2	$\bar{R}^2$	S.E.	F	D.W.	ρ
.90	.89	10,277.13	81.16	1.42	.18

Supply (OLS)

R^2	$\bar{R}^2$	S.E.	F	D.W.	ρ
.99	.98	1,175.9	1,649.80	1.62	.66

Note: Durbin two-stage method was used to correct for positive autocorrelation.

* = Significant at 10 percent level.

** = Significant at 5 percent level.

Sources: Data obtained from NAFIN, *La economía mexicana en cifras* (México, D.F.: NAFIN, 1978); various *Informes anuales* of Banco de México, S.A. (1956-72).

178

First, the given model is simultaneous because Q_{Lt} and $(r - \dot{\pi})$ are mutually or jointly determined. Thus, estimating these equations via OLS would lead to parameter estimates that are not only biased but also inconsistent. The reason for this is that the endogenous variable is included as an explanatory variable in both the supply and the demand equations. This violates one of the assumptions of OLS, which requires that the explanatory variables be uncorrelated with the error term.[51] Second, the use of 2SLS—rather than indirect least squares (ILS)—is warranted because both equations are over-identified by the order condition; each equation excludes two of the four exogenous variables, and includes one normalized endogenous variable. The results are presented in Table 5.17 along with those generated by OLS for comparison purposes.

All coefficients have the expected sign for both the OLS and the 2SLS estimates. However, in the demand equation the magnitude and the significance of the price variable increase in absolute value as we pass from the OLS to the 2SLS esti-mation procedure. A similar reversal occurs in the supply equation for the coefficient of the price variable but, unex-pectedly, its significance diminishes (as revealed by its t-value). These results cast some doubt on the role played by the real rate of interest in rationing funds among investors and savers in Mexico. Perhaps this should not come as a sur-prise, for, as we have seen in this and previous chapters, other mechanisms, such as selective controls, have played a far greater role in allocating long-term funds. Besides, many of the rates charged by NAFIN and private *financieras* are subsi-dized. Lastly, given the extreme liquidity preference of Mexican investors, it is possible that beyond some point they would rather forego additional interest than liquidity.

Turning to the remaining variables in the demand equa-tion, it is observed that the entrepreneurial activities of NAFIN—as measured by its equity investments—did exert a positive and significant influence on the demand for loanable funds during 1942-72. In addition, the coefficient for the equity variable does not change considerably under the two estimation procedures. A similar relationship is found between the demand for loanable funds and the change in gross domes-tic product. However, in this case, the coefficient experiences a substantial increase (approximately 48 percent) under the 2SLS method. Finally, the coefficients and t-statistics for the real financial resources of NAFIN and private *financieras* indi-cate that they exerted a positive and significant influence on the supply of loanable funds.

SUMMARY AND CONCLUSIONS

Several conclusions emerge from this chapter. First, the development of the financial sector has been carefully orchestrated by the monetary authorities to coincide with the economic growth priorities of the Mexican government. Second, this was particularly the case during later or sustained industrialization, when a number of policies were implemented to facilitate the flow of funds from savers to investors, so as to forestall any disruption of the process of capital formation. Among the more noteworthy policies are the establishment of obligatory reserves on the marginal deposits of commercial banks and private *financieras*; the availability of financial instruments redeemable upon request at face value; and a fixed exchange rate that ensured the convertibility of these peso-denominated bonds and deposits into dollars at any time. Third, the evidence presented in sections on evaluation and analysis suggests that the surplus funds attracted by NAFIN and private *financieras* did in fact exert a positive and significant influence on real gross domestic investment, and thereby contributed to economic growth. Finally, the creation of a very liquid market by the monetary authorities, although conducive to the investment process, is a double-edged sword; it permits periods of speculative excesses that may endanger the viability of the system. The flight of capital experienced by the Mexican financial system during the crises of 1976 and 1982 attests to this vulnerability.

NOTES

1. NAFIN, *La economía mexicana en cifras* (México, D.F.: NAFIN, 1978), pp. 247–53.
2. Ibid.
3. Ibid., p. 237.
4. Antonin Basch, *El mercado de capitales en México* (México, D.F.: CEMLA, 1968), p. 29.
5. Robert T. Aubey, *Nacional Financiera and Mexican Industry* (Los Angeles: Latin American Center, University of California, 1966), p. 61.
6. NAFIN, op. cit., p. 252.
7. Ibid., p. 323.
8. Dwight S. Brothers and Leopoldo Solis M., *Mexican Financial Development* (Austin: University of Texas Press, 1966), p. 42.

9. Basch, op. cit., p. 55.

10. Various issues of Banco de México, S.A., *Informe anual* (México, D.F.: Banco de México, 1960-65).

11. NAFIN, op. cit., pp. 311-15.

12. Banco de México, op. cit.

13. Brothers and Solis, op. cit., p. 43.

14. Ibid., p. 44.

15. Computed from NAFIN, op. cit.

16. David S. Cook, Jr., *A Guide to the Spreading and Analysis of Mexican Bank Statements* (Philadelphia: R.M.A., 1978), p. 9.

17. Ibid., p. 6.

18. Joseph S. La Cascia, *Capital Formation and Economic Development in Mexico* (New York: Frederick A. Praeger, 1969), p. 38.

19. See Brothers and Solis, op. cit., Table III-A.

20. Basch, op. cit., p. 55.

21. Cook, op. cit., p. 7.

22. Alvaro de Albornoz, *El sistema bancario y la inflación en México* (México, D.F.: Importadora y Editoria Galaxia, 1980), p. 107.

23. Ibid., p. 108.

24. Banco Nacional de Obras y Servicios Públicos, S.A., various *Annual Reports* (México, D.F.: BANOBRAS, 1960-68).

25. Ibid.

26. Albornoz, op. cit., pp. 135-42.

27. Basch, op. cit., p. 21.

28. Ibid.

29. Albornoz, op. cit., p. 133.

30. Basch, op. cit., p. 2.

31. NAFIN, op. cit., p. 245.

32. Brothers and Solis, op. cit., p. 30.

33. Antonio Gómez Oliver, *Política monetaria y fiscal de México, 1946-1976* (México, D.F.: Fondo de Cultura Económica, 1981), p. 91.

34. Basch, op. cit., p. 55.

35. Data obtained from the *Anuario financiero de México*, XXXV (México, D.F.: Asociación de Banqueros de México, 1975); Raymond W. Goldsmith, *The Financial Development of Mexico* (Paris: OECD, 1961), p. 16.

36. Goldsmith, op. cit., p. 16.

37. Rosa Olivia Villa M., *Nacional Financiera: Banco de fomento de desarrollo económico de México* (México, D.F.: NAFIN, 1976), p. 115.

38. Basch, op. cit., pp. 72-73.

39. Ibid.

40. NAFIN, op. cit.

41. Villa, op. cit., p. 117.

42. See Sidney Homer, *A History of Interest Rates*, 2nd ed. (New Brunswick, N.J.: Rutgers University Press, 1977), Table 50, p. 363.

43. Geraldo Lucas Salgado, "Performance of Public, Private and Mixed Development Banks" (master's thesis, University of Illinois, Urbana, 1974), pp. 56-57.

44. Basch, op. cit., pp. 72-73.

45. For an exhaustive treatment of this model, see R. G. D. Allen, *Macro-Economic Theory: A Mathematical Treatment* (New York: St. Martin's Press, 1967), pp. 179-219.

46. Data obtained from NAFIN, op. cit., pp. 19-47; Banco de México, S.A., various *Informes anuales* (México, D.F.: Banco de México, 1946-76).

47. Goldsmith, op. cit., p. 58.

48. R. S. Pindyck and D. L. Rubinfeld, *Econometric Models and Economic Forecasts* (New York: McGraw-Hill, 1976), pp. 374-75.

49. Ibid., p. 113.

50. K. B. Griffin and J. L. Enos, "Foreign Assistance: Objectives and Consequences," *Economic Development and Cultural Change* 18, no. 3 (April 1970): 313-27.

51. For further details see Pindyck and Rubinfeld, op. cit., pp. 132-44.

6
Summary And Conclusions

This study has assessed the economic impact of Nacional Financiera—and that of private *financieras*—on the industrial and financial sectors of Mexico for the period 1940-82. In so doing, it has contributed to a better understanding not only of the nature and functions of Nacional Financiera, but also of the role played by development banks in the period of late-late industrialization. The discussion that follows highlights some of the prominent conclusions reached by the foregoing analysis, as well as certain promising avenues for future research in the area of development banking in Latin America.

To begin with, chapter 2 developed a theoretical or conceptual framework from which to assess the performance of of multipurpose development banks such as NAFIN. The first part of the chapter addressed itself to the underlying differences between financial systems that are essentially passive (demand-following) and those in which the state plays an active role (supply-leading or demand-leading). Insofar as the latter usually arise when the prerequisites of modern industrialization are missing, they lead to what Gerschenkron calls ". . . the use of essentially different institutional instruments of industrialization."[1] It was shown, in light of the Latin American experience, that development banks often fulfill this role by engaging in operations ranging from the provision of long-term credit to the creation of key enterprises. A number of pertinent conclusions emerged in the course of reviewing the historical and institutional development of these intermediaries for some of the larger countries of the region. A sample of them is given below.

a. Public development banks far outnumber private ones.

b. They are usually older than private development banks and the size of their assets is greater.

c. Public development banks participate to a far greater extent in the transfer of technology and the provision of technical assistance.

d. They tend to be less specialized in their operations than their private counterparts.

e. Public development banks tend to engage in promotional activities more readily than private development banks.

f. They usually participate to a far greater extent in securing long-term credit from multilateral agencies and foreign private banks.

The second part of the chapter examined the question of whether the development bank can exert a positive and significant impact on the rate of capital formation. This was seen to depend on the different sets of constraints the bank faces during the periods of initial and later industrialization. It was hypothesized that multipurpose banks such as NAFIN would have a maximum impact during initial industrialization. Finally, we examined some recent trends in development banking that suggested that as a country enters the phase of later industrialization, public development banks are likely to become one of a group of specialized institutions providing financial services to leading foreign and domestic economic interests. This pattern of development not only is a trademark of the more recent institutions but also has affected the operations of the older public institutions such as NAFIN. In this regard, it would be interesting to conduct a comparative study of NAFIN and similar public development banks, such as CORFO and BNDE.

Chapter 3 traced NAFIN's institutional development in light of the historical and economic realities of Mexico. It was observed that the role of the state in fostering economic growth and political stability has a long and rich tradition that goes as far back as the Porfiriato. However, the excesses of the latter culminated in the revolution of 1910–17 and the creation of a state that no longer was used exclusively as an instrument to maintain the privileges of certain groups in society, both domestic and foreign. Under the leadership of Cárdenas, and Calles before him, the state embarked upon a number of undertakings whose ultimate objective was to legitimize the process of industrialization to the Mexican people. It was shown that these efforts culminated in the creation of a national party, a stable political system, and a number of key financial institutions, including the Bank of Mexico, the agricultural development banks, and Nacional Financiera, S.A.

The second part of the chapter dealt with four distinct but related periods in NAFIN's history. Of particular interest to this study was the period when it became not only the financial, but also the entrepreneurial, instrument for initiating many key industrial projects. Several explanations were given for the failure of the private sector to undertake such projects. We observed that in many cases private investors and bankers would initiate the project, but could not bring it to completion because of a lack of necessary capital, technical expertise, and official representation abroad; and the leaders of Mexico understood that their country needed a variety of investments that exceeded the risk-taking proclivities of the emerging private sector.

The discussion then proceeded to examine the reorientation of NAFIN's operations during the 1950s and 1960s. It was argued that this was a direct outcome of the changing size and nature of the financial requirements of the emerging industrial sector, and the implementation of financial policies designed to expedite the ongoing structural transformation of the Mexican economy. Lastly, we observed that during the Portillo years the development bank began, once again, to promote heavy industry with its own risk capital. The financing needed for these undertakings—which were by and large joint ventures—was obtained by borrowing heavily from multilateral agencies, private banks, and even by issuing variable-income securities in international markets.

Chapters 4 and 5 examined empirically the economic impact of NAFIN and related agencies on the industrial and financial sectors of the country. In these two chapters, particular attention was given to the changing role of NAFIN and private *financieras* within the limits set by the policies pursued by the Mexican government. Several conclusions emerged from this analysis. First, the development of the financial sector has been carefully orchestrated by the monetary authorities to coincide with, and to promote industrialization based on, a strategy of import substitution. Second, during initial industrialization the Bank of Mexico and national development banks such as NAFIN played a significant role in promoting industrial development and financing real gross domestic investment. By and large, the growth experienced during this period was inflationary because of the direct monetization of public-sector deficits. Third, as the country entered the phase of later industrialization, the once effective policies began to impede the economy's structural transformation along private lines. Thus, it became necessary for the Mexican government to reorient its economic policies so as to meet the pressing financial and technical requirements arising out of a growth strategy led by import-substitution industries. The stabilization policies referred to in these two chapters accomplished this by shifting the burden of financing public-sector deficits to the private banking system and relying, to an ever greater extent, on international sources of capital—both from private banks and from multilateral agencies. Of particular note was the impressive role played by private *financieras* in channeling long-term funds to certain industrial sectors once served by NAFIN.

Finally, it is ironic that some of the policies that contributed to the rapid growth rates of the 1960s and early 1970s exacerbated existing structural weaknesses endemic to the Mexican economy, and thus paved the way for the crises of 1976 and 1982. This ultimately led to their removal and, as indicated in chapter 4, a renewed participation by public credit institutions in the intermediation process.

NOTES

1. Alexander Gerschenkron, *Economic Backwardness in Historical Perspective* (New York: Praeger, 1965), p. 11.

Appendix A

TABLE A.1

Development Banks, Classified by Age and Ownership

Years in Existence	Total		Private		Public		Mixed	
	Number	Distribution (percent)	Number	Distribution (percent)	Number	Distribution (percent)	Number	Distribution (percent)
1-5	93	49	18	56	44	43	31	57
6-10	36	19	5	16	19	19	12	22
11 or more	60	32	9	28	40	38	11	21
Total	189	100	32	100	103	100	54	100

Source: Reproduced from Geraldo L. Salgado, "Performance of Public, Private and Mixed Development Banks" (master's thesis, University of Illinois, Urbana, 1974), p. 28.

188

TABLE A.2

Development Banks, Classified by Size of Assets and Ownership

Size of Assets (million $)	Total		Private		Public		Mixed	
	Number	Distribution (percent)	Number	Distribution (percent)	Number	Distribution (percent)	Number	Distribution (percent)
0.1-10.0	84	44	16	50	43	42	25	46
10.1-100.0	73	39	14	44	36	35	23	43
100.1 or more	32	17	2	6	24	23	6	11
Total	189	100	32	100	103	100	54	100

Source: Reproduced from Geraldo L. Salgado, "Performance of Public, Private and Mixed Development Banks" (master's thesis, University of Illinois, Urbana, 1974), p. 29.

189

Appendix B

TABLE B.1

Calculation of Points on Average-Cost-of-Capital Curve

	Percent of Total (1)	Component Costs (2)	Composite Cost $k = (1) \times (2) \div 100$
Debt	0	5.0*	0
Equity	100	12.0**	12.0
	100		12.0
Debt	20	5.0	1.0
Equity	80	12.6	10.1
	100		11.1
Debt	30	5.5	1.7
Equity	70	12.9	9.0
	100		10.7
Debt	40	6.5	2.6
Equity	60	14.4	8.6
	100		11.2
Debt	50	8.0	4.0
Equity	50	17.0	8.5
	100		12.5
Debt	60	13.5	8.1
Equity	40	21.4	8.6
	100		16.7

*Cost of debt (percent).
**Cost of equity (percent).
Source: J. Fred Weston and Eugene F. Brigham, *Managerial Finance*, 6th ed. (Hinsdale, Ill.: Dryden Press, 1977), p. 711.

Appendix C

STABILIZING DEVELOPMENT (1955-72)

The discussion in chapter 4 ("The Economy's Performance" section) may be rendered more precise, if not more informative, by reference to Figure C.1.

The steeper curve describes the locus of combinations of real government expenditures ($\bar{g}$) and exogenous changes in the nominal money supply ($\bar{M}$) for which the actual level of real income (y) is equal to its desired target ($\bar{y}$). More precisely, a state of equilibrium is achieved when

$$y(\bar{g}, M) = \bar{y} \tag{1a}$$

where

    M = nominal stock of money

    P = general price level

Differentiating (1a), we obtain

$$\left. \frac{dM}{d\bar{g}} \right|_{y=\bar{y}} \ (-) \ \frac{\partial y/\partial \bar{g}}{\partial y/\partial M} < 0 \tag{1b}$$

which has a negative slope, provided $\partial y/\partial \bar{g}$ and $\partial y/\partial M > 0$. The signs of the latter have been determined by obtaining the comparative static results of the following system of equations:*

---

*See section "Comparative Statics" of this appendix.

FIGURE C.1

Stabilizing Development

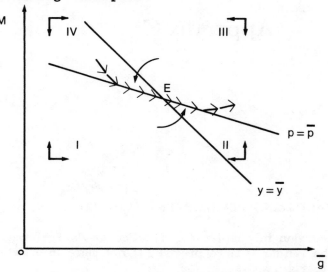

Region I: domestic recession, falling price level.
Region II: domestic excess demand, falling price level.
Region III: domestic excess demand, rising price level.
Region IV: domestic recession, rising price level.
Source: Prepared by author.

$$y - c(y, P/\bar{P}^f\bar{e}) - i(y,r) - \bar{g} - x(P/\bar{P}^f\bar{e}) = 0 \qquad (2)$$

$$0 < c_1 < 1, \ c_2 < 0, \ i_1 > 0, \ i_2 < 0, \ x_1 < 0$$

$$\ell(y,r) - \frac{\bar{M}}{P} = 0 \qquad (3)$$

$$\ell_1 > 0, \ \ell_2 < 0$$

$$B - Px(\bar{P}/\bar{P}^f\bar{e}) + \bar{P}^f\bar{e}z(y, P/\bar{P}^f\bar{e}) - K(y, r - \bar{r}) = 0 \qquad (4)$$

$$x_1 < 0 \qquad z_1 > 0, \ z_2 > 0 \qquad K_1 > 0, \ K_2 > 0$$

$$P - f(y) = 0 \qquad (5)$$

$$f_1 > 0$$

where

c = real consumption expenditures

i = real investment expenditures

x = real export expenditures

z = real import expenditures

ℓ = real money demand

K = net capital inflow

B = balance of payments (in pesos)

r = real rate of interest

$\bar{r}$ = foreign rate of interest (exogenous)

$\bar{P}^f$ = foreign general price level (exogenous)

$\bar{e}$ = fixed exchange rate (pesos/dollar)

and

$$c_1 = \partial c/\partial y, \quad c_2 = \partial c/\partial P, \quad x_1 = \partial x/\partial P, \text{ etc.}$$

Equations (2) and (3) are equilibrium conditions for the goods and loanable funds markets, respectively, and equation (5) is a simple supply function that specifies that the price level is an increasing function of the level of real income. Equation (4) gives the balance-of-payments surplus or deficit at the existing exchange rate.

The other curve describes the locus of combinations of $\bar{g}$ and M that will maintain the general price level (P) at its targeted value ($\bar{P}$). More precisely,

$$P(\bar{g},M) = \bar{P} \tag{6a}$$

Differentiating (6), we obtain

$$\left.\frac{dM}{d\bar{g}}\right|_{P=\bar{P}} = (-) \frac{\partial P/\partial \bar{g}}{\partial P/\partial M} < 0 \tag{6b}$$

which states that fiscal expansion must be accompanied by monetary contraction if the desired price level, $\bar{P}$, is to be maintained. Once again, the positive signs of the partial derivatives were obtained by totally differentiating equations (2), (3), (4), and (5), then using Cramer's rule (see next section, "Comparative Statics"). The flatter slope of this curve is explained by the assumption that fiscal policy is relatively more effective in influencing the real level of income than is monetary policy:

$$\frac{\partial y/\partial \bar{g}}{\partial P/\partial \bar{g}} > \frac{\partial y/\partial M}{\partial P/\partial M} \tag{7}$$

Put differently, a stable adjustment will be attained if fiscal policy is assigned to the level of real income.*

Thus, Figure C.1 shows that during stabilizing development, the monetary authorities pursued a policy that can be represented by the path traced by the darkened arrows. In order for economic growth to proceed with price stability, any increase in real government expenditures had to be accompanied by a decrease in the supply of real balances. In turn, this increased the real rate of interest (r) relative to that prevailing in international capital markets ($\bar{r}$), which, under a fixed exchange regime, led to a surplus in the volume of foreign reserves. These funds were not permitted to feed into the domestic money supply—not in full at least—given the nature of the open market operations: the selling of fixed-income securities to domestic and foreign investors (thereby reducing domestic liabilities). At any rate, by the late 1960s and early 1970s the monetary authorities gradually began to abandon the stabilization program, which had the effect of pushing the economy into region III.

Before concluding this discussion, it should be mentioned that Figure C.1 is somewhat misleading, since Mexican policy makers were concerned with maintaining a stable rate of inflation $\left(\frac{1}{P}\frac{dP}{dt}\right)$ —not a stable price level.

COMPARATIVE STATICS

Equations (2)-(5) can be solved to determine the effect of changes in the policy variables $\bar{g}$, $\bar{M}$ on the endogenous variables y, r, P, and B. First we take differentials, then proceed to solve the following system via Cramer's rule:

---

*See R. A. Mundell, "The Appropriate Use of Monetary and Fiscal Policy for Internal and External Stability," *IMF Staff Papers* 9 (1962): 70-79.

$$
\begin{bmatrix}
(-c_2 - x_1) & (1 - c_1 - i_1) & -i_2 & 0 \\
\dfrac{\bar{M}}{P^2} & \ell_1 & \ell_2 & 0 \\
(\bar{P}^f \bar{e} z_2 - P x_1 - x) & (\bar{P}^f \bar{e} z_1 - K_1) & -K_2 & 1 \\
1 & -f_1 & 0 & 0
\end{bmatrix}
\begin{bmatrix}
dP \\
dy \\
dr \\
dB
\end{bmatrix}
=
\begin{bmatrix}
d\bar{g} \\
\dfrac{d\bar{M}}{P} \\
0 \\
0
\end{bmatrix}
\qquad (1)
$$

The Jacobian of the system is given by

$$
J = (-) \left[(1 - c_1 - i_1)\ell_2 + \ell_1 i_2 \right] - f_1 \left[(-c_2 - x_2)\ell_2 + \frac{\bar{M}}{P^2} i_2 \right] > 0 \qquad (2a)
$$

and is greater than zero, provided

$$
(1 - c_1 - i_1) > 0 \qquad\qquad (2b)
$$

Before deriving the multipliers, we introduce the following mild restriction:

$$
(\bar{P}^f \bar{e} z_1 - K_1) > 0 \qquad\qquad (3)
$$

that is, the net effect of an increase in real income is deterioration of the balance of payments, ceteris paribus. For most of the period under consideration, this is a plausible assumption; however, in light of the massive inflows of capital toward the end of the Echeverría administration (1970-76), its validity becomes less tenable. Next, we consider the first expression in the third row of the Jacobian matrix. It may be written as

$$
[z(1 + E_z) - x(1 + E_x)] \qquad\qquad (4)
$$

where $E_x = (P/x)x_1$ is the price elasticity of demand for exports; it is negative because $x_1 < 0$. Similarly, $E_z = (P/z)z_2$ is the price elasticity of demand for imports, which is positive because a domestic price increase will stimulate demand for relatively inexpensive foreign goods. A sufficient condition for (4) to be positive is that $E_x < -1$ or $|E_x| > 1$; that is, a domestic price increase will lead to a reduction in the peso value of net exports. (It is assumed that the trade balance is initially zero $(Px = \bar{P}^f \bar{e} z)$.)

Given that these restrictions are met, we can proceed to obtain the following multipliers:

$$\left.\frac{\partial P}{\partial \bar{g}}\right|_{d\bar{M}=0} = \frac{(-f_1 \ell_2)}{\dot{J}} > 0 \tag{5a}$$

$$\left.\frac{\partial y}{\partial \bar{g}}\right|_{d\bar{M}=0} = \frac{-\ell_2}{\dot{J}} > 0 \tag{5b}$$

$$\left.\frac{\partial r}{\partial \bar{g}}\right|_{d\bar{M}=0} = \frac{(-)\left(-\ell_1 - f_1 \frac{\bar{M}}{P^2}\right)}{\dot{J}} > 0 \tag{5c}$$

$$\left.\frac{\partial B}{\partial \bar{g}}\right|_{d\bar{M}=0} = \frac{(-)\left((-\ell_1 K_2) - \alpha \ell_2\right) - f_1 \left(\left(-\frac{\bar{M}}{P^2} K_2\right) - \beta \ell_2\right)}{\dot{J}} \begin{array}{c} > \\ = \\ < \end{array} 0 \tag{5d}$$

where α and β represent expressions (3) and (4), respectively.

Similarly, for a ceteris paribus increase in the money supply we obtain:

$$\left.\frac{\partial P}{\partial \bar{M}}\right|_{d\bar{g}=0} = \frac{(-f_1 i_2 /P)}{\dot{J}} > 0 \tag{6a}$$

$$\left.\frac{\partial y}{\partial \bar{M}}\right|_{d\bar{g}=0} = \frac{-i_2 /P}{\dot{J}} > 0 \tag{6b}$$

$$\left.\frac{\partial r}{\partial \bar{M}}\right|_{d\bar{g}=0} = \frac{(1/P)[-(-c_2 - x_1)f_1 - (1 - c_1 - i_1)]}{\dot{J}} < 0 \tag{6c}$$

$$\left.\frac{\partial B}{\partial \bar{M}}\right|_{d\bar{g}=0} = \frac{(1/P)\{[-(1-c_1 -i_1)K_2 + \alpha i_2] + f_1[-(-c_2 -x_1)K_2 + \beta i_2]\}}{\dot{J}} < 0 \tag{6d}$$

Appendix D

The objective of this appendix is to provide the reader with recent economic and financial indicators for the Mexican economy. The selected statistical indicators are classified into five major categories, in the following order:

Demographic indicators

Macroeconomic indicators

Primary and industrial indicators

Monetary and financial indicators

External indicators.

By and large, the data presented here have been obtained from NAFIN, *La economía mexicana en cifras* (1984), *Annual Reports* of the Bank of Mexico and NAFIN, and various government documents and reports.

DEMOGRAPHIC INDICATORS

TABLE D.1

Mexico: Total Population by Sex, 1970–84
(thousands)

Year	Total	Men	Women
1970	49,357.0	24,629.0	24,728.0
1971	51,060.0	25,453.0	25,607.0
1972	52,796.0	26,292.0	26,504.0
1973	54,565.0	27,146.0	27,419.0
1974	56,366.0	28,014.0	28,352.0
1975	58,198.0	28,895.0	29,303.0
1976	60,060.0	29,790.0	30,270.0
1977	61,952.0	30,697.0	31,255.0
1978	63,873.0	31,617.0	32,256.0
1979	65,821.0	32,548.0	33,273.0
1980	67,796.0	33,491.0	34,305.0
1981	69,762.0	34,476.0	35,286.0
1982	71,715.0	35,456.0	36,259.0
1983	73,567.0	36,478.0	37,274.0
1984	75,567.0	37,391.0	38,176.0

Source: Compiled from NAFIN, La economía mexicana en cifras (México, D.F.: NAFIN, 1984), p. 23.

TABLE D.2

Mexico: Population by Age and Sex, 1970 and 1980
(percent)

Age	1970			1980		
	Total	Men	Women	Total	Men	Women
	100.00	49.90	50.10	100.00	49.40	50.60
0-4	16.94	8.61	8.33	16.49	8.50	7.99
5-9	16.01	8.16	7.85	15.84	8.07	7.77
10-14	13.26	6.78	6.48	13.21	6.70	6.51
15-19	10.48	5.17	5.31	10.51	5.11	5.40
20-24	8.36	4.00	4.36	8.44	3.96	4.48
25-29	6.76	3.27	3.49	6.88	3.24	3.64
30-34	5.38	2.66	2.72	5.51	2.63	2.88
35-39	5.21	2.56	2.65	5.33	2.54	2.79
40-44	4.01	1.99	2.02	4.12	1.97	2.15
45-49	3.39	1.72	1.67	3.47	1.71	1.76
50-54	2.47	1.22	1.25	2.52	1.21	1.31
55-59	2.10	1.04	1.06	2.12	1.04	1.08
60-64	1.90	0.93	0.97	1.90	0.93	0.97
65-69	1.46	0.72	0.74	1.44	0.72	0.72
70-74	1.01	0.50	0.51	0.98	0.50	0.48
75 and over	1.26	0.57	0.69	1.24	0.57	0.67

Source: Décimo censo general de población (México,
D.F.: Gerencia de Información Técnica y Publicaciones
(G.I.T.P.), 1980).

TABLE D.3

Mexico: Economically Active Population by Economic Sector, 1980-85 (thousands)

Sector	1980	1981	1982	1983	1984	1985[a]
Total	19,951.0	20,669.0	21,413.0	22,184.0	22,983.0	23,810.0
Primary sector[b]	6,384.0	6,470.0	6,552.0	6,633.0	6,711.0	6,786.0
Industrial sector	5,187.0	5,415.0	5,653.0	5,901.0	6,159.0	6,429.0
Extractive	160.0	165.0	171.0	177.0	184.0	190.0
Energy[c]	339.0	358.0	377.0	397.0	418.0	441.0
Construction	997.0	1,044.0	1,092.0	1,143.0	1,195.0	1,250.0
Manufacturing	3,691.0	3,848.0	4,013.0	4,184.0	4,362.0	4,548.0
Services[d]	8,380.0	8,784.0	9,208.0	9,650.0	10,113.0	10,595.0

[a]Preliminary figures.

[b]Includes agriculture, fishing, and livestock.

[c]Includes the petroleum industry and electricity.

[d]Includes government, commerce, and transportation.

Sources: Compiled from NAFIN, *La economía mexicana en cifras* (México, D.F.: NAFIN, 1984), p. 30; and Gerencia de Información.

MACROECONOMIC INDICATORS

TABLE D.4

Mexico: Real Gross Domestic Product by Sector, 1970-82
(millions of 1970 pesos)

Year	Total	Primary Sector*	Industrial Sector	Services
1970	444,271.0	54,123.0	260,233.0	129,915.0
1971	462,804.0	57,224.0	267,966.0	137,614.0
1972	502,086.0	57,623.0	294,685.0	149,778.0
1973	544,307.0	59,963.0	323,886.0	160,458.0
1974	577,568.0	61,486.0	344,027.0	172,055.0
1975	609,976.0	62,726.0	362,035.0	185,215.0
1976	635,831.0	63,359.0	378,021.0	194,451.0
1977	657,722.0	68,122.0	386,499.0	203,101.0
1978	711,982.0	72,200.0	422,642.0	217,140.0
1979	777,163.0	70,692.0	471,144.0	235,327.0
1980	841,854.0	75,704.0	512,220.0	253,930.0
1981	908,765.0	80,299.0	555,909.0	272,557.0
1982	903,239.0	79,822.0	546,195.0	277,222.0

*Includes agriculture, fishing, and livestock.

Source: Compiled from *El sistema de cuentas nacionales de México*, I, *1970-1982* (México, D.F.: Secretaría de Programación y Presupuesto (S.P.P.), 1983).

TABLE D.5

Mexico: Nominal Disposable Income and Its Assignment,
1977-82
(millions of pesos)

Year	Disposable Income	Public Consumption	Private Consumption	Savings
1977	1,703,426.0	198,967.0	1,226,086.0	278,373.0
1978	2,157,362.0	251,771.0	1,535,621.0	369,970.0
1979	2,817,101.0	334,316.0	1,975,879.0	506,906.0
1980	3,928,832.0	462,838.0	2,651,488.0	814,506.0
1981	5,353,899.0	684,537.0	3,583,822.0	1,085,540.0
1982	8,396,919.0	1,057,557.0	5,776,094.0	1,563,268.0

Source: Derived from NAFIN, *La economía mexicana en cifras* (México, D.F.: NAFIN, 1984), Table 2.11.

TABLE D.6

Mexico: Total Investment by Sector of Origin, 1970-81
(millions of 1970 pesos)

Year	Total	Primary Sector	Industrial Sector	Service Sector
1970	100,956.0	1,327.0	86,911.0	12,718.0
1971	96,042.0	1,600.0	85,156.0	9,286.0
1972	106,148.0	1,566.0	95,825.0	8,757.0
1973	122,327.0	1,704.0	110,074.0	10,549.0
1974	143,619.0	1,690.0	118,968.0	22,961.0
1975	150,851.0	1,719.0	130,273.0	18,859.0
1976	147,397.0	1,744.0	130,717.0	14,936.0
1977	146,938.0	1,840.0	121,883.0	23,215.0
1978	164,472.0	1,879.0	140,559.0	22,034.0
1979	193,418.0	1,892.0	169,319.0	22,207.0
1980	235,974.0	1,815.0	195,232.0	38,927.0
1981	272,782.0	2,035.0	224,036.0	46,711.0

Source: Computed from NAFIN, *La economía mexicana en cifras* (México, D.F.: NAFIN, 1984), p. 76.

PRIMARY AND INDUSTRIAL INDICATORS

TABLE D.7

Mexico: Real Gross Production of the Primary Sector, 1970-81
(millions of 1970 pesos)

Year	Total	Agriculture	Livestock	Fishing and Hunting	Other
1970	74,587.0	38,727.0	32,004.0	1,184.0	2,672.0
1971	78,750.0	41,668.0	33,127.0	1,342.0	2,614.0
1972	80,294.0	41,883.0	34,224.0	1,466.0	2,721.0
1973	84,050.0	43,733.0	35,821.0	1,637.0	2,859.0
1974	86,006.0	44,484.0	36,798.0	1,703.0	3,020.0
1975	88,601.0	45,375.0	38,286.0	1,813.0	3,127.0
1976	89,955.0	45,159.0	39,583.0	1,987.0	3,226.0
1977	96,208.0	49,677.0	40,967.0	2,201.0	3,364.0
1978	100,895.0	52,914.0	42,225.0	2,251.0	3,504.0
1979	100,132.0	50,655.0	43,110.0	2,631.0	3,736.0
1980	106,657.0	55,518.0	44,415.0	2,908.0	3,816.0
1981	113,029.0	60,180.0	45,785.0	3,239.0	3,825.0

Source: Obtained from Secretaría de Programación y
Presupuesto, *Sistema de cuentas nacionales de México*, II,
1970-81 (México, D.F.: S.P.P., 1983).

TABLE D.8

Mexico: Indexes of Agricultural Production, 1971-82
(1970 = 100)

Year	Volume of Production	Value of Production	Efficiency Index*
1971	104.46	106.33	100.68
1972	106.58	112.19	100.03
1973	110.14	145.46	101.04
1974	113.14	188.23	104.06
1975	111.76	226.19	104.31
1976	103.29	264.17	103.46
1977	117.62	365.34	103.85
1978	128.18	452.56	113.69
1979	116.21	490.97	109.61
1980	130.66	645.59	113.80
1981	147.54	916.22	116.04
1982	122.96	1,185.88	116.84

*Efficiency index is calculated by dividing the volume of production (in thousands of tons) by the cultivated surface in thousands of hectares; 1 hectare = 2.47 acres).

Sources: Calculated from NAFIN; Gerencia de información técnica y publicaciones; and La secretaría de agricultura y recursos hidráulicos (México, D.F.: Dirección General de Economía Agrícola, 1983).

TABLE D.9

Mexico: Real Gross Domestic Product of the Industrial Sector, 1970–82 (millions of 1970 pesos)

Year	Total	Mining	Manufacturing	Construction	Electricity
1970	145,070.0	11,190.0	105,203.0	23,530.0	5,147.0
1971	148,303.0	11,149.0	109,264.0	22,468.0	5,422.0
1972	163,114.0	11,663.0	119,967.0	25,316.0	6,168.0
1973	180,921.0	12,434.0	132,552.0	29,007.0	6,928.0
1974	193,901.0	14,156.0	140,963.0	30,970.0	7,812.0
1975	204,057.0	14,972.0	148,058.0	32,792.0	8,235.0
1976	214,950.0	15,881.0	155,517.0	34,310.0	9,242.0
1977	220,556.0	17,084.0	161,037.0	32,494.0	9,941.0
1978	243,597.0	19,525.0	176,816.0	36,532.0	10,724.0
1979	271,138.0	22,397.0	195,614.0	41,297.0	11,830.0
1980	296,046.0	27,391.0	209,682.0	46,379.0	12,594.0
1981	321,418.0	31,593.0	224,326.0	51,852.0	13,647.0
1982	313,163.0	34,498.0	217,852.0	49,259.0	14,554.0

Source: Data compiled from NAFIN, *La economía mexicana en cifras* (México, D.F.: NAFIN, 1984), pp. 141–42.

TABLE D.10

Mexico: Index of the Volume of Industrial Production, 1975–82
(1970 = 100)

Year	Mining	Manufacturing	Construction	Electricity	Petroleum and Gas
1975	133.8	140.7	142.1	160.2	151.2
1976	141.9	147.5	148.1	179.0	163.3
1977	152.7	151.6	143.6	196.9	179.8
1978	174.5	166.9	163.1	214.5	211.5
1979	200.1	184.4	184.7	235.3	250.4
1980	244.8	198.8	208.2	251.7	310.5
1981	282.3	213.5	232.1	272.4	362.4
1982	312.4	205.0	227.4	293.5	400.9

Source: Banco de México, Indicadores económicos
(México, D.F.: the Bank of Mexico, 1983).

TABLE D.11

Mexico: Production and Consumption of Steel, 1975–82
(thousands of tons)

Year	Production (1)	Consumption (2)	(1)/(2) (percent)
1975	5,272.0	6,444.0	81.8
1976	5,298.0	5,951.0	89.0
1977	5,601.0	7,018.0	79.8
1978	6,775.0	8,053.0	84.1
1979	7,117.0	9,175.0	77.6
1980	7,156.0	11,412.0	62.7
1981	7,673.0	12,511.0	61.3
1982*	7,048.0	8,880.0	79.4

*Preliminary figures.
Source: Computed from La camara nacional de la indus-
tria del hierro y del acero (México, D.F.: Dirección General
de Minas y Petróleos (D.G.M.P.), 1983).

MONETARY AND FINANCIAL INDICATORS

TABLE D.12

Mexico: Index of Implicit Prices for the Gross Domestic
Product and Selected Economic Activities, 1971–82
(1970 = 100)

Year	General Price Index	Price Index for Manufactured Goods	Price Index for Social and Personal Services
1971	105.9	108.0	107.8
1972	112.5	112.4	121.0
1973	126.9	123.7	141.8
1974	155.8	153.0	169.8
1975	180.3	173.4	205.3
1976	215.6	203.3	258.3
1977	281.2	273.7	334.2
1978	328.2	311.5	396.5
1979	394.8	365.4	489.7
1980	508.0	469.8	632.0
1981	643.6	578.5	810.8
1982	1,042.1	918.3	1,312.8

Source: Data obtained from NAFIN, La economía mexicana
en cifras (México, D.F.: NAFIN, 1984).

TABLE D.13

Mexico: Financial Assets of the Public
in the Banking System, 1976–82
(billions of pesos)

Year	M1[a]	M2[b]	M3[c]	M4[d]
1976	154.8	166.0	263.9	395.4
1977	195.7	209.5	323.2	521.2
1978	260.3	275.7	401.7	700.0
1979	346.5	368.6	549.2	948.3
1980	461.2	491.4	752.7	1,311.6
1981	612.4	655.2	1,012.2	1,964.9
1982	991.5	1,010.2	1,794.6	3,320.2

[a]Includes currency and demand deposits.
[b]Includes M1 and time deposits.
[c]Includes M2 and liquid instruments offered to the public with a maturity of less than 3 months.
[d]Includes M3 and long-term securities held by the public; maturities on these instruments range from 3 to 24 months.

Source: Banco de México, S.A., *Indicadores económicos* (México, D.F.: the Bank of Mexico, 1983).

TABLE D.14

Mexico: Total Financing by the Banking System
to the Public and Private Sectors, 1977–82
(billions of pesos)

| Year | Total | Public Sector | | | | Private Sector |
		Total	Federal Government	State and Local Government	Public Enterprises	
1977	890.4	565.3	362.5	5.6	197.2	325.1
1978	1,098.9	644.5	410.2	8.0	226.3	454.4
1979	1,442.2	828.8	538.9	13.2	276.7	613.4
1980	1,956.5	1,090.3	704.2	17.6	368.5	866.2
1981	2,991.5	1,793.6	1,213.9	30.1	549.5	1,197.9
1982	6,841.8	5,286.2	3,646.2	59.3	1,580.7	1,555.6

Source: Banco de México, *Indicadores de moneda y banca* (México, D.F.: the Bank of Mexico, 1983).

TABLE D.15

Nacional Financiera, S.A.: Sources and Use of Resources,
1970, 1975, 1982
(millions of pesos)

	1970	1975	1982
Total resources	42,641.0	89,290.0	950,798.0
External sources	27,924.0	58,041.0	646,778.0
Internal sources	14,717.0	31,249.0	304,020.0
Use of resources	42,641.0	89,290.0	950,798.0
Financial activities	30,827.0	62,320.0	753,404.0
Fiduciary activities	1,564.0	6,904.0	68,330.0
Underwriting activities	10,250.0	20,066.0	129,064.0

Source: Nacional Financiera, S.A.

TABLE D.16

Nacional Financiera, S.A.: Total Financing Granted,
by Economic Sector, 1977-82
(millions of pesos)

Year	Total	Infra-structure	Basic Industry	Manu-facturing	Other
1977	191,607.0	39,555.0	107,298.0	25,654.0	19,100.0
1978	225,727.0	47,226.0	133,009.0	30,883.0	14,609.0
1979	260,338.0	55,505.0	146,703.0	37,338.0	20,792.0
1980	319,699.0	68,849.0	160,506.0	48,320.0	42,024.0
1981	390,717.0	75,505.0	189,430.0	68,978.0	56,804.0
1982	858,425.0	145,920.0	363,126.0	111,518.0	237,861.0

Source: Nacional Financiera, S.A., various Informes
anuales.

TABLE D.17

Mexico: Share of the Inflows, Outflows, and Deficit of the Public Sector in the Gross Domestic Product, 1977–82 (millions of 1970 pesos)

Year	Inflows of the Public Sector (1)	Outflows of the Public Sector (2)	Deficit of the Public Sector (3)	Share of (1) in Real GDP (percent) (4)	Share of (2) in Real GDP (percent) (5)	Share of (3) in Real GDP (percent) (6)
1977	170,950.0	207,517.8	36,567.8	26.0	31.5	5.1
1978	195,468.0	233,672.0	38,204.0	27.4	32.8	5.3
1979	222,409.0	270,512.0	48,103.0	28.6	34.8	5.4
1980	280,044.6	330,705.1	50,660.5	33.3	39.3	6.5
1981	252,703.5	385,503.4	132,800.4	27.7	42.2	14.5
1982	272,987.2	432,281.0	159,293.8	30.7	48.7	17.9

Source: Computed from NAFIN, La economía mexicana en cifras (México, D.F.: NAFIN, 1984), Table 5.23.

211

TABLE D.18

Mexico: Share of Exports, Imports, and the Current
Account Balance in the Gross Domestic Product, 1977-81
(millions of 1970 pesos)

Year	Exports of Goods and Services (1)	Imports of Goods and Services (2)	Current Account Balance (3)	Share of (1) in GDP (%) (4)	Share of (2) in GDP (%) (5)	Share of (3) in GDP (%) (6)
1977	73,687.7	86,506.0	-12,818.3	11.2	13.2	1.9
1978	80,836.7	99,517.9	-18,681.2	11.4	14.0	2.6
1979	93,182.7	121,235.4	-28,052.7	12.0	15.7	3.6
1980	113,044.1	143,589.0	-30,544.9	13.4	17.1	3.6
1981	116,384.7	160,964.3	-44,579.6	12.8	17.7	4.9

Sources: Secretaría de Programación y Presupuesto,
Sistema de cuentas nacionales de México, 1981-82; Banco de
México, S.A., *Subdirección de investigación económica, Esta-
dísticas históricas de balanza de pagos, 1970-1978* (México,
D.F.: the Bank, 1983); and Banco de México, *Informe anual*,
1979-81.

EXTERNAL INDICATORS

TABLE D.19
Mexico: Distribution of Exports by Class of Goods, 1976-81
(percent)

Year	Total (millions of pesos)	Consumer Goods	Intermediate Goods	Capital Goods
1976	51,905.4	26.4	70.6	3.0
1977	94,452.5	27.2	69.8	3.0
1978	140,533.3	23.6	73.3	3.1
1979	200,646.5	17.9	79.9	2.2
1980	351,324.0	10.7	87.7	1.6
1981	475,057.5	8.2	90.0	1.8

Source: Banco de México, S.A., *Informe anual*, 1970-78.

TABLE D.20

Mexico: Distribution of Imports by Class of Goods, 1976-81
(percent)

Year	Total (millions of pesos)	Consumer Goods	Intermediate Goods	Capital Goods
1976	90,900.4	7.3	61.5	31.2
1977	126,352.0	6.6	66.8	26.6
1978	180,257.7	5.8	68.5	25.7
1979	273,336.4	8.4	61.8	29.8
1980	424,278.6	13.1	59.7	27.2
1981	566,381.2	12.0	56.9	31.1

Source: Banco de México, S.A., Estadística histórica de balanza de pagos, 1970-78 (México, D.F.: the Bank, 1983).

TABLE D.21

Mexico: Relationship Between Foreign Direct Investment and Total Net Annual Remittances Abroad, 1975-81
(millions of pesos)

Year	Direct Foreign Investment (1)	Total Net Remittances (2)	Index (2/1)
1975	2,551.3	6,817.9	2.67
1976	3,271.1	10,199.4	3.12
1977	7,383.3	11,273.7	1.53
1978	8,767.6	12,312.4	1.40
1979	15,165.6	13,288.7	0.88
1980	24,580.6	22,005.5	0.90
1981	27,997.4	35,645.8	1.27

Source: Banco de México, S.A., Estadística histórica de balanza de pagos, 1970-1978 (México, D.F.: the Bank, 1983), and Informe anual, 1979-81.

TABLE D.22

Mexico: Terms-of-Trade Index, 1971-80
(1970 = 100)

Year	Implicit Price Index for Imports (CIF) (1)	Implicit Price Index for Exports (FOB) (2)	Terms of Trade (2/1)
1971	104.5	103.1	98.7
1972	111.3	111.2	99.9
1973	126.4	128.1	101.3
1974	155.1	170.0	109.6
1975	173.1	189.8	109.6
1976	224.1	258.8	115.5
1977	349.0	437.8	125.4
1978	389.3	466.6	119.9
1979	443.3	616.7	139.1
1980	506.3	470.7	93.0

Source: Computed from NAFIN, La economía mexicana en cifras (México, D.F.: NAFIN, 1984), p. 272.

TABLE D.23

Mexico: Evolution of the Exchange Rate 1975-83
(pesos/U.S. dollar)

Year	Market Rate	
	End of Period	Average for Period
1975	12.49	12.49
1976	19.95	15.44
1977	22.73	22.58
1978	22.72	22.80
1979	22.80	22.80
1980	23.25	22.95
1981	26.22	24.51
1982	148.50	57.17
1983*	149.26	148.47

*As of September 1983.
Source: Banco de México, S.A., Informe anual, 1983.

Bibliography

BOOKS

Adler, Robert. *Public External Financing of Development Banks in Developing Countries*. Eugene, Ore.: Bureau of Business and Economic Research, 1966.

Albornoz, Alvaro de. *El sistema bancario y la inflación en México*. México, D.F.: Importadora y Editoria Galaxia, 1980.

Allen, R. G. D. *Macro-Economic Theory: A Mathematical Treatment*. New York: St. Martin's Press, 1967.

Aubey, Robert T. *Nacional Financiera and Mexican Industry*. Los Angeles: Latin American Center, University of California, 1966.

Baer, Werner. *Industrialization and Economic Development in Brazil*. Homewood, Ill.: Yale University/Economic Growth Center, 1965.

Basch, Antonin. *El mercado de capitales en México*. México, D.F.: CEMLA, 1968.

Boskey, Shirley. *Problems and Practices of Development Banks*. Baltimore: Johns Hopkins University Press, 1959.

Brothers, Dwight S., and Leopoldo Solis M. *Mexican Financial Development*. Austin: University of Texas Press, 1966.

Cameron, Rondo, ed. *Banking in the Early Stages of Industrialization*. New York: Oxford University Press, 1967.

Cockcroft, James. *Intellectual Precursors of the Mexican Revolution, 1900-1913*. Austin: University of Texas Press, 1968.

Cook, David S., Jr. *A Guide to the Spreading and Analysis of Mexican Bank Statements*. Philadelphia: R.M.A., 1978.

Cordova, Arnaldo. *La ideología de la revolución mexicana*. México, D.F.: E.R.A., 1974.

Delgado, José Hernández. *The Contribution of Nacional Financiera to the Industrialization of Mexico*. Mexico City: NAFIN, 1961.

Diamond, William, ed. *Development Finance Companies*. Baltimore: World Bank/Johns Hopkins University Press, 1968.

Diamond, William, and V. S. Raghavan, eds. *Aspects of Development Bank Management*. Baltimore: Johns Hopkins University Press, 1982.

Gerschenkron, Alexander. *Economic Backwardness in Historical Perspective*. Cambridge, Mass.: Harvard University Press, 1966.

Goldsmith, Raymond W. *The Financial Development of Mexico*. Paris: OECD, 1961.

——. *La estructura financiera y el crecimiento económico*. México, D.F.: Centro de Estudios Monetarios Latinoamericanos, 1963.

Gonzales, Hector E. *El sistema económico mexicano*. México, D.F.: La Red de Jonas Premia Editora, 1982.

Green, Rosario. *El endeudamiento público externo de México: 1940-73*. México, D.F.: Colegio de México, 1976.

Hansen, Roger D. *Mexican Economic Development: The Roots of Rapid Growth*. Washington, D.C.: National Planning Association, 1971.

——. *The Politics of Mexican Development*. 2nd ed. Baltimore: Johns Hopkins University Press, 1973.

Herzog, Jesús Silva. *Breve historia de la revolución mexicana*. Vol. I. México, D.F.: Fondo de Cultura Económica, 1972.

Hewlett, Sylvia A., and Richard S. Weinert, eds. *Brazil and Mexico: Patterns in Late Development*. Philadelphia: ISHI, 1982.

Homer, Sidney. *A History of Interest Rates*. 2nd ed. New Brunswick, N.J.: Rutgers University Press, 1977.

Huizer, Gerrit. *La lucha campesina en México*. México, D.F.: Centro de Investigaciones Agrarias, 1970.

Intriligator, Michael D. *Econometric Models, Techniques, and Applications*. Englewood Cliffs, N.J.: Prentice-Hall, 1978.

Kane, Joseph A. *Development Banking*. London: Lexington Books, 1975.

La Cascia, Joseph S. *Capital Formation and Economic Development in Mexico*. New York: Frederick A. Praeger, 1969.

Lustig, Nora, ed. *Panorama y perspectivas de la economía mexicana*. México, D.F.: Colegio de México, 1980.

Mosk, Sanford A. *Industrial Revolution in Mexico*. Los Angeles: University of California Press, 1950.

Mustaffa, Jorge, and Alberto Varillas. *Capacitación de personal en la banco de desarrollo de América latina*. Vol. I. Lima: ALIDE, 1976.

Navarrete, Jorge Eduardo, ed. *Cuestiones económicas nacionales*. México, D.F.: Banco Nacional de Comercio Exterior, 1971.

Nyhart, J. D., and E. F. Janssens. *Global Directory of Development Finance Institutions in Developing Countries*. Paris: OECD, 1967.

Oliver, Antonio Gómez. *Política monetaria y fiscal de México, 1946-1976*. México, D.F.: Fondo de Cultura Económica, 1981.

Pindyck, R. S., and D. L. Rubinfeld. *Econometric Models and Economic Forecasts*. New York: McGraw-Hill, 1976.

Reynolds, Clark W. *The Mexican Economy*. New Haven: Yale University Press, 1970.

Russell, Philip. *Mexico in Transition*. Austin, Tex.: Colorado River Press, 1977.

Shafer, Robert J. *Mexico, Mutual Adjustment Planning*. Syracuse, N.Y.: Syracuse University Press, 1966.

Solís M., Leopoldo. *La realidad mexicana: Retrovisión y perspectivas*. 11th ed. México, D.F.: Siglo xxi Editores, 1981.

Vernon, Raymond, ed. *Public Policy and Private Enterprise in Mexico*. Cambridge, Mass.: Harvard University Press, 1964.

Villa M., Rosa Olivia. *Nacional Financiera: Banco de fomento del desarrollo económico de México*. México, D.F.: NAFIN, 1976.

Villegas, Daniel Cosío. *Historia moderna de México*. Vol. VII, *El Porfiriato—vida económica*. México, D.F.: Editorial Hermes, 1965.

Weston, J. F., and E. F. Brigham. *Managerial Finance*. 6th ed. Hinsdale, Ill.: Dryden Press, 1977.

ARTICLES

Ben-Shahar, Haim. "Capital Formation and Government Policy in Developing Countries." *Journal of Development Studies* 4, no. 1 (October 1967).

Fair, Ray C., and Dwight M. Jaffee. "Methods of Estimation for Markets in Disequilibrium." *Econometrica* 40, no. 3 (May 1972).

Glade, William Patton, Jr. "Las empresas gubernamentales descentralizadas." *Problemas agrícolas e industriales de México* 6 (January 1959).

Griffin, K. B., and J. L. Enos. "Foreign Assistance: Objectives and Consequences." *Economic Development and Cultural Change* 18, no. 3 (April 1970).

Gurley, John G. "Hacia una teoría de las estructuras finacieras y el desarrollo económico." In *Estructura financiera y desarrollo económico*. Buenos Aires: Editorial del Instituto Torcuato di Tella, 1968.

Gurley, John G., and Edward S. Shaw. "Financial Aspects of Economic Development." *American Economic Review* 45, no. 1 (September 1955).

——. "Financial Intermediaries and the Saving-Investment Process." *Journal of Finance* 11 (May 1956).

——. "Financial Structure and Economic Growth." *Economic Development and Cultural Change* 15, no. 3 (April 1967).

Hamilton, Nora. "Mexico: The Limits of State Autonomy." *Latin American Perspectives* 2, no. 2 (Summer 1972).

Mamalakis, Markos. "An Analysis of the Financial and Investment Activities of the Chilean Development Corporation: 1939-1964." *Journal of Development Studies* 5, no. 2 (January 1969).

Markowitz, Harry. "Portfolio Selection." *Journal of Finance* 7, no. 1 (March 1952).

Mundell, R. A. "The Appropriate Use of Monetary and Fiscal Policy for Internal and External Stability." *IMF Staff Papers* 9 (1962).

Patrick, Hugh T. "The Mobilization of Private Gold Holdings." *Indian Economic Journal* 11, no. 2 (October-December 1963).

——. "Financial Development and Economic Growth in Underdeveloped Countries." *Economic Development and Cultural Change* 14, no. 2 (January 1966).

Solow, Robert M. "Technical Change and the Aggregate Production Function." *Review of Economics and Statistics* 39 (1957).

GOVERNMENT PUBLICATIONS AND REPORTS

Anuario estadístico de los Estados Unidos Mexicanos. México, D.F.: Secretaría de Programación y Presupuesto, 1940-53.

Anuario financiero de México. Vol XXXV. México, D.F.: ABM, 1975.

Banco de México, S.A. *Annual Report*. Mexico City: the Bank, 1950–81.

——. *Informe anual*. México, D.F.: the Bank, 1950–76.

——. *Indicadores de moneda y banca*. México, D.F.: the Bank, 1983.

——. *Informacion económica: Producto interno bruto y gasto, cuadernos 1960–77*. México, D.F. Banco de México, 1978. IPI/B6-001-00-08-78.

Banco Nacional de México, S.A. *Mexico Statistical Data, 1970–79*. Mexico City: BANAMEX, 1980.

Banco Nacional de Obras y Servicios Públicos, S.A. *Annual Report*. Mexico City: the Bank, 1960–68.

Décimo censo general de población. México, D.F.: Gerencia de Información Técnica y Publicaciones (G.I.T.P.), 1980.

Financial Monthly Report, Secretaría de Hacienda y Crédito Público, no. 5 (September 1983).

Inter-American Development Bank. *Economic and Social Progress in Latin America, 1980–81 Report*. Washington, D.C.: IDB, 1982.

Legislación Bancaria. Vol. I. México, D.F.: 1957.

Mercado de valores 24, no. 27 (July 6, 1964); 36, no. 39 (September 27, 1976); 39, no. 28 (July 28, 1979); 42, no. 20 (May 17, 1982); 42, no. 47 (November 22, 1982); 43, no. 24 (June 14, 1983).

NAFIN. *Informe anual*. México, D.F.: NAFIN, 1953–77.

——. *NAFINSA and the Economic Development of Mexico*. Mexico City: NAFIN, 1964.

——. *Statistics on the Mexican Economy*. Mexico City: NAFIN, 1966.

——. *La economía mexicana en cifras*. México, D.F.: NAFIN, 1978–84.

El sistema de cuentas nacionales de Mexico. Vol. I, *1970–1982*. México, D.F.: 1983.

United Nations. *Economic Bulletin for Latin America* 16 (1971).

OTHER

Salgado, Geraldo L. Performance of Public, Private and Mixed Development Banks (Unpublished master's thesis in Finance, University of Illinois, Urbana, 1974).

Index

foreign investment, 18, 57-58
  (*see also* direct foreign
  investment)
foreign loans, 20, 46
funds, flow of, 10
funds, sources of, 28

General Tariff on Imports,
  100
Gerschenkron, Alexander, 2,
  16, 26, 183
Gini coefficient, 129
Goldsmith, Raymond, 19, 172
government sector, 105, 110,
  149
  deficits, 129-130
  expenditures, 109-110, 130,
  133
great depression of the 1930s,
  59, 62
gross domestic investment,
  103, 104, 171, 173
  (*see also* investment)
gross domestic product (GDP),
  95, 98, 99, 101, 129, 130,
  132, 133, 148, 171, 175,
  176
  real growth rates, 96, 133
  sectoral shares, 97
Gross National Savings, 103,
  104
Gurley, John G. and Edward
  S. Shaw, 11

hacendados, 58, 63
Hernandez, Luis A., 6
historical evolution of development banking, 55-56,
  129
Honduras, 45
hospital, 63
housing, 88, 102
hypothesis of limited impact,
  2-4, 38, 116, 119

IBRD (*see* World Bank)
import-substitution industrialization (ISI), 4, 19, 65,
  98
imports, 98-99
  imports/GDP, 99

income:
  real growth, 59, 95, 132,
  133
  distribution, 46-47, 129, 130
  per capita, 59, 95, 96, 133
industrialization, 2, 3, 4, 16,
  19, 21, 26, 42, 49, 64,
  69-70, 83
  initial, 3-4, 31, 45, 94, 112,
  124
  sustained, 108-109, 111-112,
  147
industry:
  basic, 55, 56, 74, 79, 82,
  104, 135, 136, 138
  population economically
  active in, 96, 97
  growth of, 95-96
  structure, 82, 97
inflation, 46, 105, 111, 129-
  131, 135
infrastructure, and economic
  development, 20-21, 55,
  71, 74, 95, 101, 103-105,
  116
Inter-American Development
  Bank (IDB), 72, 86, 89
interest rates, 88, 106, 108
International Monetary Fund
  (IMF), 27, 131
investment, 2, 11, 13, 22, 24,
  32-33, 34, 37, 103, 104,
  159, 170-175
  (*see also* direct foreign investment; gross domestic
  investment)
irrigation, 70-71, 72, 86

Jacobian, 195
Jalisco, state of, 67
Japan, 3, 12, 16, 32, 80, 137
joint ventures and NAFIN,
  78, 79-82, 137, 185

Kane, Joseph, 2, 3-4, 25, 112
kraft paper, 67

labor force, 96
labor-intensive industry, 75
Latin America, 8, 9, 13, 17,
  19, 25, 31, 44, 45-47,
  75, 183

About The Author

MIGUEL D. RAMIREZ is an Assistant Professor of Economics at Trinity College in Hartford, Connecticut. Until 1985 he was an Assistant Professor of Economics at the University of North Florida, Jacksonville.

Dr. Ramirez has been active in research in the area of economic development. His articles and reviews have appeared in the *American Economic Review* and the *Journal of Economics and Business.*

Dr. Ramirez was born on December 17, 1956, in Santiago, Chile. In 1975 he came to Champaign–Urbana where he attended the University of Illinois. At this institution, he earned a B.A. in 1979 and a Ph.D. in 1984.